Social Networks as the New Frontier of Terrorism

Terrorism. Why does this word grab our attention so?

Propaganda machines have adopted modern technology as a means to ensure that their content is available. Regardless of the hour or time zone, information is being shared by somebody, somewhere. Social media is a game changer influencing the way in which terror groups are changing their tactics and also how their acts of terror are perceived by the members of the public they intend to influence.

This book explores how social media adoption by terrorists interacts with privacy law, freedom of expression, data protection and surveillance legislation through an exploration of the fascinating primary resources themselves, covering everything from the Snowden leaks, the rise of ISIS to Charlie Hebdo. The book also covers lesser worn paths such as the travel guide which proudly boasts that you can get Bounty and Twix bars mid-conflict, and the best local hair salons for jihadi brides. These vignettes, amongst the many others explored in this volume bring to life the legal, policy and ethical debates considered in this volume, representing an important part in the development of understanding terrorist narratives on social media with framing the legislative debate.

This book represents an invaluable guide for lawyers, government bodies, the defence services, academics, students and businesses.

Laura Scaife is a privacy practitioner and academic. She has appeared on the BBC and featured in *New Statesman* and on Radio 4. She regularly publishes scholarly articles on Social Media and is the author of *The Handbook of Social Media and the Law*, described in peer review as "the seminal text in the area".

Routledge Research in IT and E-Commerce Law

Titles in this series include:

Law of Electronic Commercial Transactions
Contemporary Issues in the EU, US and China
Faye Fangfei Wang

Online Dispute Resolution for Consumers in the European Union
Pablo Cortés

The Current State of Domain Name Regulation
Domain Names as Second Class Citizens in a Mark-dominated World
Konstantinos Komaitis

International Internet Law
Joanna Kulesza

The Domain Name Registration System
Liberalisation, Consumer Protection and Growth
Jenny Ng

Law of Electronic Commercial Transactions, 2nd Edition
Contemporary Issues in the EU, US and China
Faye Fangfei Wang

Cyberthreats and the Decline of the Nation-State
Susan W. Brenner

Balancing Privacy and Free Speech
Unwanted Attention in the Age of Social Media
Mark Tunick

Social Networks as the New Frontier of Terrorism

#Terror

Laura Scaife

Routledge
Taylor & Francis Group
LONDON AND NEW YORK

First published 2017
by Routledge

2 Park Square, Milton Park, Abingdon, Oxfordshire OX14 4RN
52 Vanderbilt Avenue, New York, NY 10017

Routledge is an imprint of the Taylor & Francis Group, an informa business

First issued in paperback 2019

British Library Cataloguing in Publication Data
A catalogue record for this book is available from the British Library

Library of Congress Cataloging-in-Publication Data
Names: Scaife, Laura, author.
Title: Social networks as the new frontier of terrorism : #terror / Laura Scaife.
Description: Abingdon, Oxon [UK]; New York: Routledge, 2017. | Series: Routledge research in information technology and e-Commerce law | Includes bibliographical references and index.
Identifiers: LCCN 2016033407 | ISBN 9781138950535 (hbk) | ISBN 9781315668680 (ebk)
Subjects: LCSH: Cyberterrorism—Law and legislation. | Online social networks—Law and legislation. | Terrorism—Prevention—Law and legislation. | Internet and terrorism. | Social media—Law and legislation. | Terrorists—Social networks. | National security—Law and legislation. | Snowden, Edward J., 1983–
Classification: LCC KZ7225.C93 S33 2017 | DDC 344.05/325—dc23
LC record available at https://lccn.loc.gov/2016033407

ISBN: 978-1-138-95053-5 (hbk)
ISBN: 978-0-367-87499-5 (pbk)

DOI: 10.4324/9781315668680

Dedications

I would like to dedicate this book to the memories of those who have lost their lives to terrorism and to their families, who quietly carry on with such dignity. I would also like to extend my thanks to those brave people who do their best to protect us from harm and ensure that our basic human rights are respected. These are not easy jobs and you have my eternal respect.

Finally, I also dedicate this book to the memory of my brother. I still think of you every day.

Contents

Acknowledgements

I am indebted to various individuals for their comments on this book. They know who they are and I extend my deepest thanks to you all for putting the materials into operational context. Although I cannot mention them by name, their contributions were invaluable. Thanks as always go to my wonderful publishers, Alexia Sutton and Jenny Olivier. I would also like to thank Stephen Anning for comments on drafts of this book, which provided invaluable insight to the challenges presented by terrorism.

My endless thanks are also extended to Peter Stapleton, who has read every iteration of these materials. He has also provided his unstinting support and encouragement for every word I bashed out on the keyboard. I also want to thank him for things that would fill a longer book than this.

Thanks too go to my family and friends for being so wonderfully supportive. They now know more about the law than they ever wanted to!

I would also like to thank two 'Man Fridays': first, Dr Richard Danbury, for his overpowering kindness and intelligence. Truly, Richard is one of the most unselfish and academically gifted individuals that I have been blessed to meet; secondly, Peter Coe, who has authored the excellent chapter on the traditional media. Peter's work is sublime and we will all be richer for reading his thoughts in this volume. Both of these stellar academics have always been a great source of unwavering support and it makes me teary eyed just thinking about it!

Foreword

'Toto, I've a feeling were not in Kansas anymore'

Judy Garland/Dorothy,
The Wizard of Oz (Metro-Goldwyn-Mayer, 1939)

When deciding how to describe this book to you, at first the words would not come. How does one even begin to explore the prolific rise of terrorism on social media?

When monoliths start by considering what the issues are in relation to a particular thorny current issue, often it is described in terms of 'unpacking the issues' to reach a conclusion. But that will not do at all for this volume, because in order to understand a little more of the extraordinary landscape that is jihad online, instead we have to embark on our journey, accepting that we may not know where the road takes us, but comforted in the knowledge that we have some kit by way of key concepts that will help us along the way should we need them, but we can't pack everything for every eventuality.

Before a traveller starts any journey it is usually a good idea to acquire a map, which is why we will begin by looking at what terrorism means to different people. So far so good, we're not in a particularly complicated place; think of it as the first leg of the gap year, where we are in central Europe, and almost everything is well marked out. We can get by as there will be some broadly familiar infrastructure in place to answer our questions such as which core legal principles govern content posted online, as well as how the security services detect information. However, when we have finished our last *café au lait* in Paris, we may decide to sojourn on to pastures new, and that is really the next phase of the book – the journey into the regulatory unknown – taking in propaganda online, surveillance, cyber hacking, media reporting and the role of the social media sites themselves.

This book does not seek to provide an 'answer' to the issues at hand, instead, it offers an opportunity to veer off the well worn paths and show the extent of the materials that are available online, from the shocking to the – at times – surreal. It aims to document a different point of view, perhaps digging a little deeper than what you may have read in the newspapers or seen on TV to reveal to you the incredible sophistication of modern terror networks and why they appeal to their online followings. You are unlikely to have read or had brought to your attention by the mainstream press the travel guide which proudly boasts that you can get Bounty and Twix bars, the best local hair salons (as well as what shampoos to avoid) or what to pack in your suitcase for a trip to Syria. These little vignettes are an important part of the story, just as much as the violent content posted online. Although superficially seemingly trivial, they assist with framing the debate as to why certain legislative or policy decisions have been taken by states and the social media companies themselves with regard to content posted online.

If you will allow me, dear reader, to indulge a little, I invite you to divert with me to a pop quiz (I am going somewhere with this . . . I promise). Pachelbel's Canon, of which the exact date of publication is not known, harks back to at least the 17th century. Its underlying sound, although you may be used to associating the tune with church services, gave birth to the following hits: Pink Floyd's *Nobody Home*, Billy Joel's *Piano Man*, Green Day's *Basket Case*, Fleetwood Mac's *Landslide*, The Beatles' *Strawberry Fields Forever*, *Hey Jude* and *Yesterday*, as well as Eminem's *Lose Yourself*. Never did violins and organs seem so exciting.

Although it may appear that I have veered off at an extraordinary tangent, the point is simply this. In this book I present a framework (my own Canon) from which you can decide how to interpret and create your own song. This book has been constructed especially to encourage you to explore your own viewpoint, whilst providing as much information and context as possible. Because of the divisive nature of the subject matter, there will likely be parts or materials with which you do not agree. However, they too are an important part of the discourse; to my mind it is important that you formulate your own views on the subject.

Do bear in mind as you go though, or perhaps even debate this text with your contemporaries that there is room for everyone to have their own interpretation in a democratic society which values freedom of expression; just because you do not like the song does not mean that others may not resonate with the meaning of the lyrics, simply because it does not chime with you. One man's *Piano Man* is another man's *Lose Yourself* (or as we will explore in this volume, one man's terrorist is another man's Facebook friend). The possibilities, my dear reader, are endless and, unless that discourse takes place, there is little chance of formulating a framework to present the unique challenges faced in this ever evolving area.

1 One man's terrorist is another man's Facebook friend

Getting information off the Internet is like taking a drink from a fire hydrant.
Mitchell Kapor

In the 21st century, the explosion of the digital age has revolutionised the way that individuals engage with mass media – putting knowledge at their fingertips.[1] It is possible (common, even) to reach an unlimited audience with the click of a mouse or the use of an internet enabled smartphone: 'we are all now connected by the Internet, like neurons in a giant brain'.[2] In particular, social networking sites accessible via smart phones have changed the way in which individuals socialise with one another, acting as a giant digital coffee shop for the exchange of ideas and connection of individuals, regardless of geographical borders.

As aptly summarised by *New York Times* columnist, David Carr:

> [w]e live in an age where there is a fire hose of information, and there is no hierarchy of what is important and what is not. Where the truth is often fashioned through a variety of digital means. Are you your avatar? Who are you in social media? What face do you turn toward the world? How much does it have in common with who you actually are?[3]

Propaganda machines have adopted modern technology as a means to ensure their content is always available. Regardless of the hour or time zone, information

1 Human Rights Committee, General Comment 34: Freedoms of opinion and expression, CCPR/C/GC/34 (12 September 2011) para 5 states: 'Internet and mobile based electronic information dissemination systems, have substantially changed communication practices around the world. There is now a global network for exchanging idea and opinions that does not necessarily rely on the traditional mass media intermediaries.'

2 J Swartz (2014), 'Stephen Hawking opens up' *USA Today* (1 December 2014) http://usatoday30.usatoday.com/MONEY/usaedition/2014-12-02-QampA-with-Stephen-Hawking_ST_U.htm.

3 J Lee (2013), 'David Carr: Truth and Lies in Life and Art' (30 January 2013) http://blogs.vancouversun.com/2015/02/12/new-york-times-david-carr-dead-at-58-his-interview-with-the-sun/.

DOI: 10.4324/9781315668680-1

is being shared by somebody, somewhere. However, propaganda is not the 'insidious, deceptive, manipulative pattern of negatively influencing behaviour that many people consider it to be'.[4] Propaganda, whilst it may conjure up images of the likes of Nazi propagandist Josef Goebbels or contemporary examples such as Osama bin Laden, can also be used for good – such as spreading public health messages. Essentially, propaganda is 'an ethically neutral idea – it is the content that varies'.[5] Arguably, the evolution and advances in social media are influencing the way in which terror groups are changing their tactics and also how their acts of terror are perceived by the members of the public they intend to influence.

The word 'terrorism' has become so entrenched in public consciousness in the post 9/11 international environment that traditional media outlets often overuse it to describe a wide spectrum of violent activity, such as insurgencies and civil war conflicts. The purpose and ultimate aim of terrorism is to frighten people into submission, often for an ideological cause. Unlike guerrilla or conventional warfare, the objective is not the violent but strategic action of seizing ground, neutralising an asset or destroying an enemy's military force, but the reaction of creating fear to influence political will or to intimidate people. An act of terrorism against a civilian target is not a political or strategic risk if people do not hear about it or see images of it, therefore understanding who did it and why. It has to be communicated to create a story and further promote the cause.

On the other hand, an attack against critical national infrastructure, such as a power station, stock exchange or port facility provides another dimension of risk that could potentially have direct economic and political impacts without the need for it to be communicated to a wide audience. A well selected and non-violent cyber-attack on a critical national infrastructure facility could, potentially, be catastrophic for the social fabric of a nation, but would not create the same level of fear, horror and trepidation as a gruesome, well documented and publicised execution.

Arguably, the modern era of live television 'terror-communication' started with the 9/11 attacks in 2001: the images of people jumping from the twin towers was bewildering and shocking to the wide Western audience who watched it unfold in their living rooms and work places. For Al-Qaeda, it was an event to celebrate and behold with joy. The 9/11 attacks achieved and provoked the reaction the perpetrators and masterminds of the attacks desired: a US and Western nation military invasion of a Muslim country, turning America's 'war on terrorism' into an Islamic Jihad.

In this chapter we will explore how terrorism has been defined and interpreted throughout history, as well as the development of social media, in order to set down the groundwork to explore the areas considered in this volume.

4 P Johnston (2013), *The Internet, Social Media and Propaganda: The Final Frontier?* (30 August 2013) http://britishlibrary.typepad.co.uk/socialscience/2013/08/the-internet-social-media-and-propaganda-the-final-frontier.html#sthash.Zas8ExR9.0lkKeumO.dpuf.

5 Ibid.

1.1 Background to the development of social media

1.1.1 Development of social media

In the era before the existence of the internet, social networking was the process of conventional human interaction that took place in key locations such as schools, market places, religious centres and sports events.[6] The potential for computer networking to facilitate newly improved forms of computer-mediated social interaction was initially suggested during the infancy of the internet.[7] The genesis of social media as we think of it today can be traced back to 1971 when the first email travelled between two computers one metre apart (many co-workers and now teenagers on social media sites continue and actually prefer to communicate this way – rather than actually talking to each other).

Efforts to support social networks through computer-mediated communication were made in many early online services, including Usenet,[8] ARPANET, LISTSERV and bulletin board services. Many proto-typical features of social networking services (SNS) were also present in online services such as America Online, Prodigy, CompuServe, ChatNet and The WELL.[9] Early social networking on the World Wide Web began in the form of generalised online communities such as Theglobe.com (1995),[10] Geocities (1994) and Tripod.com (1995).

Much of the early research on these online communities assumed that individuals using these systems would be connecting with others outside their pre-existing social group or location, liberating them to form communities around shared interests, as opposed to shared geography.[11] The early online communities focused on 'bringing people together' to interact with each other through chat rooms, and encouraged users to share personal information and ideas through personal web pages by providing easy-to-use publishing tools and free or inexpensive web space. However, other communities, such as www.classmates.com, took a different approach by simply having people link to each other by way of email addresses.

By the late 1990s, the nature of the sites began to change. User profiles became increasingly important as user demand for the ability to compile lists of connections, often referred to as 'friends', increased. The use of profiles with user data allowed users to search for and connect with other users with similar interests

6 Testimony of Evan F Kohlmann with Josh Lefkowitz and Laith Alkhouri to the UN Congress for Data Security (6 December 2011).

7 Starr Roxanne Hiltz and Murray Turoff (1978), *The Network Nation: Human Communication via Computer* (New York: Addison-Wesley, rev edn. Cambridge, MA: MIT Press 1993).

8 Michael Hauben and Ronda Hauben (1997), *Netizens: On the History and Impact of Usenet and the Internet* (Los Alamitos, CA: IEEE Computer Society Press).

9 Katie Hafner (2001), *The Well: A Story of Love, Death and Real Life in the Seminal Online Community* (New York: Carroll & Graf).

10 David Cotriss (2008), 'Where are they now: TheGlobe.com' *The Industry Standard* (29 May) 28727.

11 B Wellman, J Salaff, D Dimitrova, L Garton, M Gulia and C Haythornthwaite (1996), 'Computer networks as social networks: collaborative work, telework, and virtual community' 22 *Annual Review of Sociology* 213–38.

or shared connections. As user demand for such features grew, and sites developed increasingly sophisticated offerings that allowed users to find and manage 'friends'.[12]

In 1997, the 'next generation' social networking sites began to flourish with the introduction of sites such as SixDegrees.com. In this way they significantly changed the way in which individuals communicated, 'structured both to articulate existing connections and enable the creation of new ones'.[13] The sites began to develop certain broad commonalities, usually consisting of a representation of each user (often a profile), his or her social links and a variety of additional services. The service typically allowed individuals to create a public profile, generate a list of users with whom to share connection and view the cross-connections within the system.[14]

Today, most social network services are web-based and provide means for users to interact over the internet, such as email and messaging. Building upon this functionality, the third generation of networking sites started to appear in the early 2000s.[15] Such sites soon became part of users' regular internet consumption and, by 2005, it was reported that MySpace was getting more page views than Google.[16] In 2004, Facebook was introduced as a Harvard social networking site,[17] becoming the largest social networking site in the world in early 2009[18] and reaching the 1 billion users mark in 2012. Six hundred million of those users were accessing the site using a mobile device.[19] More than 200 social networking sites of worldwide impact are known today and this number is growing fast. Facebook now has over 1.65 billion active users.[20]

In recent years, they have become increasingly varied and they now commonly incorporate new information and communication tools, such as mobile connectivity, photo/video/sharing and blogging, creating the potential to enrich social and

12 C Romm-Livermore and K Setzekorn (eds) (2008), *Social Networking Communities and E-Dating Services: Concepts and Implications* (New York: IGI Global) 271.

13 N B Ellison, C Steinfield and C Lampe (2007), 'The benefits of Facebook "friends": social capital and college students' use of online social network sites' 12(4) *Journal of Computer-Mediated Communication* 1143–68.

14 D M Boyd and N B Ellison (2007), 'Social network sites: definition, history and scholarship' 13(1) *Journal of Computer-Mediated Communication* 210–30.

15 Makeoutclub was introduced in 2000, with Hub Culture and Friendster following in 2002. See E Knapp (2005) *A Parent's Guide to MySpace* (DayDream Publishers).

16 Steve Rosenbush (2005), 'News Corp's place in MySpace' *Business Week* (19 July) (MySpace page views figures).

17 D M Boyd and N B Ellison (2007), 'Social network sites: definition, history and scholarship' 13(1) *Journal of Computer-Mediated Communication* 210–30.

18 Andy Kazeniac (2009), 'Social networks: Facebook takes over top spot, Twitter climbs', Blog.compete.com (9 February) https://blog.compete.com/2009/02/09/facebook-myspace-twitter-social-network/.

19 D Lee (2012), 'Facebook Surpasses One Billion Users as It Tempts New Markets', BBC News (5 October 2012) http://www.bbc.co.uk/news/technology-19816709 (last accessed 26 July 2016).

20 http://www.statista.com/statistics/264810/number-of-monthly-active-facebook-users-worldwide/.

political dialogue through its ability to report, in real time, matters of public interest and concern[21] as recorded or perceived by a wide variety of stakeholders such as those close to the proximity of the event, linked to it through religious or political affiliations or merely interested in sharing their views on matters of national or, indeed, international concern. Everyone from the Pope[22] to reality television star Kim Kardashian[23] has a powerful social media presence, thereby informing social, cultural and political debate.

A powerful example of this is Edward Snowden,[24] the former NSA employee who, in June 2013, revealed classified information relating to the American National Surveillance Authority's (NSA) large-scale monitoring, covering everything from internet searches, social-media content and, most controversially, the records (known as metadata) of phone calls (including details of who called whom, for how long and from where) which, customarily, has been held for years, but may (potentially) be held forever. Many of the documents which continue to trickle out to this day specifically relate to the United Kingdom's GCHQ. The UK Government has stated that at least 58,000 'highly classified UK intelligence documents' were among those leaked. Snowden's first-ever tweet at noon on 29 September 2015 simply stated: 'Can you hear me now?'.[25] Twitter provided Snowden with an enormous platform, indeed Twitter (@Twitter) itself posted: 'Today @Snowden joined Twitter, and here's the world's response. pic.twitter.com/d6HgVvdRsf', which linked to a visual heat map of the effect of the post, across the globe.[26]

In the age of the internet, essentially anybody can become an armchair reporter or commentator. The traditional press generally covers terrorism at a rate of at least nine incidents every day worldwide, according to a pilot study undertaken by John L. Martin.[27] Martin suggests that the 'press gives terrorists publicity, but often omits the propaganda message that terrorists would like to see accompanying reports of their exploits, thus reducing terrorism to mere crime or sabotage' with regard to the ability to communicate propaganda messages. Social media can therefore be considered a 'game changer' as it is able to step beyond the restrictions of traditional reporting and selectivity and allows them to engage with the public directly, conveying their entire message. As summed up in the US case of *New York*

21 J. Oster, 'Theory and Doctrine of "Media Freedom" as a Legal Concept', (2013) 5(1) JML 57–78, 63; C Calvert and M Torres (2011), 'Putting the Shock Value in First Amendment Jurisprudence: When Freedom for the Citizen-Journalist Watchdog Trumps the Right of Informational Privacy on the Internet', *Vanderbilt Journal of Entertainment and Technology Law* 323, 344.

22 Pope Francis (@Pontifex) https://twitter.com/Pontifex (9.61 million followers as at 26 July 2016).

23 Kim Kardashian West (@KimKardashian) https://twitter.com/KimKardashian (46.9 million followers as at 26 July 2016).

24 Edward Snowden (@Snowden) https://twitter.com/snowden?lang=en-gb (2.26 million followers as at 26 July 2016).

25 Ibid.

26 'Today @Snowden joined Twitter, and here's the world's response. pic.twitter.com/d6HgVvdRsf 12:14 PM – 29 Sep 2015'.

27 J Martin (1985), *The Media's Role in International Terrorism* http://www.polisci.rutgers.edu/images/Syllabus_of_Theories_and_Strategies_of_Counter-Terrorism_Spring_2015.docx.

v Harris: 'The reality of today's world is that social media, whether it be Twitter, Facebook, Pinterest, Google+ or any other site, is the way people communicate'.[28] It continued that, whenever:

> [w]e post an opinion on Facebook, Twitter, or any other social media site, we are issuing propaganda, a piece of information designed to make those who read it think about an issue or behave in a certain way conducive to what we want them to. Corporations (and small businesses) have realised this, which is why they have such an active social media presence. Branding and advertising has become a major aspect of social media for all businesses and organisations, including terrorist groups.[29]

It is for this reason that the internet has become a core part of terrorist group communication strategies. In recent years, social media has become a dazzling jewel in their communications crown. Scarcely a day passes when there is not some new report about a post made via Twitter, YouTube or Facebook which disseminates a new extreme message from a group that identifies itself, or is attributed to an association with, terrorist causes. Owing to the phenomenal uptake in the use of modern technologies by such groups and causes, the internet is now described by some as the fifth domain of warfare.[30] William J. Lynn, US Deputy Secretary of Defence, has stated that, as a doctrinal matter, cyberspace is formally recognised as such and has become just as critical to military operations as land, sea, air and space.

Every tweet, video and sermon that is posted can be shared and thereby its reach magnified, in a way that is exceptionally difficult to track and stop. The nature of the postings is not covert: the posts are designed to be read and spread – social media presence is at the core of disseminating their message. As we will see throughout this volume, social media has played a key part on both sides of the debate in mobilising, marketing, informing, obfuscating and influencing opinions on matters of international concern, shaping the dialogue taking place across the globe, public opinion and shaping consensus of events from around the world.

In particular, as the growth of the Islamic State is followed by millions of people on Twitter, the Jihad movement has evolved into something that the US led coalition in Iraq could not have possibly imagined back in 2003. However, the communication of acts of extreme violence on social media did not originate with Islamic fundamentalists; it actually started with Mexican drug cartels. The cartels first used and invented the current day Al-Qaeda and Islamic State propaganda *modus operandi* of deliberately publishing brutal terror videos on social media.

Social media offers a new complexion, as it is not only 'official' accounts that drive the 'propaganda machine'. It is supported by hundreds of thousands of cogs,

28 *New York v. Harris*, 2012 N.Y. Misc. LEXIS 1871 *3, note 3 (Crim. Ct. City of N.Y., N.Y. County, 2012).

29 Ibid.

30 'Cyberwar: War in the Fifth Domain' *Economist* (1 July 2010).

in the form of networks of supporters, who see the internet as a kind of virtual frontline that demands as much effort and attention as the physical fight on the ground. By way of example, many supporters involved in the recent Islamic State (ISIS) discussions taking place in relation to IS's actions in Syria, who are not involved in the 'front line' battle, have talked about being involved in the 'online jihad'. According to the *Brookings Project on U.S. Relations with the Islamic World*, research conducted by researchers say that IS supporters have used at least 46,000 Twitter accounts.[31]

Such reach and the incredibly large and diverse bank of stakeholders who engage with social media undoubtedly presents difficulties in terms of what exactly we mean when we attribute the term 'terrorism' to the acts of a particular group, or label an individual as a 'terrorist'. Whilst traditionally associated with 'official' and/or 'affiliated' groups, cells or networks, 'terrorist acts' and support for such causes are now being openly expressed online by those who have never had an official or direct affiliation with terrorist organisations.

For example, in 2011 Arid Uka, an Albanian Muslim living in Germany, was watching (on YouTube) a jihadist propaganda edited video that claimed to present the rape of a Muslim woman by US soldiers. Just hours after viewing the clip he boarded a bus to Frankfurt Airport, where he wounded two people with a handgun and killed two US servicemen. After his arrest, Uka's computers were seized. His internet and social media activity showed a growing interest in Jihadist content, which snowballed his self-radicalisation. A true product of web 2.0, Uka's entire radicalisation, from early attraction to Jihadi preaching to the inspiration for his deadly mission, was accomplished online.

There are now deliberate attempts to counter the Jihadhi narrative by the US Department of Defence and UK Ministry of Defence (MoD). The MoD's creation of 77 Brigade is leading this online social media propaganda battle from the European side of the Atlantic. The UK Government counter-terrorism (CONTEST) strategy is how the UK Government aims to counter terror. Whilst much of it is classified, the PREVENT and PROTECT strands are an attempt to counter the narratives and provide a credible alternative to the terrorist message and presence.[32]

1.2 What is terrorism? An evolving concept or just a word . . .

Terrorism. Why does this word grab our attention so? A cursory examination of news reports published through popular outlets indicates that terrorist groups are

31 J M Berger and J Morgan (2015), 'The ISIS Twitter Census defining and describing the population of ISIS supporters on Twitter', The Brookings Project on U.S. Relations with the Islamic World Analysis Paper No 20 (March 2015) https://dlib.bc.edu/islandora/object/bc-ir:104188/datastream/PDF/view.

32 See https://www.gov.uk/government/publications/counter-terrorism-strategy-contest.

'embracing the web' more than ever.[33] However, in the context of this volume, such a statement is rather a case of putting the cart before the horse as we have not even begun to unpick what terrorism is and, perhaps more importantly, what it is not. Where (for instance) is the line between hate speech, extremism and terrorism to be drawn? More particularly for this work, how are these subtle distinctions to be picked apart in terms of their application to social media? In order to understand how social media and terrorism intersect, it is necessary to begin by considering the definition of terrorism itself. What do we mean when we refer to terrorism, this familiar yet distant concept? Terrorism is a bit like a *Cosmo* quiz: you can start at the top of the quiz and fall into one of many different categories, depending on your answer.

1.2.1 Types of terrorism

Although applying the label of terrorism to a particular activity is, as we have seen, a complex task, in the modern political environment experts in the field are broadly agreed on the different forms of terrorism that are found in the current modern political environment. In simplified terms, Martin[34] suggests that these definitions can be broken down into the following core typologies:

- *state terrorism*: acts committed by governments against perceived enemies
- *dissident terrorism*: acts committed by non-state groups, against governments, ethno-national groups, religious groups, and their perceived 'enemies'
- *political terrorism*: acts of political violence, e.g. Anders Breivik, Oklahoma City bombing
- *religious terrorism*: acts undertaken in the name of commitment to the glorification, defence and/or support of a religious faith
- *criminal terrorism*: acts primarily motivated by profit (as exemplified by the example of the Mexican drug cartels discussed in this chapter) who accumulate profits to sustain their movement
- *international terrorism*: acts directed towards to world stage, aimed at targeting symbols and values of international interests.

1.2.2 Defining terrorism

Although terrorism can be penned into various types, defining terrorism can be an exercise in semantics and context, most often driven by one's own perspectives, experiences and world view. Perspective is a central consideration in defining terrorism. As we will see throughout this chapter, the problem is that there exists

33 'How terrorists are using social media' *The Telegraph* (4 November 2014) http://www.telegraph.co.uk/news/worldnews/islamic-state/11207681/How-terrorists-are-using-social-media.html.

34 G Martin (2016), *Understanding Terrorism: Challenges, Perspectives, and Issues* (5th edn, Sage Publications, 2016) ch 2.

no precise or widely accepted definition of terrorism. The word 'terrorism' is an evocative one, conjuring up vivid images in the mind of the reader. However, whilst it is easy to think of acts that we would consider to be 'terrorist activity', for example bombings or plane hijacking, it is more difficult to assess the underlying rationale and ideologies which govern such activities and thereby make the act a terrorist one, rather than defined as criminal or lawful, or even subjectively perceived as heroic.

Consider, for example, the use of an improvised explosive device (IED), or a 'bomb'; in layman's terms. In wartime, this would perhaps be justified; however, to blow open a bank vault to steal money, the use would most likely be classified as criminal behaviour. On the other hand, to use an IED to kill civilians to highlight a cause could be classified as a terrorist act.

Undoubtedly the majority of the readership of this book will perceive terrorism as an aggressive and violent movement that sets out to attack their way of life. In order to understand this new era of online terrorism it is important to sit in the terrorist's chair and look at what they are viewing on their tablets and laptops. Any military commander will tell you the first part of a mission's analysis is to understand the enemy they are confronted with. As a minimum, a thorough understanding of the enemy's weapons, *modus operandi*, tactics, motivations, resources, capabilities, command structure and communications systems is needed before an analysis of their strengths and weaknesses can be conceived and understood – and then exploited. There is now a need to understand how they interact, recruit, plan and exploit the huge number of social media websites and apps available to them.

1.2.2.1 Lessons from history

In order to get to grips with this loaded word, it is useful to break it down into its component parts. An etymological line of enquiry takes us to the Latin origins of 'terror', '*terrere*', which means 'frighten' or 'tremble'. When this is combined with the suffix '*isme*' ('to practise'), it takes on a new complexion, meaning to cause the frightening (of individuals). Although the word has contemporaneously been associated with acts of the IRA or Islamic State, the concept of terror to describe the creation of a 'state of fear' takes us back to ancient times. Depending on how broadly the term is defined, the roots and practice of terrorism can be traced at least to the activities[35] of 1st-century AD Sicarii Zealots (or 'dagger-men'), an extremist splinter group[36] of the Jewish Zealots, who attempted to expel the Romans and their partisans from the Roman province of Judea.[37]

35 It should be noted that there is some dispute whether the group, which assassinated collaborators with Roman rule in the province of Judea, was in fact terrorist.

36 Nachman Ben-Yehuda (2000), 'The Masada Myth: Scholar presents evidence that the heroes of the Jewish Great Revolt were not heroes at all', The Bible and Interpretation http://www.bibleinterp.com/articles/2000/ben258001.shtml.

37 Martin Goodman (2008), *Rome and Jerusalem: The Clash of Ancient Civilisations* (First Vintage Books) 407 talks of *sicarii* practising 'terrorism within Jewish society'.

In another example drawn from Rome, following the devastation of the Arausio, fear shook the Roman Republic to its foundations and *terror cimbricus* became the watchword of the day, as Rome expected the Cimbri at its gates at any time. In this atmosphere of panic and desperation, an emergency was declared. The reflective reader may have noticed that the phrase 'terror', as understood in its ancient Latin origins, still had some maturing to do, given its extremely wide application.

To follow its development, our quest takes us to the French Revolution's 'Reign of Terror' (1793–1794). During *Le Gouvernement de la Terreur* (as it is called in its mother language) the Jacobins used the term when describing their own actions during the French Revolution. They ruled the revolutionary state by employing violence, including mass executions by guillotine, to compel obedience to the state and intimidate regime enemies.[38] Between 16,000 and 40,000 people were killed in a little over a year, with the French National Convention proclaiming, in September 1793, that 'terror is the order of the day'. Maximilien Robespierre (a key player in the revolution) declared in 1794 that 'virtue, without which terror is evil; terror, without which virtue is helpless . . . Terror is nothing but justice, prompt, severe and inflexible; it is therefore an emanation of virtue'.

The British approach to plotting a definition of terrorism is also documented by Sir Edmund Burke who, commenting on the French Revolution, warned about 'thousands of those hell hounds called terrorists'.[39] Other pre-'Reign of Terror' historical events sometimes associated with terrorism are the Gunpowder Plot of 1605, in which an attempt was made to destroy the English Parliament. Whilst at this point in time the concept of terror existed and was being used in common parlance, it was as yet devoid of a formal definition. The first official definition of terrorism is attributed to the release of the supplement for the dictionary of the Académie Française in 1798. Following on from its revolutionary origins, the term was explained as the *système, régime de la terreur* (the 'government of terror'). From this point on, the concept of terror grew in strength and was increasingly used to label the actions of revolutionary and militant groups such as the Fenian brotherhood and its offshoot – the Irish Republican Brotherhood – which were both formed in 1858 and among the earliest groups to deploy terror techniques, carrying out frequent acts of violence in metropolitan Britain to achieve their aims through intimidation.[40]

The year 1883 saw the formation of the first police unit designed to combat terrorism. Set up by the Metropolitan Police, this subset of the Criminal Investigation Department, which became known as the Special Irish Branch, was trained in counter-terrorism techniques to combat the Irish Republican Army

38 F Furstenburg (2007), 'Bush's Dangerous Liaisons', *The New York Times* (28 October 2007).

39 E Burke (1790), *Reflections on the Revolution in France* (ed C C O'Brien, London: Penguin Books, 1969); Scott Shane (3 April 2010), 'Words as Weapons: Dropping the "Terrorism" Bomb' *The New York Times*, p WK1; Joseph S Tuman (2003), *Communicating Terror: The Rhetorical Dimensions of Terrorism* (Thousand Oaks, CA: Sage, 2003).

40 R English (2007), *Irish Freedom* (Pan Books) 3.

(IRA). Steadily, its remit widened over the years before becoming what we know today as the Special Branch. However, the association with state violence only lasted until the mid-19th century, when it began to be associated with non-governmental groups. Anarchism, rising nationalism and anti-monarchism were the most prominent ideologies linked with terrorism, culminating in the assassinations of a Russian tsar.

Demonstrating its fluidity, by the 1930s the meaning had shifted again, now being used increasingly to describe the practices of mass repression employed by totalitarian states and their dictatorial leaders against their own citizens – as exemplified in Fascist Italy, Nazi Germany and Stalinist Russia. 'Terror? Never', Mussolini insisted, demurely dismissing such intimidation as 'simply . . . social hygiene, taking those individuals out of circulation like a doctor would take out a bacillus'.[41] The 1970s saw the increase in headline grabbing acts of terror, the average number of reported terrorist attacks at their peak went from 10 every week to the incredible figure of nearly 10 a day.[42]

In 2004, an important piece of research was carried out by Li and Schaub,[43] who examined international terrorist incidents across 112 countries during the period from 1975 to 1997. This research revealed that the continents suffering the highest number of terrorist attacks were as follows (in descending order); Middle East, Europe, Africa, Asia and the Americas. Although ranking the lowest in Li and Schaub's research, on 11 September 2001 America experienced one of the worst terrorist attacks on its soil, which was witnessed by the world as a result of the power and reach of global media, even in the pre social-media age. The 'Global War on Terror' (GWOT), initiated by President George W. Bush post-event, represented one of the most all-encompassing counter-terrorist campaigns in history.[44]

The 9/11 attacks demonstrated that the power of terrorist acts coupled with new media represented an opportunity to air a cause on a global scale. Since 2001, the number of terrorist attacks worldwide has increased significantly: from 2001 to 2006 alone, they rose from 1732 to 6659.[45] Some of the most recent terrorist acts committed include the post-9/11 Moscow Theatre Siege, the 2003 Istanbul bombings, the Madrid train bombings, the Beslan school hostage crisis, the 2005 London bombings, the October 2005 New Delhi bombings, the 2008 Mumbai Hotel Siege, the 2011 Norway attacks, the 2015 attacks in Tunisia and Paris and the Brussels and Orlando attacks in 2016. This book will also explore

41 W Laqueur (1987), *The Age of Terrorism* (Boston: Little, Brown) 66, quoted in Bruce Hoffman (1998), *Inside Terrorism* (1st edn, New York: Columbia University Press) 24.

42 Risks International (1985), *Major Incidents of Terrorism: 1970–1984* (Alexandria, VA: Risks International, 1985).

43 Quan Li and Drew Schaub (2004), 'Economic Globalization and Transnational Terrorist Incidents: A Pooled Time Series Analysis' 48(2) *Journal of Conflict Resolution* 230–58.

44 R Jackson (2005), *Writing the War on Terrorism: Language, Politics and Counter-Terrorism* (Manchester: Manchester University Press).

45 See Martin (n 34).

the instances of recent attacks by lone wolf individuals who commit mass murder and whether they are simply mentally unhinged individuals who cite a cause, or genuinely inspired by a terrorist movement.

1.2.2.2 Finding a consensus as to the modern definition of terrorism

Although we have explored some examples of terrorism through the ages, what still evades the reader is that ability to pin down (with a sense of certainty) what amounts to terrorism. Although we all have a vague impression, or could conjure up striking images of terrorist activity and, if asked on the street perhaps by a researcher or in a focus group we would be able to say: 'oh yes, I know what terrorism is'. However, if pressed to explain it, we would find that it is a far more difficult task to come to a concrete explanatory definition of the word, bombarded as we are with articles, live micro-blog feeds and broadcasts with reports of a wide variety of activities such as the bombing of a building, the assassination of a head of state, the massacre of civilians by a military unit and the shooting of civilians in malls, which are all described as sitting under the headline banner of 'terrorism'.

Merari found that, in the US, Britain and Germany, there are three common elements that exist in the legal definitions of terrorism:

- the use of violence
- political objectives and
- the aim of propagating fear in a target population.[46]

It has been suggested that perhaps this difficulty derives from the fact that the term is politically and emotionally charged, 'a word with intrinsically negative connotations that is generally applied to one's enemies and opponents'.[47] The meaning of terrorism is socially constructed[48] and therefore defies an 'all-inclusive' definition. Yasser Arafat, late chairman of the PLO (the Palestine Liberation Organisation), captured the issue in a 1974 speech before the United Nations, declaring that: '[O]ne man's terrorist is another man's freedom fighter'. For example, in 2001, a public opinion poll was conducted in Palestine, in which 98.1 per cent of respondents surveyed agreed or strongly agreed that 'the killing of 29 Palestinians in Hebron by Baruch Goldstein at al Ibrahimi mosque in 1994' was

46 Ariel Merari (1993), 'Terrorism as a Strategy of Insurgency' 5(4) *Terrorism and Political Violence* 213–51.

47 See Hoffman (n 41) 32.

48 Brooke Barnett and Amy Reynolds (2009), *Terrorism and the Press: An Uneasy Relationship* (New York: Peter Lang); Bruce Hoffman (2006), *Inside Terrorism* (2nd edn, Columbia University Press); Brian Jenkins (1983), 'Research in Terrorism: Areas of Consensus, Areas of Ignorance' in Burr Eichelman, David A Soskis and William H Reid (eds) *Terrorism: Interdisciplinary Perspectives* (Washington, D.C.: American Psychiatric Association) 153–77; Alex P Schmid and Janny de Graaf (1982), *Violence as Communication: Insurgent Terrorism and the Western News Media* (Beverly Hills: Sage).

terrorism. However, 82.3 per cent of the same respondents disagreed or strongly disagreed that 'the killing of 21 Israeli youths by a Palestinian who exploded himself at the Tel Aviv Dolphinarium' should be called terrorism.[49]

The question is undoubtedly a complex one straddling disciplines such as the law, sociology, economics and political science. The word, much like the etymology of so many words, has changed over time to accommodate the landscape of each successive geopolitical era. Its fluidity derives from the fact that its definition depends on whether one agrees with the message. Brian Jenkins has suggested that: 'What is called terrorism, thus seems to depend on one's point of view. Use of the term implies a moral judgment; and if one party can successfully attach the label terrorist to its opponent, then it has indirectly persuaded others to adopt its moral viewpoint'.[50]

Indeed, taking the example of the 1972 Munich Olympics massacre, in which 11 Israeli athletes were killed – the exchanges between Western and non-Western member states of the United Nations following the incident began with the proposal by the then UN Secretary-General, Kurt Waldheim, that the UN should not remain a 'mute spectator' and should take practical steps that might prevent further bloodshed. Whilst this viewpoint found support with the majority of the UN member states, a minority (including many Arab states and various African and Asian countries) derailed the discussion, arguing that 'people who struggle to liberate themselves from foreign oppression and exploitation have the right to use all methods at their disposal, including force'. The argument could have been raised during the French Revolution those hundreds of years before.

Despite the conceptual difficulties of defining terrorism, this has not prevented the most distinguished scholars in the field seeking to offer their thoughts as to how to scope the definition of this complex term. Laqueur suggests that:

> [t]errorism is the use or the threat of the use of violence, a method of combat, or a strategy to achieve certain targets . . . [I]t aims to induce a state of fear in the victim, that is ruthless and does not conform within humanitarian rules . . . [P]ublicity is an essential factor in the terrorist strategy.[51]

Hoffman suggests that:

> [t]errorism is ineluctably political in aims and motives, violent—or, equally important, threatens violence, designed to have far-reaching psychological repercussions beyond the immediate victim or target, conducted by an organisation with an identifiable chain of command or conspiratorial cell structure

49 Palestinian Public Opinion Poll No 1, Camp David Summit, Chances for Reconciliation and Lasting Peace, Violence and Confrontations, Hierarchies of Priorities, and Domestic Politics (27–29 July 2000).

50 B Jenkins (1980), *The Study of Terrorism: Definitional Problems* (The RAND Paper Series) 1.

51 Walter Laqueur (1987), *The Age of Terrorism* (2nd edn, Boston: Little, Brown) 143.

> (whose members wear no uniform or identifying insignia), and perpetrated by a sub national group or non-state entity.[52]

Sloan captures the conceptual difficulties by noting that 'the definition of terrorism has evolved over time, but its political, religious, and ideological goals have practically never changed'.[53] According to research conducted by Simon in 1994,[54] there are *at least* a mind boggling 212 different definitions of terrorism across the world. It is therefore useful to try to break down the numbers into recurrent themes to see if there are any core words or concepts associated with terrorism. Adopting a sociological approach to the issue, Schmid and Jongman[55] gathered academic and official definitions of terrorism and through careful, thorough, systematic analysis and interpretation of the content of texts (or images) to identify patterns, themes and meanings. They attempted to identify the main components, which emerged in the definitions: violence (83.5%); political goals (65%); causing fear and terror (51%); arbitrariness and indiscriminate targeting (21%); and victimisation of civilians, non-combatants, neutrals or outsiders (17.5%).[56]

Based on their research and arriving at their own definition, Schmid and Jongman suggest that:

> [t]errorism is an anxiety-inspiring method of repeated violent action, employed by (semi-) clandestine individual, group, or state actors, for idiosyncratic, criminal, or political reasons, whereby—in contrast to assassination—the direct targets of violence are not the main targets. The immediate human victims of violence are generally chosen randomly (targets of opportunity) or selectively (representative or symbolic targets) from a target population, and serve as message generators.[57]

1.2.2.3 Distinction: a path to definition?

So far in this chapter, we have explored the rich history which informs the debate as to how to define terrorism, noting that it is a fluid notion and context dependent. In order to understand the difficulties in terms of legislating for terrorist activity online, more particularly the blurred lines between what is and what is not terrorism, distinguishing terrorism from other acts of organised political activity and/or warfare is a useful exercise, not only because it assists with understanding the nuances of terrorism but also its shifting definition in recent years most

52 See Hoffman (n 48) 43.

53 Stephen Sloan (2006), *Terrorism: The Present Threat in Context* (Oxford: Berg Publishers).

54 Jeffrey D Simon (1994), *The Terrorist Trap* (Bloomington: Indiana University Press).

55 Alex Schmid andand Albert Jongman (1988), *Political Terrorism: A New Guide to Actors, Authors, Concepts, Data Bases, Theories, and Literature* (Amsterdam: North Holland, Transaction Books).

56 Bruce L Berg (2009), *Qualitative Research Methods for the Social Sciences* (7th edn, Boston: Allyn & Bacon).

57 See Schmid and Jongman (n 55) 28.

particularly in relation to the so-called Islamic State and/or the Islamic State of Iraq and Levant (ISIL or ISIS).

1.2.2.3.1 GUERRILLA WARFARE OR TERRORISM?

Guerrilla warfare often deploys tactics such as assassination, kidnapping, rape, bombing of public gathering places etc for similar purposes to that of terrorists (e.g. to create a culture of intimidation through fear). Some commentators have drawn out the widely accepted usage of the term 'Guerrilla' tactics as a way of distinguishing such warfare from terrorism, pointing out that:

> [i]t is taken to refer to a numerically larger group of armed individuals, who operate as a military unit, attack enemy military forces, and seize and hold territory (even if only ephemerally during daylight hours), while also exercising some form of sovereignty or control over a defined geographical area and its population. Terrorists, however, do not function in the open as armed units, generally do not attempt to seize or hold territory, deliberately avoid engaging enemy military forces in combat and rarely exercise any direct control or sovereignty either over territory or population.[58]

This definitional distinction highlights the fluidity of the term if one considers how, in 2014, ISIS burst on to the international scene when it seized large swathes of territory in Syria and Iraq. It has become notorious for its brutality, including mass killings, abductions and beheadings – frequently posted on social media. The group has attracted support elsewhere in the Muslim world, and a US-led coalition has vowed to destroy it. In June 2014, the group formally declared the establishment of a 'caliphate' – a state governed in accordance with Islamic law, or Sharia, by God's deputy on Earth, or caliph. It has demanded that Muslims across the world swear allegiance to its leader – Ibrahim Awad Ibrahim al-Badri al-Samarrai, better known as Abu Bakr al-Baghdadi – and migrate to territory under its control.

Mohammed Emwazi (born Muhammad Jassim Abdulkarim Olayan al-Dhafiri on 17 August 1988), a Kuwaiti-British man known more popularly as 'Jihadi John', is thought to be the person seen in several videos produced by ISIS showing the beheadings of a number of captives in 2014 and 2015, which made him one of the world's most wanted terrorists. Again highlighting the difficulty of labelling groups, some organisations defy binary classification. For example, the Islamic Jihad movement has elements of guerrilla warfare, with efforts focused on taking and maintaining control of religiously significant territory, tactical fighting grounds and controlling the local population, through brutal acts and the implementation of strict Sharia law. It also exploits marginalised elements of their host nation's political and military regime and seeks to envelope them into their fold.

58 See Hoffman (n 48).

1.2.2.4 Criminal activity

Guerrilla warfare is, however, but one example. Moving away from politicised motivations which highlight the difficulty in deciding what is and what is not terrorism, it is also useful to consider how terrorism compares to 'ordinary' criminal activity. Both criminals and terrorists have a specific goal when carrying out their acts (e.g. arson, murder etc); however, the motivation underlying the act is very different. Crime can be seen as personal to the criminal, motivated as they are by their own gain or emotions. Save for rare cases involving sexual violence or serial killings, the acts are generally not designed to spread the message of terror or create widespread fear. In contrast, the terrorist's underlying rationale for his actions is to create a widespread change to the political order. This also distinguishes the terrorist from the serial rapist or murderer as the terrorist's goal is again *political*, whilst the criminal's goal is more often intrinsically idiosyncratic, psychosomatic, egocentric and deeply personal.

In 1979, the General Assembly stated that terrorism is a *crime* which should be prosecuted within the legal system, rather than perceiving it as an act of war. Resolution 40/61 condemned 'as criminal, all acts, methods and practices of terrorism wherever and by whoever committed, including those which jeopardize friendly relations among States and their security'. Resolution 34/145, called upon states to work through the exchange of information, and creation of treaties allowing for the 'extradition and prosecution of international terrorists'. In 1987, the General Assembly, called upon states to co-operate 'on a bilateral, regional and multilateral basis, which will contribute to the elimination of acts of international terrorism and their underlying causes and to the prevention and elimination of this criminal scourge'.

The intersection between criminals and terrorists is usefully explored by reference to Hezbollah (Party of God), Iran's terrorist group in Lebanon. The group advocates Shia empowerment on a global scale and has loyalties to the cleric regime of Iran and the Ayatollah Ruholla Khomeini. Hezbollah has committed a number of acts which would amount to terrorist activity, such as the suicide truck bombings of the US embassy in Beirut in April 1983, the US marine barracks in Beirut in October 1983 and the US Embassy annex in Beirut in September 1984. However, it also runs one of the largest, most complex and sophisticated criminal networks in the world, creating a criminal syndicate of drug trafficking through some of Mexico's most well connected global drug smuggling cartels, especially the *Los Zetas* cartel.

According to Daniel Valencia in his work 'The Evolving Dynamics of Terrorism: The Terrorist-Criminal Nexus of Hezbollah and the Los Zetas Drug Cartel', this new partnership has assisted in laundering between US$850 and US$900 million.[59] Once again we are reminded that the definition of terror lies in the perception of

59 C Valencia (2014), 'The Evolving Dynamics of Terrorism: The Terrorist-Criminal Nexus of Hezbollah and the Los Zetas Drug Cartel' INSS 5390 http://academics.utep.edu/Portals/4302/Student%20research/Capstone%20projects/Valencia_Evolving%20Dynamics%20of%20Terrorism.pdf.

the individual and the nature of the cause. ISIS also makes use of dark-web cybercrime and electronic warfare to bolster its success. However, it is labelled as terrorist in the vast majority of media reporting and social media discussion, despite considering itself the 'Islamic Caliphate' (a theological empire) and having 'allegiance' pledged from different radical Islamic groups around the world who 'govern' provinces which ISIS has self-proclaimed.

1.2.2.4.1 NARCO-TERRORISM – SAME PRODUCT, OR JUST A DIFFERENT BRAND?

Mexico's infamous, sustained and affluent narcotics industry has seen violence spiral to unprecedented levels since 2000, taking on a similar level of violence as experienced during the era of the Columbian Pablo Escobar 'The King of Cocaine', before his demise in 1993. Historically, for many decades the Mexican cartels had been growing their turnover, geographical control and profits with an almost gentlemanly respect given to the competition from rival cartels and from Mexican authorities, which was generously reciprocated. Bribery, corruption and government infiltration were the cartels' preferred *modus operandi*, which the authorities generally accepted and participated in with impunity.

Although Mexican drug cartels (or drug-trafficking organisations) have existed for several decades, their influence has increasedsince the demise of the Colombian Cali and Medellín cartels in the 1990s. Mexican drug cartels now dominate the wholesale illicit drug market and, in 2007, controlled 90 per cent of the cocaine entering the United States. By the end of the Felipe Calderón administration between 2006 and 2012, the official death toll of the Mexican drug war was at least 60,000. Further estimates set the death toll above 120,000 killed by 2013, not including 27,000 missing. The non-taxable annual wholesale proceeds of Mexican narcotics production and trafficking are estimated to be in the region of US$13–50 billion.[60] Money and the will to use extreme violence has created fertile conditions to exert unprecedented power.

Many observers may be forgiven for thinking that Al-Qaeda, and subsequently the Islamic State, were the first terror organisations to use social media to create fear, in the brutal and bloodthirsty manner with which we are now all too familiar. However, as we will see in Chapter 2, the reality is that Islamic extremist groups were relatively slow starters and have allegedly copied the concept of filmed executions, violent attacks, threats and subsequent dissemination and displays of dead bodies and body parts on social media platforms. ISIS was inspired and has learned its propaganda tactics through the power of social media from equally brutal and bloodthirsty (but differentially, commercial extremists) groups such as Mexican drug cartels. For many people living in Mexico's drug cartel territories, images and videos of extreme violence on social media have been a part of everyday life since as long ago as 2005; coinciding with the advent of Facebook.

60 *A Regional Strategy for Drug Wars in the Americas* (Center for American Progress, March 2010).

From 2006 to 2012, President Felipe Calderón placed the Mexican military and authorities on a war footing against the cartels. His motivations for starting this war were not clear, but he may have wanted to use the inevitable conflict to gain political legitimacy, credibility and popularity, both at home and with the US Government. This included a media ban on using terms such as 'cartel' or 'capo' (kingpin), in an attempt to take control of the propaganda narrative. He targeted the cartel leaders and initially had some success in making some high-profile arrests and securing prosecutions. However, by 'cutting the head off the various snakes', he created a power vacuum and opportunity for the cartel middle-ranking commanders and assassins to seize control of their organisations or simply create new cartels to fight over the same key territories.

This subsequently evolved into numerous rival cartels, and also provided a catalyst for an escalation and new era of brutal violence. Currently, there are only two large cartels, Sinaloa and Los Zetas, with numerous smaller cartels scrapping for control of the leftovers. Some cartels have a long history and, in general, have previously preferred to settle their disputes peacefully. However, the newer cartels (specifically Los Zetas and La Familia Michoacana) are more violent in their approach.

Both cartels and terrorist groups use violence as propaganda. However, the main difference between these groups is in their objectives and ambitions. The cartels aim to create profits and are not motivated by ideological or political reasons, whereas ISIS desires radical changes in a state and the creation of the caliphate. Allegedly, the cartels' ultimate long-term aim may be to replace the Mexican Government; however, their short-term aim is to eliminate its interference in their drug-related activities. Violence related to drug cartels and aiming to subvert or eliminate an intended target by the threat of the use of force when deemed necessary to protect their narcotics business could be included in the definition of 'narco-terrorism'.

Some experts consider that while considering the extremely high number of victims, combined with the brutal tactics and sophisticated weaponry used by drug cartels, that it is in fact justifiable to refer to these criminal drug gangs in terms of terrorism. There is a magnitude of evidence highlighting that the state of Mexico, and its population, has deteriorated and been subverted to such a level of fear that narco-violence has become a toxic political influence. The use of propaganda to instil fear, mainly through YouTube videos and social media narco-messages could be considered to constitute a warlike propaganda tactic.

It would not, however, be advantageous for the Mexican Government to start referring to any or all of the drug cartels as narco-terrorist groups. The current administration's communication strategy not only tries to rebuff the narco-social media campaign, but also to highlight the efforts of the Mexican armed forces to capture cartel leaders. They consistently deny or ignore the assistance given and received from United States drug enforcement agencies, such as the FBI, CIA and the Drug Enforcement Administration (DEA).

The Mexican Government, of course, wants to demonstrate that it is in control of the country, without external interference and that it is winning the war on drugs. The manner in which the drug-related violence perpetrated by the drug cartels is portrayed may seem irrelevant when compared to the practical difficulties of combating the cartels; however, the media spin to the outside world is very important and has political and economic ramifications. The impact on tourism and business investment would be significant should the cartels be referred to as terrorists, as the required actions taken to fight terrorists as opposed to criminals, in reality and perception, are very different. It needs to take into account both the domestic and the international implications of labelling the cartels as terrorist organisations and deciding which counter-narcotics policies to implement. Considering the close proximity of the cartels to the US border, the Mexican Government could risk US military intervention if the situation is escalated by referring to the cartels as terrorists, which would be both embarrassing as well as economically disastrous. However, even crime can present conceptual difficulties when considering more recent Islamic-related terrorist activities.

Guerrilla warfare and narco-terrorism also demonstrate how, owing to bias or presentation, the definition and perception of terrorism can be affected. Whilst Western commentators[61] have characterised ISIS's crimes as 'unique' and 'no longer practised anywhere else in the civilised world', this is not the case; the distinction between crime and terrorism has become blurred in the social media age, if one considers the recent behaviours of drug cartels. Whilst their goals are different from ISIS, the methodologies employed by the drug cartels, most especially in Central and North America, share similarities to that of ISIS. Like ISIS, in Mexico beheading and dismembering is carried out frequently, with incidents numbering in their hundreds every year,[62] often being displayed in local towns in large piles in a bid to terrorise the public.[63]

Significantly to the rest of the discussion which informs this book, just like ISIS, the cartels use social media to post these graphic images.[64] It is not only ISIS that can hold entire cities captive, terrorising entire populations – El Mencho orchestrated the bloody siege of Guadalajara, the capital of the state of Jalisco. Similar to ISIS, the New Generation Cartel in Mexico seeks society's approval as a 'righteous' and 'nationalistic' group; indeed, Joaquín Guzmán (better known as El Chapo) threatened Donald Trump for his remarks on Mexicans, claiming

61 D Johnson and P Weiss (2014), 'Maher lumps Islam with ISIS, and CNN's Cuomo says Aslan's "primitive" tone proves Maher's point' *Mondoweiss* (6 October) http://mondoweiss.net/2014/10/aslans-primitive-proves.

62 A Lutz (2012), 'Mexican Drug Cartels Have Infiltrated All of These US Cities' *BusinessInsider.com* (16 July) http://www.businessinsider.com/this-graphic-shows-what-mexican-cartels-and-drugs-come-to-your-town-2012-7?IR=T.

63 J Tuckman (2012), 'Mexican drug cartel massacres have method in their brutal madness' *The Telegraph* (14 May) http://www.theguardian.com/world/2012/may/14/mexico-drug-cartel-massacres-analysis.

64 D Hastings (2013), 'Mexican cartels use social media to post gruesome victim photos, sexy selfies' *New York Daily News* (16 December) http://www.nydailynews.com/news/national/mexican-drug-cartel-thugs-post-atrocities-social-media-article-1.1515860.

that he gives people more jobs than the 'pinche' (damned) Mexican Government.[65] For some added El Chapo trivia, he also gave a bizarre interview to film star Sean Penn when on the run from the authorities after escaping from prison.[66]

El Chapo is perceived, by some, as a 'Robin Hood' type figure; 'for the people'. However, the two narco-terrorist kingpins, El Chapo and El Mencho, are arguably just as dangerous as Ayman Zawahiri of Al-Qaeda and Al-Baghdadi of ISIS. The cartels employ military equipment and the turf warfare, torture and killings are all very similar to those techniques employed by terror groups such as Al-Nusra, Al-Qaeda and ISIS. Like ISIS, which has sought to suppress all other smaller terror networks, in the spring of 2011, the Jalisco New Generation Cartel declared war on all other Mexican cartels, with the intention of taking control of the city of Guadalajara. Jalisco blocked roads, took down a military helicopter and set ATMs and banks on fire.

Some may attempt to draw a distinction between the cartels and ISIS in that ISIS does not deal in criminal activity for commercial gain, and therefore the cartels more squarely fit into 'criminal activity' rather than 'terrorist activity'. However, ISIS, just like the cartel, is profiting from a whole 'portfolio' of illegal activities, including human trafficking and slavery, pirating information technology and also major drug trafficking.[67] Given that, as noted above, El Chapo is perceived by some as a 'Robin Hood' type figure and is 'for the people', where is the distinction to be drawn between criminal activity and political action? Indeed, the cartels may be seen as akin to the French revolutionaries. Once again we are reminded that it is a matter of personal perception, not government labelling. They offer weapons, salaries, jobs for locals and brotherhood. Whilst it is acknowledged that there is a distinction to be drawn in that recruits to the cartels are predominantly attracted by money and power, rather than driven by ideological motivations, at least two of the cartels – La Familia Michoacana and its successor, the Knights Templar – are based on a core Christian religion.

1.2.3 Towards a framework

Although it is important to acknowledge the conceptual difficulties in defining terror, Hoffman has sought to set out themes which are common to terrorism, namely:

65 N Allen (2015), 'El Chapo Guzman "vows" to make Donald Trump swallow his words' *The Telegraph* (13 July) http://www.telegraph.co.uk/news/worldnews/centralamericaandthecaribbean/mexico/11736854/El-Chapo-Guzman-vows-to-make-Donald-Trump-swallow-his-words.html.

66 B Lee (2016), 'Sean Penn's El Chapo interview "horribly misguided" says Cartel author' *The Telegraph* (19 January) http://www.theguardian.com/film/2016/jan/19/don-winslow-cartel-author-calls-sean-penn-el-chapo-interview-horribly-misguided.

67 'Narco-Terror Expert: ISIS Moving into the Meth Business' *Fox News* (7 October 2014) http://insider.foxnews.com/2014/10/07/narco-terror-expert-isis-moving-meth-business.

- it is intrinsically bound up in political aims and motives
- there is often an element of violence or threats of violence
- the acts are designed to have far-reaching psychological repercussions beyond the immediate victim or target
- terrorism is usually allied to a particular group or cause and
- terrorism is perpetrated by a sub-national group or non-state entity.[68]

Hoffman also suggests that 'terrorist activities are conducted by an organisation with an identifiable chain of command or conspiratorial cell structure (whose members wear no uniform or identifying insignia)'. However, organisations such as ISIS have adopted flags, arguably wear a uniform and also have official Twitter accounts which bear a logo.[69] Can this element of the definition therefore survive the social media age? Or does it simply highlight again the difficulty in categorising terrorism following the advent of social media, in an age where messages are understood through imagery and users who would not traditionally be understood as terrorists, most particularly those who see themselves as part of the 'online jihad' associate themselves with identifying insignia, perhaps by following a twitter account or linking a post?

1.2.4 Legal definitions

1.2.4.1 Introduction

Following on from the socio-political definitional debate, there is also the question as to how terrorism is defined by law. The case of Hassam Yaccoub, a dual Swedish–Lebanese citizen and Hezbollah operative who was sentenced to four years in prison serves as a useful example of the difficulties of deciding where criminality ends and terrorist activity begins. Hassam Yaccoub was convicted by the Cyprus criminal courts[70] for his participation in an organised crime group and the preparation of criminal operations. The judiciary panel declared that:

> It has been proven that Hezbollah is an organization that operates under complete secrecy . . . There is no doubt that this group has multiple members and proceeds with various activities, including military training of its members. Therefore, the court rules that Hezbollah acts as a criminal organisation.[71]

68 See Hoffman (n 48) 40.

69 https://twitter.com/isis_med (note, however, that this account has now been suspended).

70 N Kulish (2013), 'Hezbollah Courier Found Guilty in Plot to Attack Israeli Tourists in Cyprus' *New York Times* (21 March) http://www.nytimes.com/2013/03/22/world/middleeast/hezbollah-courier-guilty-of-role-in-cyprus-terror-plot.html?_r=0.

71 Matthew Levitt (2012), 'Hizbullah narco-terrorism: a growing cross-border threat' (Op-Ed, Washington Institute, Washington, D.C.).

Between 1934 and 1937 a major international definitional step was taken when the League of Nations recognised terrorism as an illegal act and consequently punishable. The draft was prepared following the assassination of King Alexander of Yugoslavia and French minister Louis Barthou.[72] After the assassination, the suspects made their way to Italy and the French Government requested their extradition. However, the treaty of 1870, under which this request was made, excluded political crimes. The Italian court in Turin refused to extradite the individuals as their acts had been politically motivated. During the intervening three years, an expert committee prepared a draft convention for the prevention and punishment of terrorism, which stated that terrorist acts are 'all criminal acts directed against a State and intended or calculated to create a state of terror in the minds of particular persons or a group of persons or the general public'.[73]

1.2.4.2 International instruments

1.2.4.2.1 RUGGIE PRINCIPLES AND MULTILATERALISM

The United Nations Guiding Principles on Business and Human Rights (UNGPs) are a global standard for preventing and addressing the risk of adverse impacts on human rights linked to business activity. On 16 June 2011, the United Nations Human Rights Council unanimously endorsed the Guiding Principles for Business and Human Rights, making the framework the first corporate human rights responsibility initiative to be endorsed by the United Nations.[74] The UNGPs encompass three pillars outlining how states and businesses should implement the framework. First, states should protect human rights; secondly, there should be corporate responsibility to respect human rights and, finally, there should be a remedy for victims of business-related abuses.

The UNGP are informally known as the 'Ruggie Principles' or the 'Ruggie Framework' owing to their authorship by John Ruggie, who conceived them and led the process for their consultation and implementation. Whilst the Ruggie Principles have received wide support from states, civil society organisations and even the private sector,[75] there are difficulties with the multilateral approach to human rights, conceptualised by Ruggie as 'an institutional form that co-ordinates relationships amongst three or more states on the basis of generalised conduct for a class of action, without regard to particularistic interests or the strategic

72 B Saul (2006), 'The legal response of the League of Nations to terrorism' 4 *Journal of International Criminal Justice* 78, 81.

73 League of Nations (1991), *International Terrorism. Two League of Nations Conventions, 1934–1937* (compiled by Martin David Dubin, Millwood, NY: Fraus Microform) 18 fiches.

74 S Deva (2012), 'Guiding Principles on Business and Human Rights: Implications for Companies' 9(2) *European Company Law* 101.

75 J Ruggie (2011), 'United Nations Guiding Principles on Business and Human Rights' https://business-humanrights.org/en/un-guiding-principles.

exigencies that may exist in any specific occurrence'.[76] However, as we have seen, the notion of privacy and conceptualisation of terrorism pull states into their 'particularistic interests' and away from varying states shared objectives. Indeed, although a broadly stated norm is emerging against terrorist activity, the ongoing failure to agree a universal definition of terrorism constrains that process. Whilst principles of conduct may not be able to be specified at a general level, there is still scope to consider the specific types of responses amongst officials engaged with counter-terrorist activity. In this way, although the problem of terrorism cannot be addressed in its entirety, experts can nonetheless share their expertise on a particular issue.

The law is often responsive and arguably shaped by particular events. According to research conducted by Achayra,[77] prior to 9/11 there was a total of 13 international conventions related to terrorism in particular contexts,[78] namely: nuclear material,[79] suppression of the financing of terrorism,[80] suppression of terrorist bombings,[81] continental shelf safety,[82] taking of hostages,[83] safety of civil aviation,[84] maritime issues,[85] internationally protected persons,[86] plastic explosives,[87] suppression of unlawful seizure of aircraft,[88] offences committed on-board aircraft[89] and

76 J G Ruggie (1993), 'Multilateralism: The Anatomy of an Institution' in J G Ruggie (ed), *Multilateralism Matters* (Columbia University Press) 3, 11.

77 Upendra D Achayra (2009), 'War on Terror or Terror Wars: The Problem in Defining Terrorism' 37(4) *Denver Journal of International Law and Policy* 658.

78 M Bassiouni (1937), *International Terrorism: Multilateral Conventions 1937–2001* (Hotei Publishing 2001); see also M Bassiouni (2002), 'Legal Control of International Terrorism: A Policy-oriented Assessment' 43 *Harvard International Law Journal* 83, 91.

79 See Convention on the Physical Protection of Nuclear Material (opened for signature 3 March 1980), TIAS No. 11080, 1456 UNTS 101.

80 See International Convention for the Suppression of the Financing of Terrorism (9 December 1999), UN Doc A/RES/54/109; 39 ILM 270 (2000); TIAS No. 13075.

81 See International Convention for the Suppression of Terrorist Bombings (15 December 1997), UN Doc A/RES/52/164; 37 ILM 249 (1998); 2149 UNTS 284.

82 Protocol for the Suppression of Unlawful Acts Against the Safety of Fixed Platforms Located on the Continental Shelf (10 March 1988), UNTS 1678, I-29004.

83 See International Convention Against the Taking of Hostages (17 December 1979), TIAS No 11081, 1316 UNTS 205.

84 See Convention for the Suppression of Unlawful Acts Against the Safety of Civil Aviation (23 September 1971), 24 UST 546565, 974 UNTS 177.

85 See Convention for the Suppression of Unlawful Acts Against the Safety of Maritime Navigation (10 March 1988), 27 ILM 668 (1988); 1678 UNTS 221.

86 See Convention on the Prevention and Punishment of Crimes Against Internationally Protected Persons, Including Diplomatic Agents (14 December 1973), 28 UST 1975, 1035 UNTS 167; see also Convention on the Safety of United Nations and Associated Personnel (9 December 1994), GA Res 49/59, UN GAOR, 49th Session, Supp. No. 49, at 299, UN Doc A/49/49 (1994).

87 See Convention on the Marking of Plastic Explosives for the Purpose of Detection (1 March 1991), ICAO Doc S/22393, 30 ILM 721 (1991), [2007] ATS 259.

88 See Convention for the Suppression of Unlawful Seizure of Aircraft (16 December 1970), 22 UST 1641, 860 UNTS 105.

89 See Convention on Offences and Certain Other Acts Committed on Board Aircraft (14 September 1963), 20 UST 2941, 704 UNTS 219.

unlawful acts of violence at airports.[90] Indeed, the 1963 Tokyo Convention and the 1970 Hague Convention were adopted in response to air piracy by the Palestinians.[91]

Such conventions require the states party to the convention to take specified measures to prevent the commission of terrorist acts, such as criminalising certain conduct, matters of jurisdiction (including the principle of *aut dedere aut judicare* or 'extradite or prosecute', which, in the era of social media and the fluidity of the internet, is a particularly interesting concept) and to provide and create a framework to facilitate a legal basis for cooperation on legal assistance. In 2001, the Security Council adopted Resolution 1373, which obliges member states to take a number of measures to prevent terrorist activities and to criminalise various actions, calling on them to take measures that assist and promote cooperation.

1.2.4.2.2 UNITED NATIONS GENERAL ASSEMBLY GLOBAL COUNTER-TERRORISM STRATEGY

In 2004, the High-level Panel on Threats, Challenges and Change reported that recruitment by terrorist groups is aided by grievances borne of poverty, foreign occupation and the absence of human rights and democracy.[92] International state actors have committed, as a community, to measures to counter terrorism through the adoption of the United Nations global Counter-terrorism strategy by the General Assembly in its resolution 60/288. To combat the conditions conducive to the growth of terrorism, such as a lack of rule of law and violations of human rights. Recognising the interplay with other important international instruments and human rights considerations, the measures taken must be compliant with international legal standards relating to human rights and humanitarian law.

1.2.4.2.3 THE WORLD SUMMIT OUTCOME

In 2005, the World Summit Outcome was adopted by the General Assembly. It considered how to respect human rights whilst countering terrorism, concluding that international cooperative standards would need to be conducted in conformity with international standards such as the Charter of the United Nations. The link with human rights was also echoed by the Security Council in the declaration set out in its Resolution 1456 (2003), which stated that 'states must ensure that any measure taken to combat terrorism comply with all their obligations under

90 See Protocol for the Suppression of Unlawful Acts of Violence at Airports Serving International Civil Aviation, Supplementary to the Montreal Convention (24 February 1988), UN Treaty Series 1990 http://www.refworld.org/docid/3ddcac634.html.

91 Ikechi Mgbeoji (2005) 'The Bearded Bandit, the Outlaw Cop, and the Naked Emperor: Towards a North-South (De)construction of the Texts and Contexts of International Law's (Dis)engagement with Terrorism' 43 *Osgoode Hall Law Journal* 105, 110.

92 *A more secure world: Our shared responsibility*, Report of the High-level Panel on Threats, Challenges and Change (United Nations Department of Public Information 2004) para [21].

international law, and should adopt such measures in accordance with international law, in particular international human rights, refugee, and humanitarian law'.

This position was again affirmed in 2005 in the Security Council Resolution 1624 and by the United Nations Secretary-General in his 2006 report entitled Uniting against terrorism: recommendations for a global counter-terrorism strategy.[93] The United Nations' Secretary-General described human rights as essential to the fulfilment of all aspects of a counter-terrorism strategy and emphasised that effective counter-terrorism measures and the protection of human rights were not conflicting goals, but complementary and mutually reinforcing ones. Universal and regional treaty-based bodies have, likewise, frequently observed that the lawfulness of counter-terrorism measures depends on their conformity with international human rights law.[94]

As noted in this chapter, a predisposition to terrorism is often bred in countries where there is a lack of rule of law, or a poor human rights record. Respect for and the promotion of human rights terrorism is often a way to promote the worth of civil society through respect for the core principles that are to be protected when adopting counter-terrorist measures. For example, in the context of the International Convention for the Suppression of the Financing of Terrorism, Article 15 states that states can refuse extradition or legal assistance to another state if there are substantial grounds for believing that the requesting state intends to prosecute or punish a person on prohibited grounds of discrimination; Article 17 requires the 'fair treatment' of any person taken into custody and Article 21 makes it clear that the Convention does not affect the other rights, obligations and responsibilities of states (such as respect for human rights).

Whilst these frameworks can be applied to bombings and shootings, as we will explore in Chapter 2 with regard to social media, the task is not nearly so easy, engaging more fluid principles of human rights such as freedom of expression and privacy. In 2005 a report submitted by member states to the United Nations Counter-terrorism Committee on the implementation of UNSC Resolution 1624 (which concerned threats to international peace and security),[95] demonstrated considerable diversity in the way in which incitement to terrorism is defined and prohibited in national legislation. In relation to social media, the report noted that national responses may include or exclude broader acts such as justifying or glorifying terrorist acts and that Tweets, Facebook statuses and posts that glorify terrorist acts may fall within a category justifying prosecution.

93 UN General Assembly (2006), 'Uniting against terrorism: recommendations for a global counter-terrorism strategy: report of the Secretary-General' (27 April), A/60/825 http://www.refworld.org/docid/4786248b7.html.

94 See e.g. Annual Report of the Inter-American Commission on Human Rights 1990–1991, ch V, s II and *Digest of jurisprudence*.

95 United Nations Security Council Resolution 1624: Threats to international peace and security (Security Council Summit 2005), S/RES/1624 (14 September).

1.2.4.3 National legislation

1.2.4.3.1 TERRORISM ACT 2000

There are a number of definitions of terrorism in various sovereign state laws. However, as this volume had a decidedly Anglo-slant, the example used in this chapter of the adaptability of the definition of terrorism is the UK Terrorism Act 2000, which defines terrorism as follows:

> The use or threat of action designed to influence the government or an international governmental organisation or to intimidate the public, or a section of the public; made for the purposes of advancing a political, religious, racial or ideological cause; and it involves or causes: (1) serious violence against a person; (2) serious damage to a property; (3) a threat to a person's life; (4) a serious risk to the health and safety of the public; or (5) serious interference with or disruption to an electronic system.

In June 2015, David Anderson QC, the UK's Independent Reviewer of Terrorism Legislation, published his annual report entitled *A Question of Trust*, a report of the investigatory powers review on the operation of the UK terrorism legislation.[96] The independent reviewer suggests that it is 'time Parliament reviewed the definition of terrorism, to avoid the potential for abuse and to cement public support for special powers that are unfortunately likely to be needed for the foreseeable future'. The report, which totals 379 pages, covers a wide range of issues, including the worldwide reach of UK counter-terrorism law, and its treatment of foreign fighters in Syria[97] and focuses on the issue of the definition of terrorism.

The report notes that the UK has some of the most extensive anti-terrorism laws in the Western world, which give ministers, prosecutors and the police the powers they need to combat violence perpetrated by Al-Qaeda inspired terrorists, right-wing extremists and dissident groups in Northern Ireland. They also apply extra-territorially, enabling prosecutions to be brought for activities in other countries, including Syria and Iraq. The report states that, if these powers are to command public consent, it is important that they should be confined to their proper purpose. Recent years have seen a degree of 'creep' that Parliament could reverse, without diminishing in any way, the utility of anti-terrorism law.

Three examples of this over-breadth are given in the report. First, actions aimed at influencing the government,[98] as according to section 1(1)(b) of the Terrorism Act 2000, the politically-motivated publication of material that is thought to endanger life or to create a serious risk to the health or safety of the public is a terrorist act done for the purposes of *influencing the government*. In other Commonwealth and European countries, and under the main international

96 David Anderson QC (2015), 'A Question of Trust: Report of the Investigatory Powers Review' by David Anderson QC Independent Reviewer of Terrorism Legislation paras 6.15–6.19, 7.7–7.15.

97 Ibid paras 10.60–10.70.

98 Ibid paras 4.11–4.23, 10.35–10.43.

treaties governing the matter, the bar is set higher: there must be an intention to *coerce* or *intimidate*. This means that political journalists and bloggers are subject to the full range of anti-terrorism powers if they threaten to publish, prepare to publish or publish something that the authorities think may be dangerous to life, to public health or public safety. This means that this standard applies, even if the intention was to spread fear or to intimidate – it is enough that their work is designed to influence the government or an international organisation. Those who employ or support them, or who encourage others to do the same, could also qualify as terrorists.

As is clear from case law in this area[99] such as the celebrated judgement of *Entick v Carrington*,[100] which made it clear that it is those who are accountable to the electorate that must decide what is a risk to people's ways of life, making it a political rather than a legal question, that the protection of journalistic expression is an important sub-class of the law's more general care for free speech. However, in the 2014 case of *R (Miranda)*,[101] it was held that it was legitimate to use terrorism laws for that purpose. The High Court made it clear that, under the current law, political journalism aimed at influencing the government can be an act of terrorism when it endangers life or creates a serious risk to health or safety.

The report notes that the definition is broad enough to include a campaigner who voices a religious objection to vaccination. If this purpose is to influence the government, and if his words are judged capable of creating a serious risk to public health, then voicing support could also be a terrorist crime. Referring to the decision of the Supreme Court in October 2013 in *R v Gul*,[102] the independent reviewer noted that the court described these previous discussions of the definition of terrorism as 'very instructive' and suggested that his recommendations for reducing the width of the statutory definition of terrorism would 'merit serious consideration'.[103] The report suggests that UK law should come into line with that of other countries and with the various international treaties in this area. Terrorism should be redefined so that it applies only if there is intent to coerce, compel or intimidate a government or a section of the public. Lord Carlile QC (David Anderson's predecessor as independent reviewer) first recommended this in 2007; however, the recommendation was not acted upon by the then home secretary, John Reid. Parliament should revisit the issue in the light of recent developments.

Secondly, the report highlights the issues of hate crimes,[104] as has been noted throughout this chapter, the definitional difficulties of placing terrorism within the existing legal landscape or distinguishing it from other criminal behaviour is a

99 *R v The Central Criminal Court, ex parte The Guardian, The Observer and Bright* [2001] 1 WLR 662.

100 *Entick v Carrington* [1765] EWHC KB J98.

101 *R (Miranda) v SSHD and MPC* [2014] EWHC 255 (Admin).

102 *R v Gul* [2013] UKSC 64, [2013] 3 WLR 1207; 'A Question of Trust: Report of the Investigatory Powers Review' by David Anderson QC Independent Reviewer of Terrorism Legislation, June 2015. (n 96) 4.9–4.10.

103 *R v Gul* [2013] UKSC 64, [2013] 3 WLR 1207 at [67].

104 'A Question of Trust: Report of the Investigatory Powers Review' by David Anderson QC Independent Reviewer of Terrorism Legislation, June 2015. (n 96) paras 6.15–6.19, 7.7–7.15.

difficult task, given the subjectivity of what terrorism is. The report draws out that, whilst the criminality of certain hate crimes is obvious (and serious), if they intend harm only to their immediate victims, no purpose is served by characterising them as terrorists. The report notes that: 'the law makes a terrorist of the boy who threatens to shoot his teacher on a fascist website, and of the racist who throws a pipe bomb at his neighbour's wall'.[105]

Thirdly, the report described the difficulties created through the '*penumbra* of terrorism'. As noted throughout this chapter, terrorism is a very broad concept and is highly subjective. In the UK there are a large number of terrorist crimes, including preparatory and ancillary offences. The report suggests that there is a good case for limiting these powerful executive measures, without extending their reach still further by recourse to vague concepts such as 'terrorism-related activity'. In practice, these measures appear to be used only when a crime is believed to have been committed. To extend them further is unnecessary.

1.2.4.4 The American context

Perhaps recognising the difficulties in arising at a single definition of terrorism is to an extent reflected in the fact that the United States has not adopted a single definition of terrorism as a matter of government policy, instead relying on definitions that are developed from time to time by government agencies:

- *The Department of Defence*: 'the unlawful use of, or threatened use, of force or violence against individuals or property to coerce and intimidate governments or societies, often to achieve political, religious, or ideological objectives'.[106]
- *US Code*: illegal violence that attempts to: 'intimidate or coerce a civilian population; . . . influence the policy of a government by intimidation or coercion; or . . . affect the conduct of a government by assassination or kidnapping'.[107]
- *Federal Bureau of Investigation*: 'the unlawful use of force or violence against persons or property to intimidate or coerce a Government, the civilian population, or any segment thereof, in furtherance of political or social objectives'.[108]
- *State Department*: 'premeditated, politically motivated violence perpetrated against non-combatant targets by subnational groups or clandestine agents, usually intended to influence an audience'.[109]

105 Ibid para 10.4.

106 US Departments of the Army and the Air Force (1990) *Military Operations in Low Intensity Conflict*, Field Manual 100-20/Air Force Pamphlet 3-20 (Washington, DC: Headquarters, Departments of the Army and the Air Force) para 3.1.

107 18 USC 3077.

108 Terrorist Research and Analytical Center, National Security Division, Federal Bureau of Investigation (1996) *Terrorism in the United States 1995* (Washington, DC: US Department of Justice) ii.

109 Office of the Coordinator for Counterterrorism (1997) *Patterns of Global Terrorism 1996* (US Department of State Publication 10433 Washington, DC: State Department) vi.

1.2.4.5 Definitions adopted in other jurisdictions

Although this book will not put a focus on the global approach to the regulation of terrorist content posted on social media, it is useful at least to have in mind some of the definitions adopted in other jurisdictions that attempt to harness the meaning of terrorism. The Arab Convention for the Suppression of Terrorism defines terrorism as:

> [a]ny act or threat of violence, whatever its motives or purposes, that occurs in the advancement of an individual or collective criminal agenda and seeking to sow panic among people, causing fear by harming them, or placing their lives, liberty or security in danger, or seeking to cause damage to the environment or to public or private installations or property or to occupying or seizing them, or seeking to jeopardize a national resources.

In 2003, the Supreme Court of India described terrorist acts as the 'peacetime equivalents of war crimes'.[110] In 2014, demonstrating that criticism for overly broad definitions is not peculiar to the UK, Amnesty International and Human Rights Watch criticised[111] a Saudi Arabia terrorism law taking effect on 1 February 2014, which defined it as:

> any act carried out by an offender in furtherance of an individual or collective project, directly or indirectly, intended to disturb the public order of the state, or to shake the security of society, or the stability of the state, or to expose its national unity to danger, or to suspend the basic law of governance or some of its articles, or to insult the reputation of the state or its position, or to inflict damage upon one of its public utilities or its natural resources, or to attempt to force a governmental authority to carry out or prevent it from carrying out an action, or to threaten to carry out acts that lead to the named purposes or incite [these acts].[112]

1.2.5 What is not terrorism?

1.2.5.1 Introduction

As we have seen so far in this chapter, terrorism is highly subjective and politically charged. An understanding of the *sources* of terrorism is therefore important in order to consider what behaviours underlie terrorist acts.

110 Paul Reynolds, quoting David Hannay, former UK ambassador (14 September 2005) 'UN staggers on road to reform' *BBC News*.

111 Joe Stork (2014), 'Saudi Arabia: Terrorism Law Tramples on Rights' *Human Rights Watch* (6 February).

112 Amnesty International (3 February 2014) 'Saudi Arabia: New terrorism law is latest tool to crush peaceful expression' http://www.amnestyusa.org/news/news-item/saudi-arabia-new-terrorism-law-is-latest-tool-to-crush-peaceful-expression.

Underling terrorist activity is some types of deeply held belief system, which are often extreme. However, holding an extreme belief does not necessarily mean that the individual holding such belief is, in fact, a terrorist. Extreme behaviours can be manifested in many different ways. In order to understand the difficulty in terms of mapping out the legal regulation of social media postings, the general characteristics of the extremist foundations of terrorism must be mapped out. As will be seen throughout the following chapters it may receive its outlet through such extreme expressions of belief, finding ground in participation in debates or publications.

1.2.5.2 Extremism

Extremism, which is often seen as the precursor to terrorism, is an overarching belief system that is used by terrorists to justify their violent behaviour. Extremism is broadly defined as 'radical in opinion, especially in political matters; ultra; advanced'[113] and is characterised as intolerance toward all views other than one's own.[114] It is important to note that extremism is characterised by *what* a person's beliefs are; however, no matter how offensive or reprehensible those thoughts are, they are not by themselves acts of terrorism. It is usually understood that the act only becomes terrorist if those beliefs are violently acted on and thereby those extremist acts become labelled as acts of terrorism.

In the context of social media, the distinction can be a difficult one to draw, especially since we have noted in this chapter that many individuals now feel that they have been called to offer their help to their causes through online jihads. To understand the nature of extremist speech it is useful to consider the example of the American Knights of the Ku Klux Klan, an activist faction of the KKK that operated mostly in the Midwest and East during the 1990s. The offshoot expressed beliefs regarding racial supremacy at a series of rallies at government sites, often county courthouses. They were known for their vitriolic rhetoric. The following remarks were reportedly taken from a speech delivered in March 1998 by the Imperial Wizard at a rally held at the county courthouse in Butler, Pennsylvania, near Pittsburgh:

> Take a stand . . . Join the Klan, stick up for your rights . . . Only God has the right to create a race—not no black and white, not no nigger, not no Jew . . . Yes, I will use the word nigger, because it is not illegal . . . We are sick and tired of the government taking your money, and giving food and jobs to the niggers when the white race has to go without! Wake up America.[115]

113 *Webster's New Twentieth-Century Dictionary of the English Language* (Unabridged 2nd edn New York: Publishers Guild, 1966).

114 Roger Scruton (1982), *A Dictionary of Political Thought* (New York: Hill & Wang) 164.

115 Remarks of Jeff Berry, Imperial Wizard of the American Knights of the Ku Klux Klan, Butler, Pennsylvania (March 1998), quoted in Worth H Weller and Brad Thompson (1998), *Under the Hood: Unmasking the Modern Ku Klux Klan* (North Manchester, In: DeWitt Books) 40–41.

This language is intentionally racist, hateful and inflammatory, and yet it falls short of advocating violence or revolution.

1.2.5.3 Hate crime

As noted in *A Question of Trust*, much has also been made of as to where to draw the line between the legalistic concept of hate crime and terrorism as it is given a variety of labels and definitions. This has led to the acts perpetrated sometimes being labelled as crimes but could also fit into the definition of acts of terrorism.

In the UK, 'hate crime' has become generally classified as meaning[116] any crimes that are targeted at a person because of hostility or prejudice towards that person's:

- disability
- race or ethnicity
- religion or belief
- sexual orientation
- transgender identity.

In the USA, a similar classification is followed and the laws focus on a certain type of motive for the act, i.e. behaviour that is directed against protected classes of people (as defined in the laws) *because of* their membership in these protected classes. The question as to whether a hate crime amounts to a terrorist act has largely been determined as to whether there is an underlying political agenda. In this regard, not all acts of terrorism are hate crimes, and not all hate crimes are acts of terrorism. As terrorist acts often symbolise the causes, belief systems and lifestyles which they oppose, the distinction can be a fine one to draw, especially when acts of political violence are directed at a particular group (e.g. on the grounds of religious belief) that could fit the definitions of both hate crimes and terrorism, making the distinction unclear.

By way of example, after German reunification, 'street renegades [demanded] a new *Lebensraum* of a purified Germany whose national essence and coherence will not be weakened and "contaminated" by ethnic and racial minorities'.[117] Their targeted enemies were Turkish, Slavic and southern European foreigners and 'guest workers'. In relation to social media, this distinction is important if one considers, for instance, 'lone wolf' attacks by racially motivated individuals, most especially their online postings, which they make by way of support of the online jihad.

116 https://www.gov.uk/report-hate-crime.

117 Robert J Kelly and Jess Maghan (1998), *Hate Crime: The Global Politics of Polarization* (Carbondale: Southern Illinois University Press) 6, quoted from Benedict Anderson (1983), *Imagined Communities: Reflections on the Origin and Spread of Nationalism* (London: New Left).

1.3 Opening thoughts

As noted at the start of this chapter, defining terrorism can be an exercise in semantics and context, often driven by one's own perspectives, experiences and worldview. Perspective is a central consideration in defining *terrorism* and many factors will, therefore, shape perspectives on terror as experienced by a variety of stakeholders, such as the terrorists themselves, sympathisers, victims, the general public, states, legislators, the judiciary, the media and platform providers and analysts, as viewed through the lens of culture, political views, collective history, religion, gender, age, race, individual experience, group identity and national identity. Therefore, the perception of 'terrorist material' is intimately entwined with the participant's own experiences.

Arguably, the personalisation of media through social media concentrates this process, triggering a range of emotional responses; be it joy, sympathy, rage, sorrow, solidarity or anger. The community can also label, decry, support and/or validate acts through the use of 'likes', dislikes, re-tweets, hashtags or emoticons, using such symbols as a way to respond to particular acts, thereby assigning significance to the initial posting. For example, posts on Facebook and Flickr that document the Syrian conflict have been used as images and eulogies for murdered Jihadis. These powerful eulogies present the fighters as martyrs, thus immortalising them and creating a strong appeal to Muslims who feel marginalised in their respective societies. It has been argued that new technologies have simply allowed the dissemination of terrorist messages to reach a *'broader audience with a more concise message'*,[118] but arguably the game changer is the concentration of the message, the power and speed of dissemination of imagery. It is a useful servant but a cruel mistress.

As will be seen in this book, there has been a backlash from the social media community highlighting the role of the many stakeholders who participate in the social media cattle-pen of ideas. The oft cited aphorism that 'one man's terrorist is another's freedom fighter' in the era of social media could easily be adapted to state that someone's 'freedom fighter' is also likely to be someone's 'Facebook friend'.

This chapter began with a quote from Mitchell Kapor, who suggested that getting information from the internet was like taking a drink form a fire hydrant. In 1964, when Philip Larkin wrote his poem *Water*,[119] he posited that if he were to construct a religion he would make use of water. The delivery of his religious liturgy would employ the devout drenching of water over his congregation. Terrorism online is drenching users in information, regardless of social views in a form of digital water whose molecules are composed of all of the variations

118 Jessica Baran (2008), 'Terrorism and the Mass Media after Al Qaeda: A Change of Course?' 3(1) *The Peace and Conflict Review* 1 http://www.review.upeace.org/index.cfm?opcion=0&ejemplar=7&entrada=63.

119 Philip Larkin (1964) *The Whitsun Weddings* (London, Faber & Faber Ltd, 1964).

identified above, such as politics, religion, history, culture etc, which form who we are and how we view the world.

Aptly, Larkin finished his poem by declaring he would hold a glass of water to the East to look at how it captured the light and where such light would 'congregate endlessly'. Such are the dialogues explored in this volume, continuously offering new issues and perspectives as we turn the crystal receptacle in our hands (how you read this will depend on the unique way in which you turn the glass in your hand, as well as the glass I gave you to view it through).

So, dear reader, let us dive into cool waters contained in the crystal receptacle and explore . . .

2 Terrorism's love affair with social media

> There is always a point at which the terrorist ceases to manipulate the media gestalt. A point at which the violence may well escalate, but beyond which the terrorist has become symptomatic of the media gestalt itself. Terrorism as we ordinarily understand it is innately media-related.[1]
>
> William Gibson, Official blog (31 October 2004)

Or in other words . . .

> Fluffy velvety, and sweet. If you want to treat yourself then indulge in this full fat delight all for less than 30 pence . . . Snickers, Kit Kat, Bounty, Twix, Kinder Surprise, Cadburys – yes, yes we have it all.
>
> Abu Rumaysah al-Britani, ISIS fighter and part-time ISIS travel guide author

Terrorism is now squarely in the eye of the beholder. Nowhere is this more clearly exemplified than online. In 2002, Al-Qaeda leader Osama bin Laden remarked in correspondence to Al-Qaeda leaders: 'it is obvious that the media war in this century is one of the strongest methods; in fact, its ratio may reach 90% of the total preparation for battles',[2] as well as declaring the jihadi movement is 'in a race for the hearts and minds of our Umma'.[3]

Osama bin Laden and his highly intelligent successors and counterparts in AQI, ISIS and the Taliban have all astutely recognised how social media can skew the asymmetry of power and influence, amplify the perception of suspicion and fear to provoke reaction, and directly reach a far more receptive audience than conventional media. They have used social media to create a cult-like status for their own image as a leader. This has been and will continue to be important in

1 William Gibson, Official blog (31 October 2004).

2 Letter to Mullah Mohammed 'Omar from Usama bin Laden' (5 June 2002), Located in USMA's Combating Terrorism Centre's online Harmony Database Document: http://www.ctc.usma.edu/wp-content/uploads/2010/08/AFGP-2002-600321-Trans.pdf.

3 Letter from al-Zawahiri to Zarqawi (9 July 2005) http://www.dni.gov/letter_in_english.pdf.

DOI: 10.4324/9781315668680-2

many forms of terrorism. Often the social media presence is enhanced and amplified by the myth or actions surrounding a charismatic leader.

This is a similar phenomenon to the cult of celebrity in the West. The modern-day propaganda masterminds target their already biased social media followers, relying on their predisposition to believe and react, at face value, to their subtle mixture of imagery, misinformation and factual rhetoric. The success of committing acts of terrorism is not measured by the number of people killed, but by the amount of attention the act receives and the level of outrage or joyous reaction from the audience, depending of course on their loyalties, religion and political persuasions. The world is becoming increasingly politicised as a direct result of social media and therefore the numbers of individuals who are potentially willing to commit acts of violence to achieve their political ambitions is also likely to increase in the coming decades.

Social media lends itself well to promotion of terrorist causes, as terrorism has generally been more successful in achieving strategic or long-range goals. Terrorist actions are mainly publicity for the terrorist group and the cause, as an intermediate step in realising the cause itself. Many tactical terrorist incidents, whilst they fail in achieving their immediate objectives are highly successful in getting full publicity for the group, including extensive media explanation of their cause. Indeed, Al-Qaeda and its affiliates have moved their online presence to YouTube, Twitter, Facebook, Instagram and other social media outlets.

By way of example of the extensive use of social media by the group, in August 2013 Abu Mohammed al-Golani, the head of an Al-Qaeda branch operating in Syria called al-Nusra Front, used Facebook and Twitter to vow unrestrained rocket attacks on Alawite communities, alongside attacks on President Bashar Assad's government in revenge for an alleged chemical strike, as well as on a militant website that often broadcasts the views of Al-Qaeda and similar extremist groups. Al-Quaeda is not, however, unique in its adoption of these new methods of communication. Al-Nusra Front has its own Facebook page,[4] which contains press releases, photographs and videos from the combat in Syria; eulogies for the organisation's *shaheeds* (martyrs for Islam) and regular updates on how the fighting is unfolding.

Terrorists know they have little capability to cause significant damage to the military machine of the Western and Eastern (e.g. Russia and China) superpower countries engaged against them. They do, however, hope to create a response whereby the fear they can generate will counter-balance their lack of strength, causing an over-reaction from Western governments that will feed their narrative. This has been, and continues to be, the primary contributor to successfully achieving their aim of growing the numbers of international Islamic extremists, thus further expanding their power and global reach. Even relatively small acts of terrorism that kill only a handful of people are seen as an unacceptable threat to the legitimacy and even political survival of a state government, which fundamentally exists to protect its citizens.

4 https://www.facebook.com/public/Jalnosra-Khan.

Terrorism may well be most effectively countered by sound intelligence and covert operations directly against the perpetrators and sponsors of terrorism. However, as recent history has shown, Western political leaders face heavy pressure from their electorate and increasing media scrutiny of their decisions, for example by choosing to bomb from the air with little effect towards diminishing the global threat of terrorism, whilst counter-productively creating further damning social media opportunities. Images of 'collateral damage' and maimed or dead Muslim women and children arising from coalition airstrikes is quite simply 'Jihadi gold-dust'.

Long before Mohamed Emwazi, the media labelled 'Jihadi John' infamously identified as an ISIS star of social media, YouTube executioner and poster boy for ISIS (and hence a priority drone strike target) came to prominence, Al-Qaeda and its ideologically linked franchises were extremely successful at exploiting modern communications to spread their violent, jihadist ideology, to recruit and raise funds. A report allegedly authored by the Ministry of Information for the Islamic State of Iraq and posted on several jihadi forums in September 2007 stated that: 'Praise be to God for [the Mujahedeen's] great efforts in triggering the Jihadi awakening among the children of the Ummah. How great [are the] fingers which sit behind the computer screens, day and night, awaiting a statement or releasing a production for their Mujahideen brothers in the forums'.[5] The internet, in particular, emerged as a key weapon in Al-Qaeda's media war.[6] According to a source interviewed for this book, a large number of smart phones seized by coalition forces during surge and targeted raid operations in 2007 were found to contain Jihadhi propaganda videos.

In 2013, Zelin and Fellow predicted that it was only a matter of time before terrorists began routinely using Twitter, Instagram and other services in ongoing operations.[7] In the past three years, as part of the MEMRI Jihad and Terrorism Threat Monitor (JTTM) Project, MEMRI determined that YouTube has emerged as the leading US website for online Jihad.[8] According to the report, it has replaced (and perhaps even surpassed) websites administered by Jihadists themselves, which were previously their venue of choice.[9]

Social media and new technologies have become an essential and exciting part of how we live. We now tend to leave the TV switched off and log onto our

5 Andrew Black (2007), 'Jihadi Statement Extols Virtues of the Internet' *Terrorism Focus* (18 September), 1; and 'A Worldwide Web of Terror' *Economist* (12 July 2007).

6 Timothy Thomas (2003), 'Al Qaeda and the Internet: The Danger of "Cyberplanning"' *Parameters* (Spring); and Jarret Brachman (2006), 'High-Tech Terror: Al Qaeda's Use of New Technology' *Fletcher Forum of World Affairs* (Summer) 149–63.

7 Aaron Y Zelin (2013), 'The State of Global Jihad Online: a qualitative, quantitative and cross-lingual analysis' (Washington Institute for Near East Policy, January) http://www.washingtoninstitute.org/uploads/Documents/opeds/Zelin20130201-NewAmericaFoundation.pdf.

8 S Stalinsky and others (2012), 'Testing YouTube's "Promotes Terrorism" Flagging Feature for Videos of Osama Bin Laden, 9/11, Al-Qaeda – The Results: 58 of 100 Remain Active' (11 September 2012).

9 Ibid.

PCs intermittently. We can now check the news and social media sites as frequently as we please, using smartphones and tablets. Indeed, the time spent on social media in the United States is remarkable. It is estimated that Facebook's 1.65 billion and YouTube's 1 billion users spend an average of two hours a day on one of five other social media platforms.[10]

Social media is used to personalise and legitimise terrorist acts and status as religious warfare and soldiers. The effects of social media can simultaneously trivialise, desensitise, outrage and inflame the most hideous or innocent of acts. Anyone who wants to offer their opinion now has a voice to the rest of the world. However, as we will explore later in this book, many of the main social media platforms are capable of being closed down to terrorist users. Israeli historian Yuval Noah Harari wrote: 'People turn to terrorism because they know they cannot wage (conventional) war, so they opt instead to produce a theatrical spectacle. Terrorists don't think like army generals; they think like theatre producers'. Social media offers theatrical staging, *par excellence*. Beheadings, skewering heads on pikes and blowing up densely populated buildings are very effective ways to garner attention; in the words of Paul Wilkinson: 'when one says "terrorism" in a democratic society, one also says "media"'.[11]

2.1 Terrorism and the media *tour de force*

The relationship between terrorism and the media has long been noted.[12] As far back as 1887, inflammatory leaflets fuelled the labour protests forming part of the 'Haymarket Affair' in the USA and Russian revolutionaries in the 1920s called for terrorist acts against the ruling aristocracy. In Iran, by the 1980s, audio recordings of sermons conducted by exile Ruhollah Khomeini spread among protestors, helping in part to mobilise the nation to revolution and Ayatollah Khomeini to the supreme leader of the new Islamic Republic of Iran, leading Iranian Ministry of National Guidance official Abolhassan Sadegh to remark that 'tape cassettes are stronger than fighter planes'.

The military media propaganda process started decades ago, first with radio during the First and Second World Wars, and then with television during the Vietnam, Korea, Falkland, Bosnian and Gulf Wars. More recently, the internet has dominated audience attention over traditional outlets including the TV news channels, which arguably started with the Kosovo conflict in 1998 in the early days of websites, search engines and email blogs. The emergence and continuous improvement of social media's functionality, applications and the technology that facilitates it has now made its use pervasive in modern-day conflict. Perhaps the difference is not that terrorists can organise themselves online, but that it is an

10 L Davidson (2015), 'Is your daily social media usage higher than average?' *The Telegraph* (17 May).

11 Paul Wilkinson (1997) 'The media and terrorism: a reassessment' *Terrorism and Political Violence*.

12 Ibid.

increasingly rapid and cheap communication and propaganda tool, as the costs and barriers to getting online decrease.

Ultimately, social media has become the most far-reaching form of psychological operations (PSYOPS), hence its popularity and attractiveness to terrorist groups. According to Weimann, a dozen terrorist websites existed in 1988; fast forward to 2014 and that figure was closer to 10,000, to say nothing of their social media presence,[13] which has been nothing short of a marketing masterpiece, the explosive growth of which would be the envy of any .com start up. However, Rome was not built in a day, so where did it all begin?

2.1.1 Campaign 1: beta media

If we were writing a grand cinematic screenplay detailing the terrorists' love affair with social media, like any romantic tale it has a long and complicated back story. In this epic, the first flashback scene would surely take place during the 1980s, when jihadists produced propaganda films on video tape and printed sophisticated four-colour magazines that were akin to popular titles such as *Time* or *Newsweek*,[14] which were sent out by snail mail or distributed near mosques in lieu of the internet which, whilst it existed, was still a far off dream in terms of mass communication owing to the lack of its general availability and expense.

As technology started to take off, so did the propaganda machine. Magazines such as *Al Hussam* had high publication costs in hard copy; in contrast, sending out the e-zine *The Islam Report* is practically nothing from a costs perspective.[15] Similarly, digital video distribution took off in tandem with email efforts. Sermons, pamphlets, essays, newsletters and videotaped lectures and/or battle scenes were all posted on popular outlets such as *Al-jihad* magazine.

In the 1990s, centrally controlled websites and email grew in appeal, with the likes of Azzam Publications and al-Neda making their appearance. As the 1990s ended, the 2000s saw interactive forums administered by administrators and moderators come to the fore. Terrorism experts at the Center for Combating Terrorism at West Point (the US army officer training academy) have assessed that:

> As a repository of images, videos and stories, the Internet has come to codify a particular jihadi foundation myth, accessible to anyone, anywhere, anytime. Publishing their ideas in short forum postings, longer articles floated online or in voluminous books, jihadi strategists not only recruit new members into this worldview, but they spoon-feed recruits with their virulent (and tedious)

13 Gabriel Weimann (2014), 'New Terrorism and New Media' (Washington, DC: Commons Lab of the Woodrow Wilson International Center for Scholars) https://www.wilsoncenter.org/sites/default/files/STIP_140501_new_terrorism_F.pdf.

14 J M Berger (2011), 'Terrorist Propaganda: Past and Present' *Huffington Post* (1 August).

15 *US v. Muhammed Mubayyi, Emadeddin Muntasser, and Samir Al Monla*, Criminal Action no. 05-40026-FDS (2007), Exhibit 514A, transcript of phone conversation on 27 January 1996.

> vocabulary for expressing their anger, and provide direction to operators on the ground, both in Iraq and beyond.[16]

However, despite the increasing reach and dissemination of information, as a forum the internet has its limitations. The control by a core group of individuals meant that content posted on these forums could be deleted, users could be banned and thread topics controlled, e.g. al-Hesbah, al-Ikhlas, al-Fallujah and Shamuk. The forum allowed for like-minded individuals to disseminate materials and discuss topics of mutual interest, regardless of geographical boundaries. Indeed, after 9/11, message boards became the forum of choice for jihadists to exchange opinions though message boards grounded around core subjects, e.g. Afghanistan, Syria etc and then drilling down into specific threads, e.g. matters of national security.

Administrators and moderators police the forums, filtering content and restricting access rights for certain matters, e.g. certain topics may only be available for viewing, with the ability to comment reserved for only the inner sanctum. In this way, the forum administrators act as gatekeepers of the information posted on the forums and perhaps, more importantly, ensure that if there are concerns about security, access can be locked down.[17] At the highest levels of access to the forums, it has been reported that the medium has been used for direct communications between the most senior of jihadi officials, such as a virtual meeting which took place in 2013 on a closed circuit of an Al-Qaeda linked forum as between worldwide jihadi leaders to discuss an allegedly impending terrorist attack, which never materialised and received mixed reporting of the meeting in the media.[18]

The forums, although very useful, did generate debate amongst the higher echelons of Al-Qaeda. In a letter to Osama bin Laden, Adam Gadahn[19] complained about the elitist nature of the forums and the need to change pace to keep winning the hearts and minds of those sympathetic to the cause:

> [As for jihadist forums] it is repulsive to most of the Muslims, or closed to them. It also distorts the face of al-Qaeda, based upon what you know about bigotry and the sharp tone that characterises most of the participants in these forums. It is also biased towards [Salafists] and not any Salafist, but the jihadi

16 Similarly, the current US National Strategy for Combating Terrorism states that: 'the Internet provides an inexpensive, anonymous, geographically unbounded, and largely unregulated virtual haven for terrorists' (2008) *Harmony and Disharmony*, 51–52.

17 D Gordon (2005), 'Terrorists on the Internet' *The Connection* WBUR Boston (8 June).

18 P Cruickshank and T Lister (2013), 'Al Qaeda calling?' CNN Security Clearance blog (8 August) http://security.blogs.cnn.com/2013/08/08/al-quadea-calling/.

19 Before his apparent death at the hands of the US military in a probable drone strike in January 2015, Adam Gadahn had risen to be one of the US Government's most wanted men as he became a high-profile Al-Qaeda propagandist.

> Salafist. Salafism is but one trend among Muslim trends, and Jihadi Salfism is a small trend within a small trend.[20]

The forums, as we will again explore later in this book, can be a double-edged sword and provide the intelligence forces with critical information, or in many cases provide a means to lure an unwitting terrorist into a trap or recruit a potential espionage agent.

In this extraordinary letter, recovered from the house in northern Pakistan where bin Laden was staying when he was killed in 2011 by the US Navy's Seal Team 6, Gadahn offered 20 pages of advice on a range of other topics, from media strategy and the agendas of various global TV networks, to how to rein in off-message local groups who persisted in killing large numbers of fellow Muslims around the world. In a section of the letter devoted to Al-Qaeda's media strategy on the eve of the 9/11 attacks, Gadahn called on bin Laden and al-Zawahri to reach out to international journalists and 'explain our mission in their newspapers and channels', rather than rely exclusively on outlets such as Al-Jazeera and 'repulsive' forums:

> [t]o rely on Al-Jazeera and the jihadist forums on the internet is not useful. Al-Jazeera seems to impose conditions like other channels. Agencies and papers to cover al-Qaeda announcements, namely to include a threat or to claim responsibility for an act. As for the messages of diplomatic time in their media, as this is an aspect of al-Qaeda [they believe] should not be exposed to people . . .[21]

Gadahn was not alone in his views. Mustafa Setmariam Nasir (known as Abu Musab al-Suri) also poured criticism on the elitism promoted by the forums. In a 1600-page treatise entitled 'Call to Global Islamic Resistance', al-Suri called for producing jihadi media in languages other than Arabic, including English, and devising messages that appealed more to the masses. He also noted the power of the masses to disseminate the overarching message of the organisation, beyond the concentrated central cells:

> [t]he call for resistance is based on non-central cells. And its Jihadi detachments are based on individual operation and on the operation of small, completely separate non-central cells, so that they will not be linked, except by the mutual goal, the common name, the methodology of belief, and the way of education . . . the basic mission of this detachment is to guide and to direct

20 'Adam Gadhan lashes out against al-Quaeda affiliates, jihadist forums'. See Central Isis online (9 May 2012).

21 'Adam Gadahn lashes out against al-Qaeda affiliates'. A recent article about the American propagandist, who is wanted for treason, posted to a US military propaganda website aimed at people in Central Asia (19 May 2012) http://imgur.com/TiL0J.

> [the resistance] and to call [for resistance] by publishing the system of the call [for resistance] and its political and legal methodology, its educational methodology, its dynamic methodology, and to spread this to all levels of the Ummah. [The mission] is also to publish media statements and declarations of methodology in the name of the call and its detachments, provided that the statements include the detachments' ideas, manners of performance, and points of view. [The mission is also] to form (a separate branch of) the central detachment which actually fights on the battle front. [The mission is also] to communicate with other separate detachments, if possible, to build relationships [with them], to coordinate [with them], and cooperate [with them].[22]

Gadahn's letter makes fascinating reading, outlining as it does the need to have more control over media presence and to promote a culture of inclusion, rather than relegating all those except the elite with the highest levels of forum clearance.

2.1.2 The social network

2.1.2.1 Adoption of social media

In the wake of 9/11 the forums became increasingly vulnerable to surveillance by the intelligence services.[23] Around this time Al-Qaeda also started to turn its back on the traditional publishing of videos through news outlets such as Al-Jazeera, as monotonous lengthy videos of bin Laden lecturing on the jihadi cause were not serving the campaign effectively, having lost viewers, meaning that they were not receiving adequate media attention for the organisation and its cause.

Steadily, YouTube gained popularity as a result of the ease with which videos could be shared, with removals only being made in relation to videos 'depicting gratuitous violence, advocated violence, or use of hate speech'. For matters not falling within these narrow confines, YouTube would uphold the principles of free speech and 'allow users to view all applicable and acceptable content and make up their own minds',[24] meaning that such mediums became an important part of the campaign to radicalise and recruit. However, whilst YouTube was a valuable tool for the top Al-Qaeda echelon, it also created a more level playing-field, giving effect to al-Suri's vision of modern jihad. Prominent academic, Kohlmann, suggests that:

22 M Nasir (2004), 'Call to Global Islamic Resistance' https://archive.org/stream/TheGlobalIslamicResistanceCall/The_Global_Islamic_Resistance_Call_-_Chapter_8_sections_5_to_7_LIST_OF_TARGETS_djvu.txt.

23 See Zelin (n 7) 'The State of Global Jihad Online'.

24 Brianna Lee (2010), 'Under pressure, YouTube removes Awlaki jihadi videos' (5 November) http://www.pbs.org/wnet/need-to-know/the-daily-need/under-pressure-youtube-removes-alaki-jihadi-videos/4872/.

> YouTube has become a major alternative distribution point for jihadi propaganda, especially for home-grown militants who may not have the pedigree to gain access to the classic password-protected jihadi chat forums. If you don't have online friends who can sneak you in, and if you don't speak Arabic, then YouTube may be the best available option.[25]

One emagazine dating back to 2007 observed: 'film everything; this is good advice for all Mujahideen. Brothers, don't disdain photography. You should be aware that every frame you take is as good as a missile fired at the Crusader enemy and his puppets'.[26]

As we now know, Osama bin Laden found anonymity and security hiding in plain view for many years, living a reclusive suburban lifestyle a short walk from Pakistan's military officer training academy. He used a mixture of 'old school' messengers to run his errands and facilitate his remote online communications, through Islamabad's internet cafes. Terrorist sleeper cells are similarly able to exist in Western multi-cultural societies and communicate with each other and their leaders in the Middle East, using a combination of end-to-end encryption and their own cryptic phrases to plot and conceal the details of their next attack. Their messages are cleverly hidden within the everyday legitimate noise of the world's widely available social media and messaging app platforms.

Social media is pivotal to the success of terrorism, as it is free publicity with minimal risk if used with guile. Terrorists utilise the latest software and encryption developments and modern mobile communication technologies, combined with the more 'low tech', traditional and secure methods such as *hawala* money exchange networks, to fund their operations. The role played by third parties in the financing of a great deal of Islamic terrorism, particularly over the past 20 years, is significant but politically contentious. Wealthy foreigners (often from the oil-rich Arab states, primarily Saudi Arabia), have a huge role in funding and facilitating both terrorism and the social media presence. They are also involved in much of the technical training and facilitation that makes the online presence so effective. They do not necessarily blog or tweet, but they fund and support. This is often in support of the well documented, wider and arguably more destabilising Sunni–Shia conflict proxy war.

Although Al-Qaeda is often cited as one of the first terrorist groups to have social media super status, there were many early adopters who developed significant followings in their own right. Yemeni-American jihadist Anwar Awlaki[27] cultivated a mesmerising fanaticism within his social media following owing to his eloquence, perfect English and gift for story-telling, which earned him the

25 F Kholmann interviewed in S Shane (2011), 'Radical Cleric Still Speaks on YouTube' (4 March) http://www.nytimes.com/2011/03/05/world/middleeast/05youtube.html?_r=0.

26 See Black (n 5).

27 Anwar al-Awlaki was killed by a US drone on Friday, 30 September 2011.

reputation in some circles as the Osama bin Laden of the internet.[28] He also published 50 CDs relating the life of the Prophet Mohammed, 21 CDs on the other prophets of Islam, 22 CDs on the afterlife, at least 33 CDs on the companions of Mohammed, several important lectures concerned primarily with validating violent interpretations of jihad and open calls to violence and an explicit embrace of terrorism, as well as pieces in *Inspire* magazine.

During his life, Awlaki was considered by counter-terrorism officials to be as large a threat as Osama bin Laden and Ayman al-Zawahiri, for his extraordinary ability to nurture and cultivate home-grown terrorism. He was linked with the likes of Fort Hood shooter Nidal Malik Hasan, 'underwear bomber' Umar Farouk Abdulmutallab and, more recently, 21-year-old Roshonara Choudhury, who stabbed British legislator Stephen Timms. Choudhury admitted to having watched 'hundreds' of Awlaki's videos before deciding to go forward with her attack.[29]

Although YouTube was arguably the gateway for social media adoption, on the basis that it was similar to the release of videos through traditional media outlets such as Al-Jazeera, increasingly wider social media use of other social networking sites such as Twitter, Facebook and Ask.fm have become more widely adopted.

According to Weimann:[30]

> Terrorists have good reasons to use social media. First, these channels are by far the most popular with their intended audience, which allows terrorist organizations to be part of the mainstream. Second, social media channels are user-friendly, reliable, and free. Finally, social networking allows terrorists to reach out to their target audiences and virtually 'knock on their doors' – in contrast to older models of websites in which terrorists had to wait for visitors to come to them.

Essentially, social media provides a further layer of indoctrination potential to terror groups, in that it allows them to release messages directly to their intended audience and converse with their audience in real time.[31]

Whilst permanence, reach and spontaneity of posting is important, perhaps the difference that social media brings is that it has lowered the bar for participation – essentially, anyone with access to the internet can join in. No longer do those interested in the cause need to seek out covert forums; instead, they can simply follow terrorists online through popular social media sites. A giant digital coffee shop to discuss jihadi ideas has been created, which simply did not exist before, even during

28 J M Berger (2011), 'Gone but not forgotten' http://foreignpolicy.com/2011/09/30/gone-but-not-forgotten/.

29 V Dodd and A Topping (2010), 'Roshonara Choudhry jailed for life over MP attack' (3 November) http://www.theguardian.com/uk/2010/nov/03/roshonara-choudhry-jailed-life-attack

30 See Weimann (n 13).

31 Will Oremus (2011) 'Twitter of Terror' *Slate Magazine* (23 December) http://www.slate.com/articles/technology/technocracy/2011/12/al_shabaab_twitter_a_somali_militant_group_unveils_a_new_social_media_strategy_for_terrorists_.html.

the height of the forums. However, as we will explore later on, this also brings risks too. The element of complete control can also be lost, which may confuse, obfuscate or misdirect the message that the officials want in the public domain.

2.2 Express yourself

2.2.1 Philosophical arguments in favour of freedom of expression

In addition to legal and policy positions, philosophical arguments in favour of the protection of freedom of expression are also of importance in terms of understanding why such speech is worthy of legal protection.

The concept of freedom of expression is broadly underpinned by the following theory in, first, the 'Argument from Truth', which finds its origins in John Stuart Mill's 19th century essay 'Of the Liberty of Thought and Discussion'.[32] Such truth, Mill argues, emerges from unrestricted freedom of thought, as such uninhibited freedom of expression does not allow for autonomous thought, expression or opposition, which conversely leads to a position whereby there has to be absolute accord with such autonomous ideas and opinions.[33] Secondly, the 'marketplace of ideas', which, according to Justice Holmes's judgment in *Abrams v United States*,[34] is best tested through 'the power of the thought to get itself accepted in the competition of the market'.[35] The third theory is the 'argument from self-fulfilment', described by the European Court of Human Rights (ECtHR) in *Handyside v United Kingdom* as 'one of the basic conditions . . . for the development of man'.[36] The final theory comes from the argument of 'democratic self-governance' through citizens' engagement on political matters, where there is an uninhibited free flow of information and ideas on matters of economic, social and democratic significance.

Although it is often a matter of degree, these philosophical tenants of freedom of expression are apparent within domestic jurisprudence and that of the ECtHR.[37]

32 J Mill (1991), *On Liberty and Other Essays* (Oxford University Press); J Mill (1977), *On Liberty, Essays on Politics and Society* in J M Robson (ed), *Collected Works of John Stuart Mill* (University of Toronto Press).

33 P Wragg (2013), 'Mill's dead dogma: the value of truth to free speech jurisprudence' *Public Law* 363–85, 365.

34 250 US 616 (1919).

35 *R v Secretary of State for the Home Department, ex parte Simms* [2000] 2 AC 115at 630–31. See also *Gitlow v New York*, 268 U.S. 652 (1925), 673 (Justice Holmes).

36 *Handyside v United Kingdom* (1976) 1 EHRR 737 para [49]. See also *Bladet Tromso and Stensaas v Norway* (2000) 29 EHRR 125 para [59]; *Bergens Tidande v Norway* (2001) 31 EHRR 16para [48].

37 In *Handyside v United Kingdom* (1976) 1 EHRR 737 the ECtHR referred, at least implicitly, to these theories when it stated at para [49] that: 'Freedom of expression constitutes one of the essential foundations of such a society, one of the basic conditions for its progress and for the development of every man'. See H Fenwick and G Phillipson (2006) *Media Freedom Under the Human Rights Act* (Oxford University Press) 39.

Perhaps the most oft-quoted[38] passage of case law recognising the existence of all of these grounds is that of Lord Steyn in *R v Secretary of State for the Home Department, ex parte Simms*,[39] who observed that that freedom of expression 'serves a number of broad objectives'.[40]

2.2.2 Legal protection of freedom of expression

2.2.2.1 The Johannesburg Principles

As we saw in Chapter 1, although a framework towards international cooperation with regard to terrorist-related matters can be adopted, such conventions – designed to keep states secure – can pull in an opposite direction to other key concepts of international law, such as freedom of expression. For example, companies in democratic states have exported products and services for mass surveillance and censorship. Iran, Syria, Azerbaijan, China, Turkey Bahrain and recently overthrown regimes such as in Libya have all blocked critical websites and/or spied on protest movements using such systems. This tension is aptly summarised by Coliver:

> [t]here is little margin for error and much at stake as quick action often is necessary to thwart a genuine threat to national security but restraints on political speech can trigger an inexorable slide into tyranny. The more fragile the democracy, the less likely it is to be able to tolerate either a threat to its genuine security or the suppression of legitimate political debate.[41]

It is this inherent jarring that led to the adoption of the Johannesburg Principles,[42] based on international and regional law as well as standards relating to the protection of human rights in the context of state judgements of national courts and general principles of law. The Principles were drafted to address the extent to which it is legitimate in international law for governments to suppress freedom of expression and access to information in order to safeguard national security. The preamble to the Johannesburg Principles states that the participants involved with the drafting of the principles were:

> [K]eenly aware that some of the most serious violations of human rights and fundamental freedoms are justified by governments as necessary to protect

38 Lord Steyn's judgement has been referred to numerous times within domestic jurisprudence. For a recent example see *R (on the application of Lord Carlisle of Berriew QC and Others) v Secretary of State for the Home Department* [2014] UKSC 60 para [164] (Lord Kerr).

39 [2000] 2 AC 115.

40 Ibid 126.

41 S Coliver (1998), 'Commentary on the Johannesburg Principles on National Security, Freedom of Expression and Access to Information' 20(1) *Human Rights Quarterly* 15.

42 *Johannesburg Principles on National Security, Freedom of Expression and Access to Information*, UN Doc E/CN.4/1996/39 (1996).

> national security . . . and desiring to promote a clear recognition of the limited scope of restrictions on freedom of expression and freedom of information that may be imposed in the interest of national security, so as to discourage governments from using the pretext of national security to place unjustified restrictions on the exercise of these freedoms.

2.2.2.2 Europe

Understanding social media and the approach to its regulation in Europe is also overlaid with complex conceptual issues of law relating to privacy and freedom of expression, which long predate the rise of social networks. Freedom of expression has been described as the 'lifeblood of democracy'.[43] It is both important in its own right, and fundamental to the enjoyment and realisation of other rights. At an individual level, freedom of expression has been described as 'key to the development, dignity and fulfilment of every person'.[44] It is important for people both to be able to express views and opinions and to obtain ideas and information from others, and thus to gain a better understanding of the world around them. The United Kingdom is party to the International Covenant on Civil and Political Rights 1966 (ICCPR 1966), Article 19(2) of which provides:

> Everyone shall have the right to freedom of expression; this right shall include freedom to seek, receive and impart information and ideas of all kinds, regardless of frontiers, either orally, in writing or in print, in the form of art, or through any other media of his choice.

Article 10(1) of the European Convention on Human Rights (ECHR) also provides:

> Everyone has the right to freedom of expression. This right shall include freedom to hold opinions and to receive and impart information and ideas without interference by public authority and regardless of frontiers.

The concept of freedom of expression has been accepted by the Human Rights Committee as applying to the internet.[45] In its General Comment in 2011, the expression was deemed to include 'all forms of electronic and internet-based modes

43 *R v Secretary of State for the Home Department, ex parte Simms* (n 35) 126 (Lord Steyn).

44 Description by Article 19 www.article19.org.

45 See also 'General principles on the right to freedom of opinion and expression and the internet'; and Human Rights Council Resolution 20/8 A/HRC/RES/20/8 (16 July 2012) para 1.

of expression'.[46] In determining the weight attached to the speech, Strasbourg and the domestic courts have put varying categories of speech on a scale.[47]

2.2.2.3 America

Although this book focuses primarily on the regulation of speech in Europe, the position in America cannot be ignored, given its involvement in international counter-terrorism measures and the fact that most social media sites have American origins, meaning (ideologically) that they are closely aligned to the liberal US model of freedom of expression, which has been a core linchpin in terms of terrorists' ability to keep their content up online. The First Amendment guarantees citizens freedoms concerning religion, expression, assembly and the right to petition. With regard to freedom of expression, it prohibits Congress from restricting the press or the rights of individuals to speak freely; however, there are some forms of derogation permitted most relevant to this text, such as inciting lawless actions or matters relating to national security. The Supreme Court extended the full protection of the First Amendment to the internet in *Reno v ACLU*,[48] the court's decision extended the same constitutional protections given to books, magazines, films and spoken expression to materials published on the internet.[49]

2.3 Terror groups' use of social media

Virtually all extremist and terrorist groups have developed a social media presence, with thousands of accounts posting hundreds and hundreds of posts, which are viewed by millions of eyes, multiple times a day.

46 Human Rights Committee, General Comment 34: 'Freedoms of opinion and expression' CCPR/C/GC/34 (GC 34) (12 September 2011) at para 15 states: '[I]nternet and mobile based electronic information dissemination systems, have substantially changed communication practices around the world. There is now a global network for exchanging ideas and opinions that does not necessarily rely on the traditional mass media intermediaries'. See also M O'Flaherty (2012), 'Freedom of Expression: Article 19 of the ICCPR and the Human Rights Committee's General Comment No 34' 12 *Human Rights Law Review* 627.

47 At the pinnacle is political speech (*Campbell v MGN* [2004] UKHL 22 para [148]). Political speech is then followed by artistic speech (*Muller v Switzerland* (1991) 13 EHRR 212; *Otto Preminger v Austria* (1995) 19 EHRR 34), and then commercial expression (*Markt Intern v Germany* (1989) 12 EHRR 161). Towards the lower end of the spectrum comes celebrity gossip (*Campbell v MGN* [2004] UKHL 22 para, [149]), beneath it pornography (*Belfast City Council v Miss Behavin' Ltd* [2007] UKHL 19 para, [38]), then gratuitous personal attacks (*Gorelishvili v Georgia* (2009) 48 EHRR 36 para [40]) and hate speech (*Lehideux and Isornia v France* (1998) 5 BHRC 540 para [53]; *Norwood v United Kingdom* (2004) 40 EHRR SE 111), the latter of which attracts little, if any, protection. The case of *Fuentes Bobo v Spain* ((2001) 31 EHRR 50 para [46]) established that the court will also consider if the author has had an opportunity to prepare the content which they have written when considering if it is of high or low value and if there has been a 'possibility of reformulating, perfecting or retracting' the content of a statement before it is placed into the public domain.

48 521 U.S. 844 (1997).

49 In 2002, the court again ruled that any limitations on the internet were unconstitutional in *American Civil Liberties Union v Ashcroft* 535 U.S. 564 (2002).

2.3.1 Growth of terrorist organisations online presence

The Green revolution in 2009 almost toppled the Iranian regime through the use of social media. However, it was in December 2010 that the power of social media in relation to revolutionary activity really began to materialise on the radar of public consciousness, as the so called 'Arab Spring' unfolded. Protestors gathered to clash with police, armed with a rock in one hand and a smartphone in the other. Starting in Tunisia and Egypt, citizens were lobbying for the birth of a democratic government after years of tyrannical dictatorships. As the Arab Spring ensued, social media spread messages to which the world subscribed, followed, tweeted and retweeted. For instance, the week before Egyptian President Hosni Mubarak's resignation, the total rate of tweets about political change in Egypt spiralled tenfold. The top 23 videos featuring protests and political commentary had nearly 5.5 million views. More than 75 per cent of people that clicked on embedded Twitter links about the Arab Spring were from outside the Arab world.

According to a contemporary report:

> [s]ocial media became a megaphone that disseminated information and excitement about the uprisings to our outside world. The users of social media in the Middle East caused the world to take notice and to witness the revolution. Social media enabled these revolutionaries, change agents in their own right, to spread their messages beyond national borders to all corners of the world.[50]

However, this was no mere publicity campaign; it also provided an incredibly powerful way to mobilise tens of thousands of citizens for protest, which is a critical tool that social media facilitates (as we will see later on in this chapter). What is clear is that, from the very start, social media was the bedrock of disseminating (and sometimes distorting) information about the conflict.

The Taliban has been active on Twitter since May 2011, tweeting under the handle @alemarahweb; the Taliban tweets frequently, on some days nearly hourly[51] and has more than 8,000 followers.[52] In December 2011, Somalia-based terror cell Al-Shabab was using a Twitter account under the name *@HSMPress*[53] and amassed tens of thousands of followers owing to its frequent Tweets. In December 2011, in response to the news that Al-Shabab was using Twitter, US officials called for the company to shut down the account. Twitter executives did

50 Subcommittee on Counterterrorism and Intelligence of the committee on Homeland Security's Subcommittee on Counter-terrorism and Intelligence (2011), 'Jihadist Use of Social Media: How to Prevent Terrorism and Preserve Innovation', 112th Congress, First Session (6 December 2011).

51 Twitter, 'Twitter page of the Taliban' https://twitter.com/alemarahweb. Note, however, that this account has now been suspended.

52 https://twitter.com/alemarahweb following size accurate when accessed on 6 March 2013.

53 This account is now suspended. Notice of the suspension can be found at https://twitter.com/account/suspended.

not comply with the demands and declined to comment on the case;[54] however, the account has since been shut down by Twitter.[55] Terrorist activity has not occurred only on Twitter: shortly afterwards a series of coordinated Christmas bombings in Kano, Nigeria in 2011, the Nigerian-based terror group Boko Haram released a video statement defending their actions on YouTube.[56]

There was one group, however, very much in its infancy during these early social terror collective years, that realised the potential of the burgeoning digital landscape. Readers may not remember or have heard of the organisation Tanzim Quadat al Jihad fi Bilad al Rafidayn (or *Al Qaeda in the Land of the Two Rivers*, more commonly known in the West as Al-Qaeda in Iraq or (AQI)), but undoubtedly by 2015 everyone will have heard of its brain child ISIS. Founded in 2004 by Abu Musab al Zarqawi, who swore allegiance to bin Laden, AQI used the internet to market and further their cause in a way that Al-Qaeda Central had never quite managed to achieve. AQI took a very different approach to their media strategy, focusing less on doctrine and more on the action. They began to post violent video clips of terrorist attacks and beheadings online. Whilst such content has been available on sites such as Archive.org during the infancy of the data revolution, these were only accessed by the hardened core who knew where to look for such materials. The new wave social media, including YouTube, Facebook or Twitter, however, had popular appeal, which was an undeniable game changer. How many of us would think actively to seek out such videos? Yet how many of us have seen the beheadings by Jihadi John, thanks to social media outlets and reporting in the popular press?

For most people, ISIS burst onto the global stage in August 2014, when it conducted one of the most socially mediated conflicts in history. However, its social media origins are humbler. ISIS's first official Twitter account was set up in October 2010 under the name 'al I'tisaamm', with the handle @e3tasimo, which encapsulates the notion of maintaining Islamic tradition without deviation. Although it had 24,000 followers,[57] it did not immediately come to the attention of the media. Postings were slow and the individual members of ISIS had much more active accounts than the official presence, which had more traction with the following public.

2.3.2 Mobilisation of online battalions

In the early days, social media still followed some sort of broad hierarchy analogous to that imposed by the forums. After being posted and authenticated by ISIS officials, second tier users, who were very active on Twitter would retweet

54 Friedman, Uri (2011), 'U.S. officials may take action again al-Shabab's Twitter account' *Foreign Policy*.

55 Ibid.

56 'Boko Haram: Nigerian Islamist leader defends attacks', *BBC News* http://www.bbc.co.uk/news/world-africa-16510929.

57 Data collected from @3tassimo in December 2013.

and hashtag the posting, or upload the content onto other social networking platforms. ISIS called these second tier 'worker bees' the *mujtahdiun* (the industrious).[58] After that, a third tier of posters called the *ansar muwahideen* (general supporters) repeat the process on a larger scale.[59] In this way the collective power of the hive could create a swarm of posts across Twitter.

A key figure in the media tide turn for ISIS was a user operating under the handle @reyadiraq.[60] @reyadiraq was steadily posting more gruesome content, departing from doctrinal matters preferred by the official account to the live tweeting of an amputation of an accused thief's hand.[61] Although taken down in February 2013, the account popped up again in March of that year under the handle @dawlh_i_sh. The official account was also suspended in early 2014, and five accounts in a row were created and subsequently suspended in quick succession. The account came back as @wa3tasimu in February 2014 and began to accrue followers, gaining 18,000 in just one month.[62] As well as an essential tool for Jihadhi warriors, social media also provides a mechanism for those who sympathise with the jihadi movement but do not want actively to become involved or decamp from their comfortable Western lifestyle or to travel to the Islamic State to take up arms.

2.3.3 Strategies deployed

Although its principles are supposedly drawn from the religious norms of the 7th century, ISIS is heavily evolved in terms of its adoption of modern technology. Whilst the use of social media is present to some extent in most of the well known terrorist organisations, ISIS's social media strategy was different to the likes of Al-Qaeda, with its success no doubt partially attributable to the fact that, rather than simply posting content that would have been disseminated through traditional media outlets (e.g. a link to a video), ISIS also looked at other digital tools that could increase its visibility to the *mujtahdiun*, such as the launch of the *Dawn of Glad Tidings* app, which allowed the *mujtahdiun* collectively to engineer their efforts.

The Dawn of Glad Tidings, an official ISIS Arabic-language Twitter app promoted by some of the organisation's leading figures, has been used to give updates about the group and spread its message through user accounts. When the app is downloaded, ISIS is able to post tweets automatically on behalf of all those who have signed up. The tweets include links, hashtags and images, and the same content is also tweeted by the accounts of everyone else who has signed up for the app, spaced out to avoid triggering Twitter's spam-detection algorithms. The app first went into wide use in April 2014, reaching a staggering 40,000 tweets in one

58 ISIS Twitter strategy document (12 September 2014); Shayba al-Hamdi; http://justpasteit/h26t.

59 See n 56.

60 The account holder claimed no affiliation to ISIS.

61 J M Berger (2014), 'Twitter post' (10 January) https://twitter.com/intelwire?lang=en-gb.

62 According to a contemporary following of the account.

day during the June 2014 march on the northern Iraqi city of Mosul. The reporting online by *Dawn* app users far outstripped the reportage by the traditional media, as these users began posting thousands of tweets bearing images of an armed jihadist gazing at the ISIS flag flying over the city, with the accompanying text: 'We are coming, Baghdad'. According to statistics compiled by J M Berger, the sheer volume of posting made any search for 'Baghdad' on Twitter generate the image among its first results for that keyword.[63] Supporters also make use of mainstream accounts such as @ActiveHashtags to identify trending keywords and 'piggy back' on them to bring their posts to a more mainstream audience.

As a result of these strategies, and others, ISIS was able to project strength and to promote engagement online. For instance, the ISIS hashtag consistently outperforms that of the group's main competitor in Syria, Jabhat al-Nusra, even though the two groups have a similar number of supporters online. In data analysed in February 2014, ISIS often registered more than 10,000 mentions of its hashtag every day, whilst the number of al-Nusra mentions generally ranged between 2500 and 5000. During the 2014 World Cup, Arabic speaking fans were subject to an ISIS ambush – mixed in with football match highlights and scores were shocking images of executions of Iraqi soldiers and other atrocities perpetrated by ISIS.[64]

ISIS made use of active hashtags such as #worldcup, so that enthusiastic football fans would inadvertently come across pro-ISIS posts. Hashtags are a popular way for Twitter users to follow tweets about specific topics and for tweeters to expand their audience. Al Shabab uses a custom hashtag (#JihadDispatches) to draw attention to events in Somalia. Unsurprisingly, other favourites of jihadists are #jihad and ال جهاد (jihad in Arabic). ISIS also organises hashtag campaigns, skewing trending terms by encouraging supporters repeatedly to tweet various hashtags such as #AllEyesonISIS or #CalamityWillBefallUS.

The use of such apps is not always successful: when the insurgents overcame Mosul, ISIS hinted at its plans to change the name of its organisation. Like many brands before them, ISIS employed an activist to promote a hashtag carefully crafted to resemble a grassroots initiative, demanding that ISIS leader Abu Bakr al-Baghdadi declare not an Islamic state in Syria and Iraq, but the rebirth of an Islamic caliphate. ISIS used hashtags to focus-group messaging and branding concepts, very much akin to the media stages employed by large Western corporates when rebranding. The question of when and how to declare a new caliphate is highly controversial in jihadi circles, and the hashtag produced a great deal of angry and divisive discussion. It never announced a name change. The app was terminated on 17 June 2014, just days before the announcement of the caliphate, which struck a blow into the heart of the ISIS media machine at a critical time.

63 J M Berger (2014), 'How ISIS games Twitter', *The Atlantic* (16 June) http://www.theatlantic.com/international/archive/2014/06/isis-iraq-twitter-social-media-strategy/372856/ (last accessed 31 July 2016).

64 See Berger (n 61).

The app was just one way ISIS uses Twitter to magnify its message. Other methods used by ISIS to spread its message through social media have included organised Twitter hashtag campaigns, professionally produced promotional videos and a call for support through its 'one billion campaign'. Through the 'one billion campaign' the radical fundamentalists have sought support from Muslims around the world to join their cause and post videos onto YouTube and pictures to Instagram with messages that 'proudly support the Muslim cause'. The hashtag campaigns encourage users to tweet hashtags repetitively at certain times of day, so that they trend on social networks so that more users are exposed to ISIS's messages. ISIS has also attempted to branch out to alternate social networks such as Friendica, Quitter and Diaspora, but with limited success;[65] Friendica and Quitter in particular were quick to remove the group's presence from their sites.[66]

As we have seen above, ISIS has had a long history on social media, but the gruesome beheading of James Foley[67] sparked global outrage as the whole sickening event played out in real time to a global audience. ISIS had found its media footing, mixing high production values with slick but horrifying content with Jihadi John representing to those minded to seek it in their leader a 'jihadi cool' aesthetic. As time has gone on, the videos stop short of showing the actual beheading, as the producers have realised that too much graphic violence can be counter-productive in their target audience. The videos undoubtedly cause shock, outrage and fear in the Western world, in a way scarcely felt since 9/11 and again creating imagery that will define, change and shape our understanding of terrorism. A beheading is a far concept from the twin towers, even if the underlying cause and desire to promote fear remains the same goal.

According to Nasswer Balochi, a member of ISIS's social media team: 'this is a war of ideologies as much as it is a physical war. And just as the physical war must be fought on the battlefield, so too must the ideological war be fought in the media'.[68] The fact that ISIS even has a dedicated team says everything that needs to be understood in terms of the importance that ISIS attaches to its utilisation of social media propaganda content, as part of the cause.

2.3.4 Image is everything

It is crucial, when considering the phenomena of social media and terrorism, not to approach it through the lens applied by the Western media. English-language forums are far less active than Arabic-language forums, which suggests that jihadi

65 http://blog.adl.org/extremism/isis-faces-resistance-from-social-media-companies.

66 This is considered in Chapter 3.

67 Following the beheading of former US Army Ranger Peter Kassig, there have now been five recorded executions of Westerners taken captive in Syria. James Foley, David Cawthorne Haines, Alan Henning and Steven Sotloff are also among the men kidnapped and executed by ISIS.

68 Mark Townsed and Toby Helm (2014), 'Jihad in a Social Media Age: How can the West win an online war?' *Guardian* (23 August) http://www.theguardian.com/world/2014/aug/23/jihad-social-media-age-west-win-online-war.

ideological penetration into the West is limited.[69] There are also distinctions between what is posted for consumption in the West and the Arabic-language content. Inevitably, the distortion in terms of what we consume as a Western audience, wittingly or unwittingly, affects our understanding of how we think ISIS uses social media. In order really to understand ISIS, one has to step beyond the reporting in the media and consider all of the posting activities of these types of organisations, and why, as a consequence, they are gaining such strong and loyal followings.

Extreme violence is not enough to keep an audience engaged for a prolonged period and, unlike the world of the forums, the wider breadth of followers attached to social media content may not be as doctrinally committed as those who were active on the forums, differing in intellectual sophistication and formatively influenced by diverse cultures, meaning that they need something more from terrorist propaganda to keep them interested in the content. ISIS in particular understands this concept. It is creating a goodwill factor which draws individuals to the ISIS brand and is starting to develop a unique selling point (USP) to differentiate itself from its peers. The terrorists are renaissance men of the media, business, finance, technology and warfare. However tempting it is to write off these individuals as merely psychopathic, religious zealots with sharp knives and a video camera, that would be an extreme under-estimation of the sophistication of their efforts and the danger they present.

Much of ISIS propaganda focuses on trying to make the organisation appear as a normally adjusted community. As will be seen throughout this chapter, there are numerous examples of such propaganda with postings showing members 'chowing down' on bananas with Nutella or playing the popular videogame *Call of Duty*. As noted by one commentator: 'Most of the pictures by ISIS are not . . . [of] a fighter holding a gun, it's more about eating couscous or hummus . . . trying to show that it's a normal life. . . . They're trying to show that life continues even if everyone is against them'.[70] The most bizarre of these 'everyman' posts might be *Cats of Jihad*, which gave ISIS fighters a chance to put images of their cats with their guns on sites such as Instagram.

ISIS has even launched a *Call of Duty* style game by hijacking and modifying the popular video game *ARMA III* to create characters based on ISIS militants, which allows users to play the role of ISIS fighters on a mission to murder Westerners, serving as a recruitment and radicalisation tool aimed at impressionable individuals. ISIS had previously hijacked *Grand Theft Auto 5* for the same purpose.[71]

69 See Zelin (n 7).

70 Y Tadjdeh (2015), 'U.S. Government Trying to Counter ISIL "Twitter Consensus"' http://www.nationaldefensemagazine.org/archive/2015/April/Pages/USGovernmentTryingtoCounterISILTwitterConsensus.aspx.

71 J Hall (2015), 'The video game that allows you to play as an ISIS fighter slaughtering Westerners: Islamists give away combat simulator in a bid to recruit children and young men' *Daily Mail* (3 February) http://www.dailymail.co.uk/news/article-2937641/ISIS-fighters-distributing-video-game-allows-players-play-role-Islamist-kill-Westerners.html.

In September 2014, ISIS uploaded a video to YouTube bearing the black ISIS flag that showed violent scenes from the game – including police officers being gunned down and lorries being blown up by suicide bombers. The stark message with on the video reads: 'Your games which are producing from you, we do the same actions in the battlefields (sic)!!'. As characters are killed and bombs explode in-game, players can be heard chanting Islamist slogans and music can also be heard, which is designed to emulate the terror group's real-life footage. Films have also been produced that mock up *Call of Duty*'s gameplay using tools such as HD helmet cameras, freeze-frame footage and heavily edited audio, all designed to make the real-life massacre at Kobane look like a game.

In May 2015, Siddhartha Dhar, a popular British ISIS fighter known as Abu Rumaysah al-Britani, authored a 46-page guide for prospective immigrants to the Islamic State, a sort of travel guide, which makes the *Times* travel pages and *Wish you were here* look like Nelly the Elephant. Amongst the content he clarifies:

> This book does not contain any information on how to perform acts of terrorism, nor does it provide any instructions on how to migrate to the Islamic State. It is simply my take on unravelling events that have transpired in the Islamic State's first year of governance.

In the guide he tackles important issues:

> If you were worried about leaving behind your local Costa Coffee [a British coffee chain] then you will be happy to know that the Caliphate serves some of the best lattes and cappuccinos around. The milk is truly delightful – creamy and fresh. As for the tea then, the distinctive pekoe leaves of Layalina are, at the moment, the frontrunners.

He also has some domestic goddess-worthy views on ice cream, penning: 'Fluffy, velvety, and sweet. If you want to treat yourself then indulge in this full fat delight all for less than 30 pence . . . snickers, kit kat, Bounty, Twix, Kinder Surprise, Cadburys – yes, yes we have it all'. Of a more healthy disposition? Fear not:

> The great thing about food in the Caliphate is its freshness. You can be sure that the vegetables you crunch down on basked gloriously in the sunshine before reaching your dinner plate. And what about olive groves. Yes, there are plenty of them and the pickles and rich oils that spring from them beat anything from your local Tesco's [British grocery store] or Walmart. If nothing here tickles your taste buds then remember we have only scratched the surface; as more Muslims flock to the Caliphate from Europe, Asia, the Caribbean Islands and elsewhere you can be sure to find your mouth watering morsels somewhere. I cannot help but think that in the near future we will be eating curries and chow meins on the streets of Raqqah and Mosul. Lastly, another great perk about food in the Caliphate is that everything is 100% halal. No squinting at the back of food packets looking for those dreaded

> 'E' numbers, alcohol additives or pork gelatine; all the meat here is thoroughly checked and approved for consumption.

On issues of technology, he writes: 'the Islamic State's deft use of media and hi-tech weaponry to further its aims also shows that Islam is not an enemy to modern technology, and in many ways it has propelled the Caliphate brand into something that is stylish and cool'. The fighter assures readers that the Caliphate is equipped with Western technology: 'Inside the Islamic State you will have access to the usual gizmos such as laptops, mobile phones, and of course the internet. Keep in mind that mobile networks are still in the making, but apps such as Skype, Kik, WhatsApp and Telegram, to name but a few, are great alternatives'. He adds:

> As far as the future is concerned, the renewable and non-renewable energy is one place where the Caliphate can move [in] leaps and bounds. Nestled in an energy hotspot, Islamic State scientists will, no doubt, think of innovative ways to tap into the vast amount of resources locked into their surroundings, including amongst others, wind, sunlight, fossil fuels, timber, earth minerals, metal ores, and fresh water; however, this is just one idea amongst a sea of others, and I would still advise keeping your eyes firmly on the battlefields for the real movers and shakers.

From reading this guide, an impressionable reader may be taken away though the florid women's magazine writing style to day-dreaming of munching on a Bounty bar on the cosmopolitan streets of Syria, bought into a false feeling of belonging, not fully taking in the final chapter's chilling prophecy, reminding non-susceptible readers of the underlying message of evil, even if thinly veiled in a Western cloak of domestic civility that pervades the rest of the guide and draws in those vulnerable to such cheap rhetoric:

> when we descend on the streets of London, Paris and Washington, the taste will be far bitterer, because not only will we spill your blood but we will also demolish your statues, erase your history and, most painfully, convert your children, who will then go on to champion our name and curse their forefathers.

Authors such as Al-Britani are also active on social media sites including Twitter and Ask.fm. Responding to issues such as 'what to pack if making the journey to Syria', these individuals also entice and influence jihadists to go to Iraq using similar rhetoric to that in the excerpts in the guide above. Fighters also hold Q&A sessions on discussion boards, where they frankly discuss the ups and downs of their jobs.

The reality of Syria, as reported by one ex-fighter, is that in February 2015, just a few months before the guide was published, citizens were suffering from a lack of water and electricity as the generators that operate them only worked for three to five hours every two days. The price of cooking gas has soared to the equivalent of £50 a cylinder; a litre of petrol costs £2.70 and a bag of flour more than £65. ISIS blew up the mast for mobile phones in late 2014, meaning that only a very small number of civilians have managed to obtain satellite internet lines.[72] The words of Adolf Hitler chime though the ages to these new mediums, when he declared: 'by the skilful and sustained use of propaganda, one can make a people see even heaven as hell or an extremely wretched life as paradise'.

There has been some dissent talk online, demonstrating the instability that social media can bring; however, it is not from the corners one might have thought. So, what is it that has caused online grumblings? One answer is Jihadi brides' lack of quality shampoo. On 8 July 2015, a woman called Muhajira tweeted a photo of local shampoo and wrote: 'No good at all . . .'. Other delightfully childish complaints include 'rubbish' mobile phone reception, crumbling buildings,[73] malicious gossip, the blazing heat and being pestered by terrorist fighters. @OumHaarith posed to her followers on 20 May 2015 (in Carrie Bradshaw fashion): 'When you're in your iddah [mourning period] and the first thing people ask is "Do you want to marry if ure finished?"#GettingTired! Let it be clear. NOHO!!'.

The content is *Dynasty*-worthy, also featuring online rows between Sally Jones, the widow of prominent British ISIS hacker Junaid Hussein, and another jihadi: 'They all sit there gassing [gossiping] in internet cafes when they should be out on Ribat [guard duty]'. ISIS fighter Abu Malik Al Qatari responded to Jones's post, writing: 'You needn't be so rude. I do [did] my share of fighting for the last year and 7 months. This is my ijazah. I just thought I hd 2 point out before I'm accused. We all know who never fired a bullet on [an] enemy [a reference to Jones's deceased hacker husband]'. Step aside, Alexis and Crystal . . .

In order to show its softer side and, as the vast majority of non-Arabic propaganda distributed by ISIS is designed to get attention, often tweeting information at members of the media and government and to enhance the group's image and encourage Westerners to support and join the organisation, ISIS has embarked on 'corporate social responsibility' campaigns to rival charitable aid organisations and multi-national corporates the world over. Several Twitter feeds maintained by ISIS (as well as accounts on Facebook and other social media outlets belonging to ISIS or its supporters) regularly distribute images of militants engaging with children, distributing food and performing other social services. Even more extraordinary, in April 2014, ISIS released a video featuring former German rapper-turned-ISIS-militant Denis Cuspert engaged in a snowball fight with fellow extremists, stating in German: 'Now you see . . . here in Syria, we also can

72 P Cockburn (2015), 'Life under Isis: The everyday reality of living in the Islamic "Caliphate" with its 7th century laws, very modern methods and merciless violence' *The Independent* (15 March) http://www.independent.co.uk/news/world/middle-east/life-under-isis-the-everyday-reality-of-living-in-the-islamic-caliphate-with-its-7th-century-laws-10109655.html.

73 See @GreenBirdDabiq https://twitter.com/account/suspended. Note that this account has now been suspended.

have fun! . . . That's jihad, jihad makes fun . . . and we have fun here with the children . . . Come on, we invite you to jihad!'.[74]

The ISIS social network is not all about snowball fights and charity; other propaganda focuses on the work the organisation is doing to establish a supposedly model Islamic state, which is after all one of the missions of this organisation. However, the power of lengthy videos extolling the virtues of scripture and Arabic teachings had waned to all except the most committed. The key thing that ISIS has grasped, however, is how to take a message and make it appear attractive to the masses.

The issue is summarised aptly thus: '[a]ll propaganda has to be popular and has to accommodate itself to the comprehension of the least intelligent of those whom it seeks to reach'. These are the words, again, of Adolf Hitler. Sven Mary, the Belgian attorney of the suspected and now captured Paris terrorist attacker Salah Abdeslam, commented of his client:

> He's a little a**hole from Molenbeek, who started off as a petty criminal – more of a follower than a leader. He has the intelligence of an empty ashtray, he's utterly vacuous. He's the perfect example of generation GTA [Grand Theft Auto], who think they live inside a video game. He and his friends have succeeded in making an entire religion look bad.[75]

ISIS has also learned the power of making an audience want more, tapping into the desire to view more content and anticipate the next posting. June 2014 saw the start of a YouTube mini-series of short videos called 'Mujatweets' (named ostensibly for their brevity). The videos depict ISIS as a charitable organisation, beloved by civilians and establishing a better society. Episode 1 depicts an apparent European recruit singing a song in German praising ISIS. The second episode shows clips of children having fun with ISIS militants. The third episode features an apparent Syrian chef – an everyday civilian – who explains how good life is now that ISIS controls his region. If this series was focused on the day-to-day happenings of a call centre, political group, hotel or charity, it would not be out of place on the BBC or Channel 4. However, the fourth episode, released in July 2014, took a different tack. Now that viewers had been eased into the world of ISIS, this instalment started a subtle call to action by following an apparently German ISIS member who visits supposedly wounded militants in a hospital, telling viewers: 'Come to the land of honour and search for *shahada* (martyrdom)'.

By August 2014, ISIS had released eight Mujatweet episodes in total. ISIS has also released highly popular short films such as *Khairah Ummah*, in which an ISIS

74 R Sanchez (2014), 'Tweeting at terrorists: inside America's social media battle with online jihad', *The Telegraph* (21May) http://www.telegraph.co.uk/news/worldnews/al-qaeda/10829355/Tweeting-at-terrorists-inside-Americas-social-media-battle-with-online-jihad.html.

75 Vice.news(27April2016)https://news.vice.com/article/suspected-terror-mastermind-salah-abdeslam-is-dumb-as-an-empty-ashtray-his-lawyer-says.

member 'reminds' shopkeepers to go to the mosque on Friday and not to display mannequins with women's clothing, amongst other things. In the 15-minute feature, the presenter explains and creates 'the best *Ummah* [community] produced for mankind'. However, the video takes a sinister turn towards the end, showing how ISIS found and executed a person it claimed to be a sorcerer – a scene meant to show the extent to which it is working to eradicate evil and implement Islamic law and values. *Khairah Ummah* was designed to have high impact and audience reach, being released in multiple versions for Western audiences, with subtitles in several languages, including English, French, Russian and Turkish. Throughout the winter of 2013–2014, ISIS also released a number of propaganda posters explaining the 'virtues of swords', 'virtues of seeking martyrdom' and the benefit of 'racing towards jihad'.

In a video entitled *Messages to the Media Knights*,[76] several ISIS members discuss the role of social media:

> *Interviewer*: Brother, do you feel that the work on the internet by the supporters of the Islamic State is effective?
>
> *ISIS Fighter 1*: By Allah, they have a great and clear impact. Anyone who denies this is ungrateful. Sometimes, when we hear lies about the Islamic State, we are preoccupied in battle. But when we tune in to the media, and see that our brothers defended us and our honour, it makes us happy. May Allah reward them.
>
> *ISIS Fighter 2*: The work of our brothers in the jihadi media has a great impact on the war on the ground. They deliver the message of the *mujahideen* to the nation of Islam. This makes the Muslims sympathize with their brothers, the *mujahideen*. . . . I advise my brothers in the jihadi media to double their efforts. The war is fierce and is about to become fiercer. Their mission is one of great importance, for as we fight the enemies of Allah upon the Earth, they defend the Islamic State, and wage war upon the infidels and the nations of heresy, through the media. Their efforts have a great impact, which is palpable upon the ground, in the war against the infidels and the Crusader coalition.

2.3.5 Refer, recruit, reward

Having a strong presence and following is one thing, but the conflict in Syria requires people actively to join the cause, whether as foot soldiers or as part of the online jihad. Without doubt, there is a massive amount of radicalised activity online, allowing sympathisers to participate without the physical risks of being killed fighting or trapped in a brutal regime without the freedoms that a Western democracy allows.

76 http://www.memrijttm.org/isis-militants-commend-work-of-supporters-on-the-internet.html.

Jihadists such as Neil Prakash, who goes by the fighting name of Abu Khaled al-Cambodi, act as Islamic State's top recruiters, appearing on a select list of key contacts for would-be foreign fighters wanting to join the terror group in the Middle East. Prakash operates one of about 16 Twitter accounts that can be contacted by individuals wanting to travel to Syria or Iraq. Along with Prakash, there are also prominent account holders such as Muhammed Abdullahi Hassan, known as 'Mujahid Miski', an American who encouraged the recent terrorist attack in Texas, and British recruiter Abu Faris al-Britani. The page containing the Twitter contacts states: 'These people live in the Islamic State. They have Surespot and other private messaging apps. If their Twitter is banned, they will always make a new one', whilst another says: 'See you in the Caliphate!'. As well as his Twitter presence, he also provides details of his Surespot account on his Twitter page, so that potential jihadists can communicate with him through the encrypted service without those communications being read by authorities.

Social media efforts have focused on ISIS's military strength and called on followers to join in the fighting. The *Ya Junod Al-Haqq Hayya* video,[77] released early in June 2014, featured prominently displayed English subtitles of a song bragging about ISIS's military conquests and its ability to instil fear in its enemies. Later in the same month, a video called *Haya alal-Jihad* or 'Let's go for Jihad!' featured a song in German, with prominent English subtitles, with the lyrics: 'Brothers join us/We slaughter until the day of Judgment', and proclaims that ISIS members 'love to die'. The song was accompanied by images of explosions, casualties and fighting ISIS members. In February 2015, President Obama stated, during a Washington summit on countering violent extremism: 'Terrorist groups like Al-Qaeda and ISIL deliberately target their propaganda in the hopes of reaching and brainwashing young Muslims, especially those who may be disillusioned or wrestling with their identity'.[78]

The sense of campfire camaraderie embodied in the approach to recruitment may feel fresh but ISIS has done its research, drawing on techniques employed by Al-Qaeda's *Inspire* magazine, which in the early days encouraged Americans to join terrorist training camps abroad and also looked for ways to weave traditional doctrine at length. Reporting on their highly successful short and sharp social media campaigns in publications such as the *Islamic State Report* is therefore also disseminated via Twitter. The Home Office has gone so far as to issue a report on the use of social media by ISIS to recruit both men and women, although its promotion of images of success, the ISIL slogan 'Baqiyah wa-Tatamaddad' (remaining and expanding) presents the group as one that consistently achieves success, whilst portraying their 'Caliphate' as an ideal, utopian state where Muslims will find status and belonging, together with ISIS propaganda output

77 http://blog.adl.org/international/new-terrorist-video-rails-against-jews.

78 Remarks by the President in closing of the Summit on Countering Violent Extremism (18 February 2015) https://www.whitehouse.gov/the-press-office/2015/02/18/remarks-president-closing-summit-countering-violent-extremism.

insisting that it is the personal duty of Muslims to support them and travel to the 'Caliphate'.[79]

Increasingly, terrorist groups and their sympathisers are using youth dominated communities like Facebook, MySpace and Second Life, as well as their Arabic equivalents to recruit. Counter-terrorism expert, Anthony Bergin, says that terrorists view these websites as recruitment tools 'in the same way a paedophile might look at those sites to potentially groom would-be victims'.[80] The reality of life in such organisations is, however, a stark contrast to the world presented by ISIS on social media. In an interview given to the *Independent*, one fighter recalled how, in Fallujah, he and fellow fighters captured Shia soldiers of the Iraqi Army:

> [t]his was the first time that I witnessed a beheading. I had been shown some videos made with impressive visual and audio skill. After watching many of these, we were being taken to attend public executions . . . However, the problem was that I was a little bit shaken after attending those executions. I don't like Shia but when it came to killing them, I was shocked. Although they were showing us videos of Shia militias killing Sunni people, we were troubled when we attended real executions . . . I left them because I was afraid and deeply troubled by this horrible situation. The justice they were calling for when they first arrived in Fallujah turned out to be only words.[81]

2.3.6 Jihadi whispers: is it official yet?

As discussed at the start of the chapter, the real game changer social media brings is that it levels out the playing-field in terms of participation. Although there is still an element of hierarchy, the accounts not controlled or officially endorsed by a terrorist group have a great deal of sway. ISIS official Twitter accounts are supported by people who have accounts that have quasi-official status. Think of Twitter account holders such as Markaz al Islam or local government or a franchise of a fast food chain. However, whilst the beehive formed by apps such as *Dawn of Glad Tidings* are useful for spreading the message, the more you dilute the command network for posting, the more the risk that your message changes or you can't control the timing. When it comes to terrorist on social media, it is not Chinese whispers anymore: it is *Jihadi whispers*.

79 https://www.gov.uk/government/uploads/system/uploads/attachment_data/file/440450/How_social_media_is_used_to_encourage_travel_to_Syria_and_Iraq.pdf. Islamic scholars have clearly dismissed this and have made clear there is no such obligation.

80 'Facebook terrorism investigation'. *The Advertiser* (5 April 2008, 10 March 2009).

81 P Cockburn (2015), 'Life under Isis: Why I deserted the "Islamic State" rather than take part in executions, beheadings and rape: the story of a former jihadi', *The Independent* (16 March) http://www.independent.co.uk/news/world/middle-east/life-under-isis-why-i-deserted-the-islamic-state-rather-than-take-part-in-executions-beheadings-and-10111877.html.

2.3.6.1 #Error

Perhaps one of the best reported Twitter blunders, which highlighted that rather than just a PR crisis, social media has the potential quite literally to lead the enemy to your door from the comfort of their living room is that of Mark John Taylor (who reportedly now goes by the name of Mohammad Daniel or Abu Abdul Rahman). Taylor, who slipped out of New Zealand in May 2012, despite being subject to travel restrictions, surfaced in Syria in June 2015. 'My current location is in Syria and my commitment is for jihad for Allah, and his Messenger', he said in a YouTube video posted that month.

Taylor failed to turn off the location service on his Twitter account, thereby identifying his whereabouts every time he tweeted. Now, whilst the greatest consequence of this for the general public is that you get caught at your secret lover's address, or out partying when you have told your boss you are sick – on their blog, iBrabo, an open source intelligence research group located in Ontario, Canada, wrote that they had been able to track Taylor's activities through his Twitter account as he moved from Kafar Roma to the desert and then to Isis stronghold Al Tabqah. One tweet states that his mission to Syria was a 'one-way trip' and featured a picture of his burnt passport.[82]

Taylor, realising his error and demonstrating a naivety as to the 'recordability' of postings online, deleted 45 tweets from his account @M_Taylor_Kiwi, but not before screenshots had been captured by iBrabo. The research group was also able to pinpoint a specific house in Al Tabqah where Taylor stayed between 3–10 December 2014. Taylor has been placed on a watch list after visiting another New Zealand radical, Muslim bin John, in Yemen in 2009. John was killed by a drone strike in Yemen in November 2013 along with an Australian, Christopher Harvard.

If it is some small comfort to Taylor that his blunder played out in the international press, he is not the only account holder to undermine the strategic aims of ISIS. After Anwar al-Awlaki and Samir Khan were killed in airstrikes in Yemen during September 2011, English language propagandist Omar Hammami[83] (also known as Abu Mansur al-Amriki), an al-Shabaab American commander, poised to become the most important and influential English-speaking jihadi in the world, flummoxed his bid to rise through the ranks on 16 March 2012, when he took to YouTube to upload a video titled *Urgent Message*, stating that: 'To whomever it may reach from the Muslims . . . I record this message today because I fear

82 M Safi (2015), 'New Zealander Accidentally Tweets Location' *The Guardian* (1 January) <http://www.theguardian.com/world/2015/jan/01/new-zealander-syria-isis-accidentally-tweets-locations.

83 Hammami was born in Alabama to a Native American mother and a Syrian-born father. He was the president of his American college's chapter of the Muslim Students Association, whose websites were monitored by police. He dropped out of college in 2002, travelled with a friend to Somalia and then joined the terrorist group. He previously mocked the United States after false reports that a drone attack had killed him.

my life may be endangered by [al-Shaba] because of some differences that occurred regarding matters of the Sharia and of strategy'. This was swiftly followed by confirmation by A. R. Sayyid, the editor and writer of the *Somali War Monitor*, that there were no conversations in Somali on the al-Qimmah Islamic network.[84]

The Islamic Awakening Forum silenced discussion on the matter and conversation on the subject was also completely banned on the Ansar al-Mujahidin English forum. Much like corporate organisations when they have a reputational crisis, the only content allowed on the forums regarding this matter was the official response and statements from al-Shabaab, which down-played the controversy by claiming the group was surprised by the video and looking into its content, maintaining that Hammami was safe.[85]

As seen from this example, social media can prove an unpredictable medium and difficult to control. A video that allegedly showed the execution of Steven Sotloff emerged online before it was officially scheduled to be released through a Twitter account. The video contained a message directly addressing President Obama on matters concerning the Caliphate. User @Khattabyaz warned the first account there had been a mistake, and failed to stop the beheading video from being disseminated, the website reported. ISIS then wrote on *Justpasteit*:

> A clarification about the mistake was made by 'Uyun al-Ummah' account, that has published the video before the official time. The user saw a tweet with the video and thought it was published officially. We tried to remove the video after we understood that his was published by mistake, and we are sorry to the followers of the Islamic State.[86]

In a later Twitter message, those responsible apologised and asked fellow jihadis not to 'reproach' them.

The cases discussed above show a few examples of the instability that using the internet can bring. In terms of the online and social media timeline, the erosion of the command and control network has been ongoing since 2001. Despite repeated efforts by Al-Qaeda Central, the grandfather of ISIS, Abu Musab al Zarqawi, could not be reined in. In a letter dating back to July 2005, Zawahiri reproved Zarqawi for his videotaped beheadings of hostages, a self-declared 'all-out war' against Shiites, and to launch indiscriminate attacks against Muslim civilians. It was felt, by Zawahiri, that these actions were causing alienation and preventing the success of the broader media war. Quite simply in his opinion:

84 Interview with A R Sayyid via Twitter (17 March 2012) https://twitter.com/SomWarMonitor/status/181087306097246209.

85 See Zelin (n 7); http://webcache.googleusercontent.com/search?q=cache:Kz8fxQ_tGiMJ:www.washingtoninstitute.org/uploads/Documents/opeds/20130201-NewAmericaFoundation.pdf+&cd=1&hl=en&ct=clnk&gl=uk.

86 http://justpaste.it/gxlp.

'[w]e don't need this'.[87] However, given Zarqawi's behaviour over the subsequent year, it was also wholly ineffective and, despite the criticism levelled at him, jihadi guerrilla operations in Iraq have, on balance, been spectacularly successful and have had numerous viewings.

2.3.7 The command and control network

Social media is not simply a tool of propaganda or a recruitment machine; it is also a means to organise attacks. Recently, an aspiring suicide bomber and his secret wife, who had a 'common interest' in violent jihad, have been found guilty of planning an ISIS-inspired terror attack on London after testing lethal bombs in their back garden. Mohammed Rehman, 25, planned to blow up either Westfield shopping centre or the London Underground to coincide with the 10th anniversary of the 7/7 bombings. He and his wife immersed themselves in ISIS and Al-Qaeda propaganda, and idolised 7/7 bomber Shehzad Tanweer. Tweeting under Silent Bomber (@InService2God), Rehman was caught after posting: 'Westfield shopping centre London underground? Any advice greatly appreciated'. The tweet – sent from a profile showing a photograph of Jihadi John – was accompanied by a link to the Al-Qaeda uncensored media release about the 7/7 atrocities. When officers raided their home they found 10 kg of nitrate explosives, twice the amount used in the failed 21/7 London bombings. Officers also found videos of test explosions filmed in Rehman's garden. In the court case, again, the prosecution said that the would-be bomber was just days away from completing the device, which would have caused multiple casualties in the capital.

The Rehmans are not alone. In March 2016, Mohammed Mohsin Ameen went on trial for sending thousands of tweets glorifying acts of terror and encouraging extremism under 42 different Twitter handles, with names including 'Anti-coconut-01', which celebrated the 9/11 attack on New York's Twin Towers as well as tributes to 'martyred' ISIS fighters. Ameen pleaded guilty at the Old Bailey to five counts of encouraging the commission, preparation or instigation of acts of terrorism on Twitter. As well as general propaganda activities, he admitted a further charge of inviting support for Islamic State, and disseminating a terrorist publication relating to a link to a video entitled *For the Sake of Allah* on Twitter.

Ameen made posts such as: '#TheMagnificent19 May you all get accepted in the highest ranks and multiply your kind! #Happy 911 – includes image of 9/11 bombers'. Another read: 'The #ISIS fighter who chose to drive a truck filled with tons of explosives instead of his Rolls-Royce #Kirkuk #Iraq'. Ameen's home was first raided in December 2013 when police found a one-way ticket from Luton to Istanbul and, in June 2014, anti-terror 'Prevent officers' interviewed him about his possible desire to leave the country to join ISIS. He took to Twitter in March 2015, amassing more than 8000 tweets before he was arrested on 21 October 2015 under

87 Letter from al-Zawahiri to Zarqawi (n 3) 4–5, 10.

section 41 of the Terrorism Act 2000.[88] The question for the future is: when will the use of social media be subject to the Terrorism Prevention and Investigation Measures (TPIM)?

2.3.8 Will social media replace the forums?

Although social media is undoubtedly a powerful medium to communicate terrorist materials and propaganda, Al-Qaeda continues to release content through online forums so that it can maintain control over content and authorship. This is why Al-Qaeda accredited forums such as Shamukh al-Islam and al-Fida al-Islam remain the first locations where new releases will appear. According to research conducted by the Washington Institute, when these forums went down in March 2012, no new outlets appeared until Shamukh al-Islam came back up on 4 April 2012, but users did turn to second tier forums such as AMAF and social media accounts such as Ansar al-Mujahidin Arabic Forum (@as_ansar) and the Somali al-Qimmah Islamic Network (@AlqimmahNetwork), which did report on matters in the interim. Others also joining Twitter have included: Ansar al-Shariah in Yemen's media outlet Madad News Agency (@W_mdd); Asad al-Jihad2 (@AsadAljehad2), a prominent online jihadi essayist; Minbar at-Tawhid wa-l-Jihad (@MinbarTawhed), a library of jihadi scholarly materials; Jabhat al-Nusrah (@JbhatALnusra), the premier jihadi organisation active in Syria; and Muhammad al-Zawahiri (@M7mmd_Alzwahiri), the brother of Ayman Al-Qaeda Central's leader and an influential Egyptian jihadi in his own right.[89]

Whilst Twitter has brought jihad further into the public consciousness for strategic missions, it is unlikely to replace the protected world of the forums entirely, even with the evolution of encryption standards offered by social network services. The ease and availability of social media does offer user flexibility and instantaneous reporting but, as we have seen in this chapter, with such freedom comes risks as a consequence of the lack of control that can be exerted over postings made by non-official account holders. Media attention has focused, perhaps not unreasonably, on ISIS's use of social media. However, it is important to acknowledge that these activities are supported by sophisticated online machinery.

88 L Crossley (2016), 'ISIS fanatic, 23, pleads guilty to trying to recruit support for the terror group with thousands of tweets' *Daily Mail* (31 March) http://www.dailymail.co.uk/news/article-3517065/ISIS-fanatic-23-pleads-guilty-trying-recruit-support-terror-group-thousands-tweets.html#ixzz44UM88LHF.

89 See Zelin (n 7).

3 Freedom of the newsfeed

> I believe in censorship. I made a fortune out of it.
>
> Mae West, Actress

> You announce daily that you suspend many of our accounts, and to you we say, 'Is that all you can do?' You are not in our league. If you close one account we will take 10 in return and soon your names will be erased after we delete your sites, Allah willing, and will know that we say is true.[1]

These are the words fired across cyberspace to Silicone Valley giants Facebook CEO Mark Zuckerberg and Twitter CEO Jack Dorsey by of one of the world's deadliest terrorist groups, ISIS. In a 25-minute video entitled 'Flames of the Supporters', uploaded to the discerning jihadists' choice of social network 'telegram', the tech giants are pictured against images of bullet holes.

As discussed in Chapter 2, there is terrorist group content available online that ranges from the bone-chilling to the ridiculous. So, if social media fans the flames of violent extremist speech online causing the spread of its fire to grow by its very accessibility and though the use of 'shares', 'hashtags' and 'likes', it could (perhaps) be suggested that the only way to put out the fire it is to cut off the oxygen that fuels it, that is to say, to cut off the access to social media platforms on which comments are posted. As we have seen in Chapter 2, the incredible ease with which would-be terrorists and jihadists are recruited online presents the authorities with a rather sticky conundrum: do you shut down the networks where the conversations and conversions are happening, or do you let them go on, given that such postings are also a veritable treasure trove for law enforcement officials in terms of knowing what terrorists are up to? As the director of Europol has claimed: '[w]e know much less than the private sector. All recent cyber-crime operations you've heard about on the news were launched on the basis of information provided by the private sector'.[2]

1 The video was discovered by Vocativ. See http://www.vocativ.com/news/289402/isis-threatens-mark-zuckerberg-and-jack-dorsey/.

2 R Wainwright (2014), 'Cybercrime and the challenges for law enforcement', speech to LIBE Committee, European Parliament (11 November).

DOI: 10.4324/9781315668680-3

As social networking sites are private corporations with their own commercial goals, they can (in theory) allow anybody who so wishes to use their platforms. That said, there will, of course, be situations where (just like any other organisation or citizen) they are required to comply with the law or requests made by law enforcement agencies. In the context of terrorist content, such platform providers have faced real difficulties in applying their moderation policies in a way that does not amount to censorship or infringement of people's right to freedom of expression. In the USA and Europe, in particular, where speech is protected by the First Amendment and the European Convention on Human Rights (ECHR) respectively, this has led to significant discussion at the highest level.

As we saw in Chapter 1, one man's terrorist is arguably another man's freedom fighter (or Facebook friend), so how do the sites decide what speech is extreme; what speech amounts to credible terrorist threat; and what are there mere postings of 'plastic' wannabe jihadists – who are all talk and no action? The very notion of freedom of expression as we know it in a democratic society is, potentially, under threat. Furthermore, what should the response be if the next Jihadi John or Osama bin Laden post is a video about knitting or the benefits of yoga home practice alongside radicalisation videos? Just because it's a post by a terrorist, does not necessarily mean their right to freedom of expression should be curtailed if their posts are not 'terrorist' in nature or promoting violent extremism.

Who too should sit in judgement of the removal of such content? Should it be the state or will social media sites preside over censoring such content? What will become clear from the examples explored in this chapter is that, even if the social media sites adopt an approach of taking down terrorist content, it is still very difficult to know where to draw the line. In a bid to stop bushfires you can't cut down all the trees, as there would be no trees to generate the oxygen that everyone breathes in order to survive and give breath to their expression.

3.1 Freedom of the newsfeed

So what is the situation now with regard to moderating online content and the responsibilities of the social media sites? It seems that the jury is still out. Whilst there is active lobbying activity both in the UK and across the channel, there is not a consensus as to what these privately owned sites need to do in practice. They are caught between a rock and a hard place – giving effect to freedom of expression, whilst not being seen as arbiters of state censorship through the backdoor or as a mouthpiece for terrorists and thereby facilitating terrorist causes. As we saw in Chapter 2, individuals have a right to freedom of expression but with such rights come certain restrictions, which were developed long before the creation of social networks. So, how is speech regulated online and protected from undue interference by the state?

3.1.1 Takedown requests made by the state

3.1.1.1 Restrictions on freedom of expression

In Europe, states party to free speech provisions must ensure that there is legal and administrative governance in place, sufficient to address the regulation of such mediums in a manner which is consistent with Article 19(3) of the International Covenant on Civil and Political Rights 1966 (ICCPR), which provides that:

> The exercise of the rights provided for in paragraph 2 of this Article carries with it special duties and responsibilities. It may therefore be subject to certain restrictions, but these shall only be such as are provided by law and are necessary: (a) For respect of the rights or reputations of others; (b) For the protection of national security or of public order (ordre public), or of public health or morals.

This is reflected in Article 10(2) of the ECHR, which states that:

> [t]he exercise of these freedoms, since it carries with it duties and responsibilities, may be subject to such formalities, conditions, restrictions or penalties as are prescribed by law and are necessary in a democratic society, in the interests of national security, territorial integrity or public safety, for the prevention of disorder or crime, for the protection of health or morals, for the protection of the reputation or rights of others, for preventing the disclosure of information received in confidence, or for maintaining the authority and impartiality of the judiciary.

The United Nations (UN) report entitled 'Comprehensive Study on Cyber-crime'[3] noted that the increasing use of social media and user-generated internet content has resulted in regulatory responses from governments, including the use of criminal law and calls for respect of rights to freedom of expression. For example, in the UK the Metropolitan Police's Counter-terrorism Internet Referral Unit (CTIRU) is charged with reviewing terrorist and violent extremist material online and contacting the relevant internet hosting company to ensure that content which breaches terror legislation is taken down. Each week on average the unit makes 1100 requests about such sites and about 80 per cent of the postings are Syria- or Iraq-related.[4] In 2012, the United Nations Human Rights Council's panel discussion on the promotion and protection of freedom of expression on the internet stated:

> Online content has particular features – including the fact that the impact and longevity of information can be multiplied when placed on the internet, that content is easily accessible to minors, and that developments in social

3 United Nations Office on Drugs and Crime, 'Draft Comprehensive Study on Cybercrime' (2013).

4 M Townsend and T Helm (2014) 'Jihad in a social media age: how can the west win an online war?' *Guardian* (23 August).

media and user-generated internet content have begun to challenge traditional monopolies over information.[5]

In 2011, the European Court of Human Rights (ECtHR) Research Division stated that the interpretation of human rights provisions must take into account the specific nature of the internet as a means of imparting information, given that social media (and the internet) have become increasingly important aspects of political activity and socio-cultural expression.[6]

3.1.2 The margin of appreciation

Described as being 'as slippery and elusive as an eel',[7] the human rights doctrine of the 'margin of appreciation' allows for a certain amount of leeway to EU Member States in determining the boundaries of acceptable expression in line with their own cultures and legal traditions.[8] It is regarded as one of the most prominent judge-made legal constructs in European human rights jurisprudence, ensuring a minimum level of human rights protection is met in all contracting states, whilst at the same time allowing some latitude for the particularities of each jurisdiction subject to the ECHR.

The margin of appreciation is illustratively employed in respect of qualified rights of the Convention, such as freedom of expression contained in Article 10 of the ECHR. As set out above, Article 10(2) of the ECHR acknowledges the possibility of limitations to the protected right, where 'prescribed by law' or 'in accordance with the law' they meet a legitimate aim and are 'necessary in a democratic society'. Articles of the ECHR such as Article 10, that require balancing with other rights, or need to be weighed up against other aspects of the public interest, are largely devolved to national courts, in recognition of their expertise regarding matters pertaining to national law.[9] Although this subsidiarity to national law can be inferred from these qualified rights, the margin does not, however, provide blanket exemptions to overcome the application of convention rights; rather, it allows convention rights to remain mindful of national context, as located in the rights as set out by the Convention.[10]

5 United Nations Human Rights Council (2012) 'Summary of the Human Rights Council panel discussion on the promotion and protection of freedom of expression on the internet. Report of the Office of the United Nations High Commissioner for Human Rights' A/HRC/21/30 (2 July).

6 ECtHR Research Division (2011), 'Internet: Case-law of the European Court of Human Rights'.

7 A Lester (1998), 'Universality vs Subsidiarity: A reply' 1 EHRLR 73, 75.

8 A Legg (2012), *The Margin of Appreciation in International Human Rights Law* (Oxford: Oxford Monographs in International Law).

9 *Handyside v United Kingdom*, Application no 5493/72, ECtHR (7 December 1976).

10 As noted by Sir Nicolas Bratza, former president of the ECtHR, the margin is therefore a 'valuable tool devised by the Court itself to assist it in defining the scope of its review, . . . it is a variable notion which is not susceptible of precise definition' in 'Reforming the European Convention on Human Rights: *Interlaken, İzmir, Brighton* and beyond – A compilation of instruments and texts relating to the ongoing reform of the ECHR Directorate General Human Rights and Rule of Law' (Council of Europe, 2014) 82.

The margin is not necessarily applied consistently in every case and has been criticised for its unclear nature and unpredictability.[11] However, whilst not technically bound by its own precedent, the ECtHR does, in practice, respect it. In 1976, in *Handyside*,[12] the Court made it clear that there is a sequential process involved when securing human rights: (i) an assessment of the compatibility of national measures with the Convention is best made by national courts; and (ii) subsequently, if required, a review of this assessment is undertaken by the ECtHR. With regard to Article 10 in particular, the ECtHR has acknowledged that national authorities are, with their knowledge of contextual considerations, e.g. standard relation to public morals, able to assess the content limitations that may be placed on ECHR rights, as well as the degree to which the limitations imposed are necessary.

It is not the Court's role to standardise views across the Member States, but rather to coordinate the protection of human rights in light of their differences. In *Handyside*, the word 'necessary' was judged to mean that there was a 'pressing social need' for the interference.[13] The adoption, in May 2015, of Protocol No 15 to the Convention added explicit references to both the margin of appreciation and to the principle of subsidiarity to the Convention's preamble, meaning that the margin will no longer be purely founded in case law, but will (according to the explanatory report which accompanies the protocol) remain 'consistent with the doctrine of the margin of appreciation as developed by the Court and its case law'.[14]

However, this is not to suggest that national courts have free rein to decide when rights can be restricted. Closely tied to the margin is the principle of proportionality, that is to say, a consideration as to whether the national measures are appropriate and do not go beyond what is necessary to meet a specific objective. For example, in the *Vereinigung Demokratischer Soldaten Österreichs und Gubi* case,[15] the Court decided that a prohibition on the dissemination of a journal to soldiers was a disproportionate restriction because the contents of the articles were not a serious threat to military discipline, even though they were critical of military life.

11 See House of Lords House of Commons Joint Committee on the Draft Voting Eligibility (Prisoners) Bill Session 2013–14 HL Paper 103 HC 924 (18 December 2013) para [60].

12 *Handyside v United Kingdom* (n 9).

13 R Gordon, T Ward and T Eicke (2001), *The Strasbourg Case Law* (London: Sweet & Maxwell) 1125–38.

14 Council of Europe, 'Explanatory note to protocol no. 15 amending the Convention for the protection of Human rights and fundamental freedoms' CETS no 213, para 7 www.echr.coe.int/Documents/Protocol_15_explanatory_report_Eng.pdf. Article 1 of protocol no 15 provides that the following text will be added to the final paragraph of the Convention's preamble: 'Affirming that the High Contracting Parties, in accordance with the principle of subsidiarity, have the primary responsibility to secure the rights and freedoms designed in this Convention and the Protocols thereto, and that in doing so they enjoy a margin of appreciation, subject to the supervisory jurisdiction of the European Court of Human Rights established by this Convention'.

15 *Vereinigung Demokratischer Soldaten Österreichs und Gubi v Austria*, Judgment of 19 December 1994.

The increasing use of social media and user-generated internet content has resulted in regulatory responses from government, including the use of criminal law, and calls for respect for rights to freedom of expression.[16] Although, as acknowledged by Article 10(2) of the ECHR, there are many instances in which freedom of expression can be restricted, and the potential implications of such restrictions are arguably most illustratively explored by reference to the criminalisation of such expression.[17]

3.1.3 Legislation restricting freedom of expression

In the UK, cases involving criminal behaviour can be prosecuted under an umbrella of legislation. Sections 4A and 5 of the Public Order Act 1986 (POA) make it an offence for a person to use threatening, abusive or insulting words or behaviour that causes (or is likely to cause) another person harassment, alarm or distress.[18] Section 127 of the Communications Act 2003 makes it an offence to send a message by means of a public electronic communications network which is grossly offensive, or of an indecent, obscene or menacing nature.

With regard to terrorism-related offences specifically, section 1 of the Terrorism Act 2006 criminalises the 'encouragement of terrorism', which includes making statements that glorify terrorist acts, as well as disseminating terrorist publications under section 2 of the Act, which is punishable by up to seven years' imprisonment.[19] It is an offence even if the person or group making the statement does not intend to encourage terrorism. The Act also makes it an offence to collect, make or possess material that could be used in a terrorist act, for example bomb-making manuals.[20] In the USA, current statutes make it a crime to provide 'material support' – including expert advice or assistance – to organisations designated as terrorist groups by the State Department,[21] which feels at odds with the First Amendment guarantee of free speech. Whilst there are special derogations for

16 United Nations Office on Drugs and Crime (2013), 'Comprehensive Study on Cyber-crime' ch 4: 'Criminalization' 107.

17 A Bailin (2011), 'Criminalising Free Speech? *Criminal Law Review* 705; and Council of Europe (2003), 'Convention on Cybercrime 2001, ETS 185 and its Additional Protocol concerning the criminalisation of acts of a racist and xenophobic nature committed through computer systems' (ETS 2003) 189.

18 In 2006 the Racial and Religious Hatred Act amended the Public Order Act to make it an offence punishable by up to seven years' imprisonment to use threatening words or behaviour intended to stir up religious hatred.

19 Under section 1(7) and section 2(11)(a) respectively, a person guilty of an offence under this section shall be liable (a) on conviction on indictment, to imprisonment for a term not exceeding seven years or to a fine, or to both; (b) on summary conviction in England and Wales, to imprisonment for a term not exceeding 12 months or to a fine not exceeding the statutory maximum, or to both.

20 Home Office, Office for Security and Counter-terrorism, 'Safeguarding Online: Explaining the Risk Posed by Violent Extremism' http://cms.walsall.gov.uk/officers-esafety-leaflet-v5.pdf at 3.

21 Gregory McNeal (2008), 'Cyber Embargo: Countering the Internet Jihad' (2007–2008) 39(3) *Case Western Reserve Journal of International Law* 792.

materials such as child pornography, there is no consensus as to how to deal with terrorism content per se, unless of course there was a clear case to incite violence, intent is not always easy to infer, as will be seen from the case of *Chambers*, discussed below. In the 1960 case of *Brandenburg v Ohio*, the court held that the government cannot punish inflammatory speech unless it is inciting or likely to incite imminent unlawful action.[22]

So what does this mean in terms of categorising speech as criminal? The United Nations Committee on Crime Prevention and Control[23] has stated that: 'crime is what is defined by law as such. On the other hand, the definition must take into account the existence of, and respect for human rights and not merely be the expression of arbitrary power'.[24] In other words, national criminal laws are not to be excluded from the oversight of international human rights law.[25] The UN report entitled 'Comprehensive Study on Cyber-crime' acknowledges that there are diverse national approaches to the criminalisation of internet and social media content, which can be accommodated by international human rights law, within certain boundaries.[26] However, this is not to suggest that criminalisation may fall within the margin of appreciation in every case. Indeed, the UN, in the same report, suggests that criminalisation may not be justified if it concerns criminal

22 *Brandenburg v. Ohio*, 395 U.S. 444 (1969) www.oyez.org/cases/1960-1969/1968/1968_492/.

23 The Committee was established by resolution of the United Nations Economic and Social Council in May 1971. See United Nations Economic and Social Council, Resolution 1548(L) (1971).

24 M López-Rey (1978), 'Crime and Human Rights' 43(1) *Federal Probation* 10–15, 11.

25 The human rights contained in customary international law, the nine core international human rights treaties and their protocols, as well as the treaties of the three regional human rights mechanisms, and the authoritative interpretations of these instruments by mechanisms established thereunder, or otherwise for the purposes of their promotion and implementation, are taken as the principal expression of 'international human rights law'. These include: ICCPR, ICESCR, ICERD, CEDAW, CAT, CRC, ICRMW, CPED and CRPD. In addition, Optional Protocols to ICESCR, ICCPR, CEDAW, CRC, CAT, and CRPD cover areas such as the abolition of the death penalty (ICCPR-OP2), the involvement of children in armed conflict (OP-CRC-AC), and the sale of children, child prostitution and child pornography (OP-CRC-SC). At the regional level, customary international law includes: ECHR and its 15 Protocols, including on protection of property and the right to education, freedom of movement, abolition of the death penalty, and a general prohibition on discrimination, the ACHR in the Americas, and in Africa, the ACHPR. At present, there is no Asia-wide convention on human rights. With some notable exceptions (such as the obligation to make all acts of torture a criminal offence and the prohibition of retroactive criminal offences), international human rights law has not traditionally specified directly what should, or should not, be a criminal offence in national law. However, this is not to suggest that international human rights law jurisprudence does not increasingly face the question of whether the criminalisation of certain conduct is compatible with, or even required, by individual human rights and in doing so can act both as a 'shield' and a 'sword', either neutralising or triggering the criminal law. See F Tulkens (2011), 'The Paradoxical Relationship between Criminal Law and Human Rights' 9(3) *Journal of International Criminal Justice* 577–95.

26 United Nations Office on Drugs and Crime (n 16) 116. These include permissible criminal prohibitions on: child pornography; direct and public incitement to commit genocide; advocacy of national, racial or religious hatred that constitutes incitement to discrimination, hostility or violence; incitement to terrorism; and propaganda for war.

offences relating to defamation, obscene material and insult.[27] These types of activity are likely to face a high threshold test, even within the margin of appreciation, in order to demonstrate that the measures conform to the principle of proportionality, are appropriate to achieve their protective function, and are the least intrusive instrument amongst those which might achieve protection.[28]

3.1.4 Offensive content and hate speech

Although there are situations where the material in question will clearly amount to terrorist-related activity, such as uploading a YouTube video describing how to make a bomb, one area that has caused much debate in terms of the restriction of speech online is what amounts to offensive content, as opposed to hate speech. With regard to hate speech, Article 20 of the ICCPR provides that: '(1) any propaganda for war shall be prohibited by law; (2) any advocacy of national, racial or religious hatred that constitutes incitement to discrimination, hostility or violence shall be prohibited by law'.

The UN has suggested that, whilst Article 20 ICCPR is engaged, as it imposes an obligation to combat such expression,[29] in order to meet the threshold, *restrictions* on such speech must meet the following three-part test of: (i) legality; (ii) proportionality; and (iii) necessity. The severity of the hate speech, which may justify restricting freedom of expression, must also be considered. The UN has indicated this should include an assessment of: (i) the context of the statement; (ii) the position or status of the speaker; (iii) the intent (negligence and recklessness should not suffice); (iv) the content or form of the statement; (v) the extent of the statement; and (vi) the degree of risk of harm resulting.[30]

These non-binding principles further highlight that the terms 'hatred' and 'hostility' used in ICCPR Article 20 refer to 'intense and irrational emotions of opprobrium, enmity and detestation towards the target group'.[31] Therefore, speech can be restricted in circumstances where, for example, there is advocacy of national, racial or religious hatred that constitutes incitement to discrimination, hostility or violence; incitement to terrorism; and propaganda for war.[32]

At the European level, the ECtHR emphasises the need for genuine and serious incitement to extremism to be present. For example, in the United Kingdom,

27 Ibid.

28 United Nations Human Rights Committee, General Comment No 34 art 19: Freedoms of opinion and expression CCPR/C/GC/34 (12 September 2011) para [34].

29 United Nations Office on Drugs and Crime (n 16) 113.

30 United Nations Office of the High Commissioner for Human Rights (2012), 'Rabat Plan of Action on the prohibition of advocacy of national, racial or religious hatred that constitutes incitement to discrimination, hostility or violence'. Conclusions and recommendations emanating from the four regional expert workshops organised by OHCHR in 2011 and adopted by experts in Rabat, Morocco on 5 October 2012.

31 United Nations Human Rights Committee, General Comment No 34 art 19; Camden Principles on Freedom of Expression and Equality, Principle 12.

32 United Nations Office on Drugs and Crime (n 16) 113.

'encouraging' terrorism is criminalised by section 1 of the Terrorism Act 2006, as opposed to ideas such as those such as speech prosecuted under the Communications Act 2003, that simply offend, shock or disturb others.[33]

In *DPP v Chambers*,[34] a case that can only be described as a key moment of British eccentricity, Mr Chambers posted a joking tweet on Twitter about blowing up Robin Hood Airport. Mr Chambers was motivated by love: using Twitter the appellant met another Twitter user (identified as 'Crazycolours') online. She was a woman who lives in Northern Ireland. The pair started communicating using Twitter, and a romance developed. The appellant was due to fly to Belfast from Doncaster Robin Hood Airport to meet 'Crazycolours' on 15 January 2010. On 6 January 2010, following an alert on Twitter, the appellant became aware of problems at Doncaster Robin Hood Airport, owing to adverse weather conditions. He and 'Crazycolours' had a dialogue on Twitter: '@ Crazycolours: I was thinking that if it does then I had decided to resort to terrorism': '@ Crazycolours: That's the plan! I am sure the pilots will be expecting me to demand a more exotic location than NI'. Some two hours later, when he heard that the airport had closed, he posted the following message: 'Crap! Robin Hood Airport is closed. You've got a week and a bit to get your shit together otherwise I am blowing the airport sky high!!' The joke was taken seriously and he was arrested, charged with sending a grossly offensive message by way of a communications network under section 127 of the Communications Act 2003 (which will be explored in more depth later in this chapter).

After a long and much-debated case, Mr Chambers was eventually acquitted by the High Court, with comedians Al Murray and Stephen Fry in tow to support the erstwhile Tweeter's right to make a joke, albeit a very foolish one. In *Chambers*, the court took the view that English law had long been tolerant of satirical and even distasteful opinions about matters of both a serious and trivial nature. The court also noted that the 2003 Act predated the advent of Twitter. The Lord Chief Justice, Lord Judge, expressed the view that:

> The 2003 Act did not create some newly minted interference with the first of President Roosevelt's essential freedoms – freedom of speech and expression. Satirical, or iconoclastic, or rude comment, the expression of unpopular or unfashionable opinion about serious or trivial matters, banter or humour, even if distasteful to some or painful to those subjected to it should and no doubt will continue at their customary level, quite undiminished by this legislation.[35]

33 Council of Europe (2012), 'Factsheet – Hate speech' (July) http://www.echr.coe.int/Documents/FS_Hate_speech_ENG.pdf.

34 [2012] EWHC 2157.

35 [2006] UKHL 40 at [28].

It would appear, from a reading of the case transcripts, that the prevalent judicial attitudes arise from a desire to restrict the scope of free speech to speech that is civil or palatable (termed 'pro-civility').[36] However, it is suggested that (from cases such as *R v Collins*) censorship in the context of racist hate speech where, despite unpopularity or otherwise, the speech is outlawed,[37] repression may be acceptable when that suppression is based on the 'rights of others' because it accords with the principles underlying free speech.[38] However, pro-civility cannot be an acceptable starting point to determine criminal liability in *every* case of distasteful speech that does not necessarily amount to hate speech and may merely be distasteful rather than grossly offensive (whatever that may mean, given the varying approaches taken in the case law).

The UK is not the only jurisdiction to take such an approach to the regulation of speech online. For example, on 14 January 2015, the French comedian Dieudonné M'bala M'bala was arrested, reportedly on suspicion of publicly condoning terrorism.[39] Publicly condoning (*faire publiquement l'apologie*) acts of terrorism is a crime under Article 421-2-5 of the French Criminal Code, and is punishable with up to five years' imprisonment and a fine of €75,000. Harsher penalties for the offence are available when it is committed online, allowing for up to seven years' imprisonment and a fine of €100,000. The arrest was believed to be connected to a Facebook post saying 'tonight, as far as I'm concerned, I feel like Charlie Coulibaly', a reference to Amedy Coulibaly, who it is alleged killed four hostages at a kosher supermarket shortly after the Hebdo attacks. Justice Minister Christiane Taubira said words of hatred and contempt had to be fought with the 'utmost vigour'. Dieudonné had already been convicted for inciting anti-Semitism and the courts banned several of his one-man shows in 2015. It has been argued, by some commentators, most notably by the Article 19 human rights watchdog that: 'Jokes posted on Facebook about terrorist atrocities, even if distasteful or offensive, are protected by the right to freedom of expression if they

36 A Geddis, 'Free speech martyrs or unreasonable threats to social peace?' [2004] *Public Law* 853, 855. See also examples of this attitude in *Percy v DPP* [2001] EWHC Admin 1125; [2002] ACD 24; *Connolly v DPP* [2007] EWHC 237 (Admin); *Novartis Pharmaceuticals UK Ltd v Stop Huntingdon Animal Cruelty* [2009] EWHC 2716 (QB); [2010] HRLR 8.

37 See Public Order Act 1986 Pt III and, in particular, s 18; see also Crime and Disorder Act 1998 ss 28(1)(b) and 31(1)(c) in relation to Public Order Act 1986 s 5. See also ECHR art 17, discussed in *Norwood v UK* (2005) 40 EHRR SE 111; *Glimmerveen and Hagenbeek v Netherlands* (1982) 4 EHRR 260; *DPP v Collins* [2006] UKHL 40; [2006] 1 WLR 2223. In international law, see art 4 of the Convention on the Elimination of all Forms of Racial Discrimination 660 UNTS 195 (entered into force 4 January 1969); art 20(2) of the International Covenant on Civil and Political Rights 993 UNTS 3 (entered into force 3 January 1976).

38 S Foster, 'Free speech, insulting words or behaviour and Article 10 of the European Convention on Human Rights' (2004) 9(1) *Coventry Law Journal* 68, 71; F Schauer, *Free Speech: A Philosophical Enquiry* (Cambridge, Cambridge University Press, 1982) 3–15.

39 Ben Morris (2015), 'Paris attacks: Dieudonne held as France tackles hate speech' (14 January) http://www.bbc.co.uk/news/world-europe-30811401. Ahmed received 240 hours' community service.

fall short of actual incitement to terrorist acts', given that those at Charlie Hebdo were standing up for the very principle that the authorities wanted to suppress in this case.[40]

The UN Human Rights Committee has expressed concern that people can be found guilty of this offence, even when they did not intend directly or indirectly to encourage members of the public to commit acts of terrorism.[41] In 2012, Azhar Ahmed[42] was prosecuted for posting a message on Facebook about the deaths of six British soldiers in Afghanistan, which read: 'All soldiers should die and go to hell'. Ahmed was charged after the mother of one of the soldiers read the comments and was so upset she called the police. The police described the tweet as a 'racially aggravated public order offence'. However, applying the factors above, it is likely that such a post would fall short of racist activity, as the tweet itself did not refer to any racist content. District Judge Jane Goodwin said the law should not stop legitimate political opinions being strongly voiced, but the test was whether what was written was 'beyond the pale of what's tolerable in our society'.

It is questionable whether this benchmark alone was the standard by which Mr Ahmed was to be judged, as the court made reference to the damage to commercial reputation of Mr Ahmed's previous employer, Fox's biscuits, which was taken into account when determining the sentence to be delivered to Mr Ahmed and the impact of his actions. In the sentencing remarks, the district judge noted that:

> Mr Oakland of Fox's Biscuits described how the company received numerous calls and e-mails regarding your involvement with the company. Fox's Biscuits have a strong local heritage in West Yorkshire and such was the impact that the matter had to be referred to the parent company and CEO to prevent serious damage to their reputation.[43]

3.1.5 General blocking

Prosecution of individuals who have posted the material aside, there is also the issue of removing the content from the platform on which it was posted. When it comes to government requests, Twitter (for example) functions on a country-by-country basis. So, if the government has a legally binding order and makes it clear that the content in question is against the law, then the service is obligated to

40 T Hughes (2015), 'France: Social Media Investigations and Arrests Violate the Right to Freedom of Expression' (14 January) https://www.article19.org/resources.php/resource/37822/en/france:-social-media-investigations-and-arrests-violate-the-right-to-freedom-of-expression.

41 European Commission for Democracy through Law (Venice Commission) (2010), 'Report on Counter-Terrorism Measures and Human Rights' adopted by the Venice Commission at its 83rd Plenary Session (Venice, 4 June) Study no 500/2008 para [33].

42 Huddersfield Magistrates' Court, before District Judge (Magistrates' Court) Goodwin (9 October 2012, unreported).

43 Ibid.

take it down or block it. Twitter blocked the neo-Nazi account @hannoverticker[44] after a request from the German Government, which argued that the account violated its laws against hate speech. Twitter began releasing transparency reports in 2012. In the first report,[45] Twitter noted that there has been a steady increase in government requests for content removal and copyright notices. Twitter stated that in the majority of cases it had not complied with the requests to take down the content. The reports state that, on some occasions, requests are not complied with as the content which the government institution seeks to remove has not been sufficiently identified; however, it does not state why other content that has been identified is not removed.

Whilst there may be arguments to remove specific content online, such blocking or takedown requests may not always be targeted towards specific content and, as will be explored later in this chapter, it is difficult to determine where to draw the line in terms of content management and freedom of expression and can (at times) feel like a jurisdiction lottery. In 2015, according to its online 'transparency report', Twitter honoured 42 per cent of the 1003 removal requests from governments, law enforcement and courts worldwide, and withheld 158 accounts and 2354 tweets. More than two-thirds of the requests came from Turkey.[46]

Relating to state censorship more generally, in the Turkish case of *Cengiz and Others v Turkey*,[47] the ECtHR was asked to consider whether the blocking of the popular video-sharing website YouTube constituted a violation of users' Article 10 Convention rights. In 2008, legal academics Serkan Cengiz, Yaman Akdeniz and Kerem Altıparmak were lecturing at universities throughout Turkey when the Turkish Government blanket blocked access to the popular video-sharing website YouTube. The ban was justified pursuant to legislation that prohibited 'insulting the memory of Ataturk'. YouTube contained approximately 10 videos that were deemed to fall within such a category and, consequently, the domestic court issued the blocking order. The ban commenced on 5 May 2008, but was not lifted by the public prosecutor's office until 30 October 2010 after a long-fought campaign in the domestic courts based on arguments surrounding the freedom to receive and impart information, as well as the public interest in accessing an information sharing website such as YouTube. These arguments were rejected by the Turkish Courts and the matter was therefore referred to the ECtHR. The Strasbourg Court found a violation of the professors' right to freedom of expression under Article 10 of the ECHR.

In formulating this conclusion the Court considered *Akdeniz v Turkey*, in which access to music websites was blocked. The Court in *Cengiz* distinguished it from

44 Communications Act 2003. See further ch 4.

45 https://transparency.twitter.com/removal-requests/2012/jan-jun.

46 J Stempel and A A Frankel (2016), 'Twitter sued by U.S. widow for giving voice to Islamic State' *Reuters* (14 January) http://www.reuters.com/article/us-twitter-isis-lawsuit-idUSKCN0US1TA.

47 *Cengiz and Others v Turkey* Application no 48226/10 Judgment (Merits and Just Satisfaction) [2015] ECHR 1052 http://hudoc.echr.coe.int/eng?i=001-158948.

Akdeniz, as the YouTube ban resulted in a popular platform for political discussion being banned, which could not be easily accessed through other media, as opposed to *Akdeniz* where access to the music contained on the site was available from other outlets.[48] The Court referred to the importance of YouTube as a vessel for political discourse, which is ignored by mainstream media. The potential for interference with the applicants' freedom of expression having been established, the Court went on to assess if there had actually been a violation of the applicants' Article 10 rights. The Court found that, although the blocking of YouTube was not applied to the applicants directly, it did interfere with their right to receive and impart information and ideas.

It is important to note that the ban was illegitimate as the legal basis on which the ban had been established only allowed for the banning of the specific publications, in case an offence was suspected.[49] It is significant that, although the applicants were not the direct target of the blocking order, as regular internet users it did facilitate the opportunity to challenge such a ban.

3.2 Self-regulation

3.2.1 Introduction

As far back as 2011, a report of the United States Subcommittee on Counter-terrorism and Intelligence of the Committee stated that, if real progress is to be made towards cleansing online social networks of terrorists and their supporters, 'the U.S. Congress must bring pressure to bear on commercial providers who are themselves being victimized in the process to start acting more like aggrieved victims instead of nonchalant bystanders'.[50] The report suggests that pause for thought must be given to the curbing effect that this may have on freedom of expression, but contends that official terrorist recruitment material should be of equal concern as pornography. Congress stated that: 'if such companies are to be trusted to self-police their own professed commitments to fighting hate speech, then they must be held to a public standard which reflects the importance of that not unsubstantial responsibility'.[51]

48 Ibid para 1.

49 Judge Lemmens was of the view that the ban did have a legal basis: 'For my part, I think it did have a legal basis to block access to websites, namely Article 8 §§ 1 b) and 2 of Act No. 5651 of 4 May 2007. Under this provision, blocking access to broadcast on the internet publications can be ordered by a judge. This provision has been the basis for the measure ordered in the present case the criminal proceedings Ankara court, and therefore formed the basis of the measure in national law'. *Cengiz and Others v Turkey* (n 47) para 1.

50 United States Subcommittee on Counterterrorism and Intelligence of the Committee on Homeland Security's Subcommittee on Counterterrorism and Intelligence, 'Jihadist Use of Social Media – How to Prevent Terrorism and Preserve Innovation', 112th Congress, First Session (6 December 2011).

51 Ibid.

It is a fine line to tread for private sector companies trying to facilitate open dialogue on their platforms, whilst preventing terror-related content from infiltrating them. Caught as a 'piggy in the middle', one camp is lobbying for legislation that would require social media companies to report any terror-related activity on their platforms[52] and, across the way, the other camp is threatening to assassinate tech CEOs who are perceived as curbing free speech.[53] As if that was not enough, in January 2016 a law suit was filed against Twitter by the widow of an American killed in Jordan. She accused the social media company of giving a voice to Islamic State, and that Twitter knowingly let the militant Islamist group use its network to spread propaganda, raise money and attract recruits.[54] According to the complainant: 'without Twitter, the explosive growth of ISIS over the last few years into the most-feared terrorist group in the world would not have been possible'.[55] She also claimed a triple damages award from Twitter for violating the US federal Anti-Terrorism Act by having provided material support to terrorists.

How did these sites – designed to keep in touch with friends and share cute videos of cats doing the silliest things – become the breeding ground for evil? It is enough to make the silicon valley techies hang up their sandals, board shorts and Hawaiian shirts.

3.2.2 Locating social media sites within an existing statutory framework

Admittedly, delving into some black letter law may not feel the most exciting of activities in the overall context of terrorism in all its gory 'as reported by the media' glory. However, it is important to think about how the existing law has shaped the way that the policy approach to moderating online content has developed. In the UK there is a suite of existing legal and regulatory frameworks such as the Regulation of Investigatory Powers Act 2000 (RIPA 2000), EU classifications of 'information society service' (ISS)[56] and 'electronic communications service' (ECS)[57] into which social networking sites have been categorised. An ISS provider is defined in the Directive for Electronic Commerce 2000[58] as 'any service normally

52 E Weise (2015), 'Twitter pressured to do more to halt terrorists' *USA Today* (11 December) http://www.usatoday.com/story/tech/2015/12/07/facebook-twitter-social-media-terrorism-lawmakers-feinstein/76948528/.

53 C Garling (2015), 'Twitter CEO Dick Costolo on Receiving Death Threats from ISIS' *Vanity Fair* (October) http://www.vanityfair.com/news/tech/2014/10/twitter-ceo-death-threats-isis.

54 *Fields v Twitter, Inc.*, US District Court, Northern District of California, No. 16-00213.

55 http://www.reuters.com/article/us-twitter-isis-lawsuit-idUSKCN0US1TA.

56 Directive 2000/31 on electronic commerce [2000] OJ L178/1. See Recital 17 for paraphrasing of the definition of an ISS.

57 Directive 2002/21 on a common regulatory framework for electronic communications networks and services (Framework Directive) art 2(c) [2002] OJ L108/33.

58 Directive 2000/31/EC of the European Parliament and of the Council of 8 June 2000 on certain legal aspects of information society services, in particular electronic commerce, in the Internal Market ('Directive on electronic commerce') (Framework Directive) art 2(c) [2002] OJ L108/33.

provided for remuneration at a distance, by means of electronic equipment for the processing (including digital compression) and storage of data, at the individual request of a recipient of the service'.[59]

SNSs are accepted by the Article 29 Working Party (Working Party)[60] to fall within the terms of an ISS.[61] The Working Party notes that the definition of information society services already exists in community law in Directive 98/34/EC of the European Parliament and of the Council of 22 June 1998. It also lays down a procedure for the provision of information in the field of technical standards and regulations and of rules on information society services.[62] Directive 98/84/EC of the European Parliament and of the Council of 20 November 1998 on the legal protection of services based on, or consisting of, conditional access states this is any service normally provided for remuneration, at a distance, by means of electronic equipment for the processing (including digital compression) and storage of data, and at the individual's request.

An ECS is defined in the UK Communications Act 2003 as 'a service consisting of, or having as its principal feature, the conveyance by means of an electronic communications network of signals, except in so far as it is a content service'.[63] The Information Commissioner's Office, which oversees data protection rights in the UK, has stated that an electronic communications service is any such service that is provided so as to be available for use by members of the public.[64] In terms of the application of ECS to social networking, having regard to the above, it has been suggested by some commentators[65] that SNSs constitute ISSs, but not ECSs. This is supported by the fact that retention obligations in the Data Retention (EC Directive) Regulations 2009 do not currently extend to any SNS communications.[66]

59 Ibid recital 17.

60 EU art 29, Data Protection Working Party (DPWP), Opinion 5/2009 on online social networking (12 June 2009) 4.

61 Directive 2000/31 on electronic commerce [2000] OJ L178/1. See Recital 17 for paraphrasing of the definition of an ISS.

62 [1998] OJ L204 of 21 July 1998 at 37, as amended by Directive 98/48/EC ([1998] OJ L217 5 August 1998 at 18).

63 Communications Act 2003 s 32.

64 http://ico.org.uk/for_organisations/privacy_and_electronic_communications/the_guide/security_of_services?hidecookiesbanner=true.

65 D Ormerod and M O' Floinn (2011), 'Social Networking Sites, RIPA and Criminal Investigations' 10 *Criminal Law Review* 766.

66 Directive 2006/24 on data retention [2006] OJ L105/54. See further, responses of Mr Vernon Coaker to questions posed during the discussion of the Draft Data Retention (EC Directive) Regulations 2009 (Fourth Delegated Legislation Committee (16 March 2009)), and Data Retention Expert Group (Commission Decision 2008/324/EC) on webmail and web-based messaging: DATRET/EXPGRP (2009) 2 – FINAL – ANNEX- 03 12 2009. For critique of the directive see I Brown, 'Communications data retention in an evolving internet' (2011) 19(2) *International Journal of Law and Information Technology* 95. Many countries have expressed concern over the directive and the ECJ is soon due to rule on its legality following a referral from Ireland. See further opinion of the European Data Protection Supervisor at https://secure.edps.europa.eu/EDPSWEB/webdav/site/mySite/shared/Documents/EDPS/PressNews/Press/2011/EDPS-2011-06_Data%20Retention%20Report_EN.pdf.

Whilst the case of *Chambers*, discussed above, is very interesting from a freedom of expression perspective (and satisfied a common prurient interest in modern romance online), a ground-breaking element of the Court of Appeal's judgment in this case came from its agreement with the crown court's analysis that the internet itself constitutes a public network. The crown court held that:

> [t]he 'Twitter' website although privately owned cannot, as we understand it, operate save through the internet, which is plainly a public electronic network provided for the public and paid for by the public through the various service providers we are all familiar with . . . The internet is widely available to the public and funded by the public and without it facilities such as 'Twitter' would not exist. The fact that it is a private company in our view is irrelevant; the mechanism by which it was sent was a public electronic network and within the statutory definition . . . 'Twitter', as we all know is widely used by individuals and organisations to disseminate and receive information. In our judgment, it is inconceivable that grossly offensive, indecent, obscene or menacing messages sent in this way would not be potentially unlawful.[67]

In defining the internet thus, the court stated that the internet 'is plainly a public electronic communications network provided for the public and paid for by the public through the various service providers we are all familiar with' and that 'potential recipients of the message were the public as a whole, consisting of all sections of society'.[68] Judge Jacqueline Davies' reasoning, with which the Court of Appeal agreed, derived from an analysis of the internet's network infrastructure as a series of links. These links cover networks of networks and services linking individuals, service providers, network providers, platform providers and content providers.

However, if, as in *Chambers*, these groupings of networks are considered as a single entity, then it has the potential to cast a net over networks previously considered 'private' or 'bespoke'. Such examples could include networks unavailable *to* the public, which are (nevertheless) able to connect *with* the public, as well as their supporting platforms and applications, e.g. Facebook and Twitter. However, the definition of a 'public electronic communications network' is derived from an EU concept developed for the purposes of regulation. The European Framework for Electronic Communications is designed around the distinction between public and private networks and services. The former attracts comprehensive regulation, which non-public networks are not required to conform to, e.g. rights and obligations to negotiate interconnection with other public network providers. The similar term, 'public communications network', entails further requirements to ensure the availability of the public network, such as taking necessary measures to maintain the perpetual effective functioning of the network and disaster plans for system breakdowns.

67 [2006] UKHL 40 at [23].
68 Ibid at [24].

Stringent guidelines also apply with regard to the protection of consumers, including the obligation to publish quality of service information, if instructed to do so by Ofcom, and offering contracts with specified minimum terms to end-users. Most significantly, in terms of the future regulation of social media sites and the role of platform providers, there are additional requirements with regard to data retention and lawful intercept requirements, such as the relevant government authorities requiring operators of public networks to retain communications data relating to the traffic passing over its network and information about subscribers, to be made available to authorities on request. A public network provider may also be instructed to maintain the capability to intercept communications over its network at the direction of the government.

By describing and defining the internet as a 'public electronic communications network', the judgement appears to have cast a net over a wide range of network and service providers within the scope of EU and UK communications law. It leaves open the possibility, for example, that Twitter could be bound by the above regulatory requirements, which could potentially place significant burdens on the operators of such sites in the future. The potential implications of the judgement of the divisional court on the future landscape of policing the online environment will remain to be seen as they have not as yet received positive or negative judicial treatment.

3.2.3 Contractual terms

Whilst there have been accusations from some corners that social media sites do not do enough to police their data waves, most of the major sites do, in fact, have contractual terms that tackle illegal content. For example, under point 8 of its terms 'Restrictions on Content and Use of the Services',[69] Twitter operates its site in a way that satisfies applicable laws and regulations. In January 2015, Twitter suspended the account of the Somali-based Al-Qaeda-linked terrorist group Al-Shabaab. The account was taken offline after the group posted a video on Twitter threatening to kill two Kenyan hostages unless the Kenyan Government met its demands. Twitter did not comment on the account deletion.

It is suggested that Al-Shabaab's account was suspended and access to the postings on the pages wall removed as the account had violated Twitter's terms of service, which prohibit direct threats of violence. The relevant term states: 'you may not publish or post direct, specific threats of violence against others'.[70] Twitter is not alone in its attempts to be all things to all men. In December 2010, in response to growing demands that YouTube should pull video content from terrorist groups from its servers, the company created a new category through which viewers could 'flag' offensive content. The category is called 'promotes

69 http://twitter.com/tos.
70 https://support.twitter.com/articles/20169997#.

terrorism', and now appears as an option under the 'violent or repulsive content' category.[71]

3.2.4 Filtering and content blocking

Whilst the immediate danger may appear to be that the platforms will not do enough to police their sites, there is a converse risk that if the platform providers or search engines are quick to respond to complaints, this may create a feeling amongst users that too little weight is being afforded to the protection of an individual's expression, simply moderating site content because there has been an open objection to it.

In June 2011, the Special Rapporteur, together with the Special Rapporteur for Freedom of Expression of the Inter-American Commission on Human Rights of the Organization of American States, the Representative on Freedom of the Media of the Organisation for Security and Cooperation in Europe, and the Special Rapporteur on Freedom of Expression of the African Commission on Human and Peoples' Rights, issued a joint declaration establishing guidelines to protect freedom of expression on the internet, reinforcing the need to protect freedom of expression, even in the online context.

It is suggested that the report's findings are of equal applicability to social media sites. On the issue of censorship, the mandatory blocking of websites are extreme actions that may only be justified in accordance with international standards. The Rapporteurs stated that content-filtering systems that cannot be controlled by users, imposed by governments or commercial providers, are also actions that are incompatible with freedom of expression. It is noted that in relation to the criminal law this has caused significant difficulties in the UK regarding the time when filtering and content removal should occur. The report considered this issue in some depth, noting that, while the state (which is party to human rights treaties) has an obligation to establish criminal law and systems sufficient to deter and respond to attacks on individuals,[72] it must not go so far as to deny individual rights by its criminalisation of particular conduct.[73]

In order to undertake an impact assessment, states must therefore assess criminal provisions on a 'right-by-right' basis.[74] By approaching an analysis of

71 Craig Kanalley (2010), 'YouTube Gives Users Ability to Flag Content that Promotes Terrorism' *The Huffington Post* (13 December) http://www.huffingtonpost.com/2010/12/13/youtube-terrorism-flag_n_796128.html.

72 See, for example, *Osman v United Kingdom* Application No 23452/94 ECtHR (28 October 1998), in which the court stated that the right to life (ECHR, art 2(1)) included the obligation to put in place 'effective criminal law provisions to deter the commission of offences against the person backed up by law enforcement machinery for the prevention, suppression and sanctioning of breaches of such provisions'.

73 United Nations Commission on Narcotic Drugs, Commission on Crime Prevention and Criminal Justice (2010), 'Drug control, crime prevention and criminal justice: A Human Rights perspective' Note by the Executive Director, E/CN.7/2010/CRP.6–E/CN.15/2010/CRP.1 (3 March).

74 Ibid.

the provisions in this way, it is possible to test whether its contents infringe a range of individual rights – such as the right not to be subjected to arbitrary or unlawful interference with privacy, family, home or correspondence,[75] the right to freedom of thought, conscience and religion,[76] or the right of peaceful assembly.[77]

Putting it crudely, removing postings after they have been uploaded is a case of shutting the stable door after the horse has bolted. In the USA in particular the issue of screening and filtering has been hotly debated, with industry officials telling law-makers that they already ban content relating to things such as beheadings and alert law enforcement officials about credible threats if they are aware of them. However, in the summer of 2015, a bill was still put before congress by Senator Dianne Feinstein (D-Calif) as part of the intelligence authorisation bill,[78] with provisions similar to the laws that require companies to report child pornography. Determining what constitutes child pornography is, technically speaking, a simple task as a criminal photograph can be digitally analysed and assigned a unique identifier, which can then be used to detect similar images. As such, identifiers cannot be assigned *en masse* to terrorist content.

There has been concern from tech quarters that any legislation which requires social media giants actively to police their sites may result in overly broad legislation that might mean that a missed tweet or photo could result in legal repercussions and also make it hard to determine what should be referred up to law enforcement officials. This is because context is everything with such content. For instance, a news article or video clip used by CNN or the BBC could end up having the same identifiers as a posting made by an ISIS member – so how does the algorithm calculate what is propaganda and what is not?

The difficulty of content filtering is usefully explored though consideration of the postings of radical Muslim cleric, Adnan Awlaki, who (as noted in previous chapters) has a very active presence on YouTube, posting everything from daily teachings right through to inciting terrorist behaviour. Should materials about what makes a good marriage, his account of the final moments of the Prophet Muhammad or Awlaki's counsel on the proper diet for a good Muslim be removed from the internet? These videos do not contravene any particular YouTube standard and his postings have also been used in newscasts by CNN and Al Jazeera. Although not directly advocating terrorism in these particular videos, there is evidence that Mr Awlaki's sermons were the gateway materials that lured in individuals who went on to commit violent terrorist activity. An example of this is the 21-year-old British student who confessed to police that she had stabbed a member of the UK Parliament after watching more than 100 hours of Awlaki videos. Also, according to a senior source investigating the case, 'she was inspired

75 ICCPR art 17.

76 Ibid art 18.

77 Ibid art 21.

78 Note that this is yet to be approved by the Senate.

by his sermons, and radicalised by watching them. His message is "do anything, whatever you can"'.[79]

So how does one remove traces of Awlaki and bin Laden from the net? Should all of their postings be removed, including all references to them in the various ways in which their materials are shared and re-used, given that individuals also have a right to receive ideas as well as to impart them? Discussions surrounding issues which have terrorist organisations and leaders as part of their focus inform an important part of individual ability to explore their ideas.

In 2015, as part of its 'Year in Review', Facebook analysed the past year's conversations on Facebook.com to create statistics that revealed the most talked-about global topics by its account holders. They were not, however, about trivial matters or celebrities; instead, there was a strong focus on politics, terrorism, economics, natural disasters and human rights. The top 10 topics included:

1 US presidential election
2 13 November attacks in Paris
3 Syrian civil war and refugee crisis
4 Nepal earthquakes
5 Greek debt crisis
6 Marriage equality
7 The fight against ISIS
8 Charlie Hebdo attack
9 Baltimore protests
10 Charleston shooting and flag debate.[80]

These examples (it can be argued) indicate that such channels have now become an increasingly important source of news,[81] but also form part of powerful socio-political dialogue. Unlike traditional media, which is dominated and controlled by a small number of established institutions that disseminate information to their audience,[82] social media enables anyone to publish or access information, without editorial limit or control, by adding further complex dimensions to reporting, such

79 'Stephen Timms attacker guilty of attempted murder' http://www.theguardian.com/uk/2010/nov/02/stephen-timms-attacker-guilty.

80 http://newsroom.fb.com/news/2015/12/2015-year-in-review/.

81 See L Durity (2006), 'Shielding Journalist-"Bloggers": The Need to Protect Newsgathering Despite the Distribution Medium' 5 *Duke Law & Technology Review* 1; J S Alonzo (2006), 'Restoring the Ideal Marketplace: How Recognizing Bloggers as Journalists Can Save the Press' 9 *New York University Journal of Legislation and Public Policy* 751, 754.

82 See F Webster (2014), *Theories of the Information Society* (4th edn, Oxford, Routledge) 20; I Barron and R Curnow (1979), *The Future with Microelectronics: Forecasting the Effects of Information Technology* (Pinter); G Mulgan (1991), *Communication and Control: Networks and the New Economies of Communication* (Polity).

as in interactivity, reach, frequency, immediacy and permanence.[83] Essentially, anybody can become an armchair reporter or commentator. According to statistics published by Twitter, it has 320 million active users[84] and every second, on average, around 6000 tweets are tweeted on Twitter, which corresponds to more than 350,000 tweets sent every minute, 500 million tweets every day and around 200 billion tweets every year.[85]

By way of example, the elimination of Osama bin Laden accounted for 80 per cent of the news links on blogs in the week following his death and half the news links on Twitter from 26 May 2011, making it one of the top 10 Twitter stories in the past two years.[86] A poll conducted by Mashable found more than half of those polled learned about Bin Laden's death on Twitter or Facebook.[87] In the early hours of 1 May 2011, many turned to social media to share their reaction to the news. Indeed, media reports have generally credited Keith Urbahn – chief of staff to former defence secretary Donald Rumsfeld, who tweeted the news about bin Laden's death – as being the first person to break the news.[88]

Social media is undeniably a powerhouse for the facilitation of political discussion. A user who possesses a sphere of influence or credibility must be particularly mindful of their duty to report responsibly: the very fact that Urbahn took to social media to report the news and did not have his tweet deleted or censored is a powerful argument in favour of freedom of expression online. This initial posting and re-reporting by media outlets had a huge impact; however, – more interestingly – bloggers and Twitter and Facebook users in the subsequent weeks were all very busy sharing new developments in the basic narrative of the raid on the Pakistan compound, as well as scepticism as to whether bin Laden had actually been killed. Of the many postings 14 per cent specifically involved the question of which president deserved more credit for bin Laden's demise. Should such postings be censored, given that they relate to Al-Qaeda? To what extent and by whom?

Even if the grand marine vessel *Censor Ship* could be successfully charted though the choppy waters of freedom of expression, there is also a question of the extent to which social media sites can police their platforms. As King Canute found out, it is not possible to hold back a tide. Modern day Canutes such as YouTube have stated that, for every single minute of the 24 hours in a day, it receives an

83 N Morgan, G Jones and A Hodges, 'Social Media: the Complete Guide to Social Media from the Social Media Guys' http://www.yumpu.com/en/document/view/5539277/the-complete-guide-to-social-media-the-social-media-guys. Note, however, that this link is no longer available.

84 Twitter publishes Twitter usage and Company acts via its corporate website https://about.twitter.com/company.

85 http://www.internetlivestats.com/twitter-statistics/.

86 P Hiltin and S Tan (2011), 'Social Media React to Bin Laden's Death' *PEJ New Media Index* (2–6 May).

87 J O'Dell (2011), 'How the Social Web Reflected on Bin Laden's Death', *Mashable* (2 May) http://mashable.com/2011/05/02/social-media-bin-laden/.

88 See Hiltin and Tan (n 86).

average of 35 hours of video from millions of contributors.[89] Essentially, this boils down to a very simple concept: it is not possible to pre-screen material prior to uploading and actively policing is just not possible or practical. Instead, these sites must rely on their own communities to police content through reporting materials that infringe the YouTube community guidelines.[90]

Even if such materials can be moderated, there is the risk that materials will slip through (given the sheer volume of material that would need to be screened) or that censoring of materials may be cast too wide. Social media sites commonly use algorithms to 'flag' accounts that might need to be suspended, as there are not sufficient resources or time to conduct a thorough review of all content posted online of every item that might attract a small number of complaints. These algorithms can, however, be exploited through 'flag spamming campaigns', as was evident though their use to push critics of the Russian and Vietnamese Governments off Facebook. For example, shortly after their video *'If I Wanted America to Fail'* went viral, Free Market America found themselves kicked off Twitter.[91] Companies such as Google have sought to grant enhanced flagging privileges to non-governmental *'trusted users'* who have the ability to report offensive material and obtain swift action from service providers. However, whether this is more of an affront to freedom of expression than state interference is debatable.

3.3 Does takedown work?

3.3.1 Whack-a-mole!

The use of social media by terrorist groups, most notably ISIS, has been prolific. As explored in this chapter, the result of increased focus on the postings coming out of *their* social media accounts has meant that social media companies and states alike have been deploying measures to shut down accounts in a bid to frustrate propaganda distribution mechanisms. Operational, philosophical and legal arguments aside, do such measures work?

As we saw in Chapter 2, there is a whole host of social media platforms available to such individuals, which extend far beyond the mainstream offerings of Facebook, Instagram and Twitter. As far back as July 2014, ISIS announced[92] that

89 'Statistics' YouTube Press Office https://www.youtube.com/yt/press/statistics.html.

90 See http://www.youtube.co.uk/t/community_guidelines. In the case of terrorism-related material, objections could fall in the categories 'violent or repulsive conduct', including subcategories for 'physical attack' or 'promotes terrorism'. *Recognising* that there are shades of grey and not all videos may be specifically calling individuals to commit terrorist activity, content can also be reported if it amounts to 'hateful or abusive content' that 'promotes hatred or violence'.

91 J Hayward (2012), 'If I wanted America to Fail' *Human Events* (Monday, 23 April, 9:45 am) http://www.humanevents.com/2012/04/23/if-i-wanted-america-to-fail/.

92 Anti-Defamation League Extremism and Terrorism Blog (2015), 'ISIS Faces Resistance From Social Media Companies' (23 July) http://blog.adl.org/extremism/isis-faces-resistance-from-social-media-companies.

several of its main accounts would be shunning Twitter in favour of Friendica, which was promptly adopted by many of its followers. However, Friendica had a surprise in store for ISIS when, on 20 July, the content posted by ISIS on @Ale3tisam, an official ISIS media outlet, was deleted and replaced with a banner at the top of the account page, stating that 'Islamic State not welcome on friendica. eu'. Undeterred, ISIS made its move to Quitter and Diaspora. Whilst ISIS found some success with keeping the content up on Diaspora (initially), Quitter shut down the ISIS accounts and replaced them with a picture promoting peace and coexistence, a link to a website selling books about Mahatma Gandhi and text in English and Arabic, stating that 'When you fight evil with evil – evil wins'.[93] In August 2014, following ISIS's online release of a video depicting the beheading of an American journalist, Diaspora removed ISIS accounts.

With its tail between its legs, Ale3tisam went back to Twitter; however, Twitter had continued to shut down accounts for ISIS regional commands. The issue does not stop at official accounts; as we saw in Chapter 2, ISIS supporters remain very active on social media and regularly share official propaganda. Twitter has adopted a more active policy of removing ISIS and pro-ISIS accounts but the situation remains an elaborate game of cat and mouse as ISIS has been adept at quickly reinstating its Twitter accounts.

Even if social media sites take down terrorist pages and content, there is no guarantee that they will not re-emerge in the same platform in an elaborate game of 'whack-a-mole'. For example, in December 2015 in Pakistan, Facebook suspended the account of the Pakistani Taliban's media branch, Umar Media. The page was taken down because it violated Facebook's rules on fan pages that promote terrorism. Two weeks later, a new Umar Media account had been created on Facebook, although it was unclear if it belonged to the same group. The Electronic Frontier Foundation, a US-based internet activist organisation, has also reported on a growing number of requests by US government officials for Twitter to suspend accounts of alleged terrorist groups. According to MacKinnon, 'Facebook is less transparent about how they are responding to government requests or what kinds of requests they are receiving from what governments, so it's kind of difficult to know'.[94]

Furthermore, even shutting down sites or trying to remove content from social media outlets, does not guarantee success that such postings will be put beyond access to users, given the scale and complexity of posting online. As discussed in Chapter 2, although prominent YouTube poster Anwar Awlaki had many of his YouTube videos removed by the site and even though he was killed by a US drone on 30 September 2011, a quick search of YouTube today for 'Anwar al-Awlaki' finds hundreds of his videos, most of them scriptural commentary clerical advice and a few on diet, although scores of the videos include calls for

93 https://quitter.se/ale3tisam/replies.

94 D Kjuka, 'How Social Networks are Dealing with Terrorists' http://www.rferl.org/content/twitter-facebook-terrorists/24906583.html (19 February 2013).

jihad or attacks on the United States. Even if YouTube did delete every video of Awlaki's, regardless of its approach to censorship, scores of other non-YouTube affiliated sites still bear the content.

As noted by John B. Morris, Jr., general counsel at the Center for Democracy and Technology (a non-profit group in Washington): 'There's no way as a practical matter to wipe this material off the face of the Internet, it's very unrealistic to believe that any action of any American company or American politician can keep this material off the Web'.[95]

3.3.2 Jurisdiction

A further issue that compounds the difficulties surrounding the regulation of speech online is that the internet has no borders. Put simply, it is not possible to set up roadblocks to pen the joyriders in (something footballer Ryan Giggs found out during the flouting of the super injunction relating to his affair, which created a field-day on websites and Twitter). Couched in more techie speak, if an ISP shuts down a site, it can (with relative ease) migrate to another hosting service and obtain a new domain name.

As discussed briefly above, in 2012 Twitter blocked the account of @hannover ticker, a neo-Nazi group accused of inciting hatred towards foreigners. In Germany, minority groups are protected by law. The move came after an investigation into about 20 members of the neo-Nazi group in Lower Saxony, northern Germany, after they were charged with inciting racial hatred and forming a criminal organisation. The group was banned in October 2012 by the state's interior ministry. In particular, the group (which is estimated to have around 40 active members), stands accused of being behind a threatening video that was sent to the social affairs minister of Lower Saxony, Aygül Özkan.

German police requested that Twitter close the account immediately, without opening a replacement account. Twitter stated, at the time, that the company aimed to comply with the law as well as retaining its status as a platform for free speech and announced on Twitter that they 'never want to withhold content; good to have tools to do it narrowly & transparently'.[96] Besseres-Hannover had been watched by the authorities for the past four years after drawing attention to itself through various anti-foreigner campaigns. Its account, @hannoverticker subsequently carried the notice 'withheld'. However, Dirk Hensen, a Twitter spokesman, said the contents of Besseres-Hannover tweets were still available outside Germany because the German police did not have the jurisdiction to request bans overseas, demonstrating the importance of national courts in determining where the margin of appreciation will fall. The group's website has also been blocked.

95 S Shane, 'Radical Cleric Still Speaks on YouTube' *New York Times* (4 March 2011) http://www.nytimes.com/2011/03/05/world/middleeast/05youtube.html?_r=0 Accessed 8 August 2015.

96 'Twitter blocks neo-Nazi account to users in Germany' (18 October 2012) http://www.bbc.co.uk/news/technology-19988662 .

As a consequence, Twitter announced changes to its censorship policy, stating that it would now be censoring tweets in certain countries when the tweets risked breaking the local laws of that country.[97] The reason behind the move was stated on its website as follows:

> As we continue to grow internationally, we will enter countries that have different ideas about the contours of freedom of expression. Some differ so much from our ideas that we will not be able to exist there. Others are similar but, for historical or cultural reasons, restrict certain types of content, such as France or Germany, which ban pro-Nazi content. Until now, the only way we could take account of those countries' limits was to remove content globally. Starting today, we give ourselves the ability to reactively withhold content from users in a specific country – while keeping it available in the rest of the world. We have also built in a way to communicate transparently to users when content is withheld, and why.[98]

The move drew criticism from many Twitter users, who said the move was an affront to free speech and open web practices.[99] Twitter produced an update on 27 January 2012, noting that it believed 'the new, more granular approach to withheld content is a good thing for freedom of expression, transparency, accountability—and for our users. Besides allowing us to keep Tweets available in more places, it also allows users to see whether we are living up to our freedom of expression ideal'.[100] Twitter explained that it does not filter content owing to the sheer volume of tweets posted every day and that it would be taking a re-active approach to post removal or moderation, only withholding specific content, when required to do so in response to what Twitter believed to be a valid and applicable legal request.[101]

In 2012, the Union of French Jewish Students (UEJF) pursued a claim against Twitter for nearly US$50 million after it refused to turn over the names of people who had tweeted racist and anti-Semitic remarks, as ruled by a French court. The case revolved around a hashtag – #unbonjuif (translation: 'a good Jew') and #UnJuifMort (translation: 'a dead Jew'), which became the third-most popular on the site in October. In October 2012, Twitter agreed to remove the offensive hashtags. But its lawyer, Alexandra Neri, told the court that users' details would not be handed over. She said that Twitter's data on users was collected and stocked in California, and French law could not be applied. She said

97 'Tweets still must flow' (Thursday, 26 January 2012) (@twitter) https://blog.twitter.com/2012/tweets-still-must-flow.

98 Ibid.

99 Omar El Akkad, 'Why Twitter's censorship plan is better than you think' *The Globe and Mail* http://www.theglobeandmail.com/technology/digital-culture/social-web/why-twitters-censorship-plan-is-better-than-you-think/article543062/.

100 'Tweets still must flow' (n 97).

101 Ibid.

that the only way the site could be forced to hand over details would be if the French justice system appealed to American judges to push for the data.

Twitter stated: '[W]e're not fleeing our responsibility. Our concern is not to violate American law in cooperating with the French justice system. Our data is stored in the US, so we must obey the rule of law in that country', adding that Twitter had no obligation to hand over data in France.[102] Fleur Pellerin, minister for the digital economy in France, stated that because Twitter was opening an office in France and seeking to establish itself in Europe, 'it's in their interest to adapt to the legal, philosophical and ethical culture of the countries in which they're seeking to develop'. She said the French Government was in 'permanent' discussion with Twitter, which was receptive to its ideas as 'they know that they have to adapt to other cultures, legal [systems] and to appreciate the fundamental freedoms of the countries where they operate and I think they're open to discussion'.[103]

More recently, Mark Zuckerberg, CEO of Facebook, speaking at a conference in Berlin, stated that social networks need to do more to prevent hate speech against migrants. It was reported in January that German authorities were working with Facebook, Google and Twitter to make sure the law took priority over company policy. When asked to clarify Facebook's position directly, Zuckerberg said: 'There's not a place for this kind of content on Facebook. Learning more about German culture and law has led us to change the approach',[104] but did not specify what measures Facebook would take.

3.3.3 A question of trust?

According to a report published by the National Security Preparedness Group: '[w]e know that individuals in the United States are increasingly engaging in "virtual" radicalisation via the internet . . . while there are methods to monitor some of this activity, it is simply impossible to know the thinking of every at-risk person'.[105] Therefore, it is questionable whether censorship is ever going to be an effective response to terrorist content online, if the end goal is to eradicate terrorism itself and/or reduce the far-reaching effects of its propaganda.

For example, there is not one 'type' of ISIS supporter, but social media offers access to a veritable treasure trove of material from which to assess who is a hardened convert as opposed to a hanger on. According to a report prepared by

102 A Chrisafis, 'Twitter under fire in France over offensive hashtags' *Guardian* (9 January 2013) http://www.theguardian.com/technology/2013/jan/09/twitter-france-offensive-hashtags.

103 Ibid.

104 BBC Newsbeat (2016), 'Facebook wants to crack down against hate speech on migrants' (27February) http://www.bbc.co.uk/newsbeat/article/35677435/facebook-wants-to-crack-down-against-hate-speech-on-migrants.

105 The National Security Preparedness Group, 'Preventing Violent Radicalisation in America' (July 2011) http://bipartisanpolicy.org/wp-content/uploads/sites/default/files/NSPG.pdf. Accessed 10 October 2015.

George Washington University, which analysed those arrested in the US on terrorism-suspected charges, a typical follower is on average 26 years old, although some have been as young as 15.[106] Many are male but 15 per cent of women make up the arrests as they increasingly take on a more prominent role. Converts to Islam are over-represented, comprising 40 per cent of those arrested.[107]

The majority of suspects charged are US citizens or legal residents, 'underscoring the home-grown nature of the threat', according to the report, which said some clusters are organised around ethnicity. This presents an unprecedented challenge for law enforcement officials and the value of data that allows for the easy identification of groups clustered around specific interest, age bands or locations is obvious. 'This is not your grandfather's al-Qaida', FBI Director James Comey told the Senate Judiciary Committee in July 2015 that: 'This is a group of people using social media to reach thousands and thousands of followers, find the ones who might be interested in committing acts of violence, and then moving them to an (end-to-end) encrypted messaging app'.[108]

There is a distinction to be drawn between the trust placed in private companies as opposed to the government, with research indicating that the government is trusted.[109] However, concern has been expressed regarding the government's use of data,[110] particularly in terms of profiling or leaks.[111] In 2005, it was reported that the FBI was purchasing data from a data broker to help keep track of suspected terrorists. This led to concerns that limitations placed on governments to carry out surveillance were being avoided by the use of private companies.[112]

In December 2015, Twitter warned its users by email that a number of profiles may have been the target of state-sponsored hacking. More than 20 users of the social network received a letter from Twitter saying that the accounts were part of a 'small amount' of profiles singled out by an unnamed state actor. The notes said: 'We believe that these actors (possibly associated with a government) may have been trying to obtain information such as email addresses, IP addresses and/or

106 L Vidino and S Hughes, 'ISIS in America: From Retweets to Raqqa' (The George Washington University, December 2015) https://cchs.gwu.edu/sites/cchs.gwu.edu/files/downloads/ISIS%20in%20America%20%20Full%20Report.pdf.

107 D Barrett and N Hong, 'ISIS Sympathizers in U.S. Prefer Twitter Among Social Media' *Wall Street Journal* (1 December 2015) http://www.wsj.com/articles/islamic-state-sympathizers-in-u-s-prefer-twitter-among-social-media-1448982000.

108 'Could Twitter stop the next terrorist attack? ISIS uses social media to recruit' *Associated Press* (24 July 2015) http://www.syracuse.com/us-news/index.ssf/2015/07/twitter_stop_terrorist_attacks_isis_social_media.html.

109 See Ipsos MORI: ESRC/ONS; Deloitte; Eurobarometer and Executive Office of the President, 'Big Data: Seizing Opportunities, Preserving Values' (May 2014) in which law enforcement and intelligence agencies were ranked low in terms of public trust.

110 See Ipsos MORI: ESRC/ONS, Deloitte and Eurobarometer.

111 See Ipsos MORI: ESRC/ONS and Deloitte.

112 'FBI, Pentagon pay for access to trove of public records', Government Executive website (11 November 2005).

phone numbers. At this time, we have no evidence they obtained your account information, but we're actively investigating this matter'.[113]

It is a difficult situation, and one which has led to friction between the authorities and the social media sites, with accusations being levied by the UK's Metropolitan Police Assistant Commissioner that some internet firms were deliberately 'undermining' counter-terrorism investigations by refusing to hand over potential evidence or threatening to tip off suspects, describing it as a 'growing Achilles' heel'.[114] Whilst this language may seem inflammatory, given the difficult line that social media sites tread, the criticism has resulted in part from policies maintained by the sites that they will inform users about government requests for data about that user.[115]

For these legal and technological reasons, it is harder to obtain access to information on corporate-owned sites (e.g. Facebook) compared to Al-Qaeda-owned forums, leading to suggestions that the first priority should be monitoring and not taking down content.[116] This leads neatly onto the next act in our drama, entitled 'surveillance' which, if you thought Acts 1 and 2 of the play had been mildly diverting, is about to get a whole lot more interesting. It may not exactly be as binge-worthy as the TV series *Breaking Bad* but it has just as much action as *Spooks* or *The Night Manager*, so buckle your seatbelts . . . we're off on a trip to Cornwall . . .

113 C Johnson 'Twitter warns of government "hacking"' (13 December 2015) http://www.bbc.co.uk/news/business-35089309. Accessed 29 March 2016.

114 T Whitehead (2015), 'Police losing track of terror plots because of "irresponsible" social media firms' *The Telegraph* (5 October) http://www.telegraph.co.uk/news/uknews/terrorism-in-the-uk/11912779/Police-losing-track-of-terror-plots-because-of-irresponsible-social-media-firms.html.

115 T Whitehead (2015), 'Twitter and other firms could tip off terror suspects that they are under watch by spies, report reveals' *The Telegraph* (11 June) http://www.telegraph.co.uk/news/uknews/terrorism-in-the-uk/11668999/Twitter-and-other-firms-could-tip-off-terror-suspects-that-they-are-under-watch-by-spies-report-reveals.html.

116 United States Subcommittee on Counterterrorism and Intelligence of the Committee on Homeland Security's Subcommittee on Counterterrorism and Intelligence (n 50) Expert Testimony of William F. McCants.

4 The spy who liked my tweet: counter-intelligence and the terrorists' reaction to Snowden

Spying among friends is never acceptable.

Angela Merkel

Whilst surveillance thwarting technology was once the preserve of governments and Tom Cruise in *Mission Impossible*, the reality nowadays is that almost anyone can communicate securely using an untraceable throwaway smartphone, purchased online through the likes of Amazon. Once the phone arrives, the user is only a few clicks away from getting close to some very dangerous causes. According to the *Homeland Security Newswire*, about 200,000 people worldwide are exposed to 'terrorist messaging' daily from ISIS supporters through direct messaging, online videos or social media posts.[1] Interception per se is not necessarily of universal value to security services. Indeed, the chief terrorism investigator in the French judicial system said of the Kouachi brothers, who perpetrated the 2015 Charlie Hebdo shootings: 'The phone tapping yielded nothing. . . . No one talks on the phone anymore'.

Arguably, in the age of the smartphone traditional phone tapping is old hat. Thanks to the development of communications tools such as WhatsApp, Facebook and Twitter, the data that is processed on an average smartphone is a veritable cornucopia of information, ranging from the fantastic to the benign, extending well beyond phone call logs and SMS, which are of genuine value to the security services in terms of tracking criminals and persons of interest.

According to a freedom of information request submitted by the *Financial Times*, which surveyed 34 police forces and authorities, the UK Government paid telecoms companies including BT, Vodafone, EE and Virgin Media more than £37 million for data on customers and their activities in the past five years.[2]

1 http://www.homelandsecuritynewswire.com/dr20150610-dark-internet-inhibits-law-enforcement-s-ability-to-identify-track-terrorists.

2 Daniel Thomas (2016), 'UK police pay millions of pounds for telecoms surveillance' (8 January) http://www.ft.com/cms/s/0/1728997e-b3b3-11e5-8358-9a82b43f6b2f.html#axzz3xDSgOdSl.

DOI: 10.4324/9781315668680-4

Arrangements in the USA between the National Surveillance Authorities Special Source Operations division and third-party sector data providers have cost in the region of millions of dollars.[3]

In addition to communications data, the Federal Bureau of Investigation (FBI) has arrested nearly 40 people since last summer on the suspicion of seeking to support terrorist groups and the vast majority of those people communicated their intentions through social media.[4] According to an unclassified field analysis report published in May 2015 by the Department of Homeland Security, messaging is amplified through a sophisticated use of social media tailored to a global audience' and is used to 'propagate its message and benefits from thousands of organized supporters globally online—primarily on Twitter—who seek to legitimize its actions while burnishing an image of strength and power'.[5]

According to the guide:

> Leveraging news stories, media reports and postings on social media sites concerning Homeland Security, Emergency Management, and National Health for operationally relevant data, information, analysis, and imagery is the first mission component. The traditional and social media teams review a story or posting from every direction and interest, utilizing thousands of reporters, sources, still/video cameramen, analysts, bloggers and ordinary individuals on scene. Traditional Media outlets provide unmatched insight into the depth and breadth of the situation, worsening issues, federal preparations, response activities, and critical timelines. At the same time, Social Media outlets provide instant feedback and alert capabilities to rapidly changing or newly occurring situations. The extensive information from these resources to provide a well rounded operational picture for the Department of Homeland Security.[6]

Items of interest are wide-ranging, from trafficking and board control right through to natural disasters. Unsurprisingly, terrorism is listed as the first item, noting that items of interest include: 'activities of terrorist organizations both in the United States as well as abroad. This category will also cover media articles that report on the threats, media releases by al Qaeda and other organizations, killing, capture, and identification of terror leaders and/or cells'.[7]

3 Ewan MacAskill (2013), 'NSA paid millions to cover Prism compliance costs for tech companies' (23 August).

4 '"Dark Internet" inhibits law enforcement's ability to identify, track terrorists' (20 June 2015) http://www.homelandsecuritynewswire.com/dr20150610-dark-internet-inhibits-law-enforcement-s-ability-to-identify-track-terrorists.

5 Department of Homeland Security, Unclassified field report (2015), 'Assessing ISIL's influence and Perceived Legitimacy in the Homeland: a State and Local Perspective' (5 May) https://info.publicintelligence.net/DHS-AssessingLegitimacyISIL.pdf (cached).

6 Department of Homeland Security National Operations Center, 'Media Monitoring Capability Desktop Reference Binder' section 1.1.1 'Leverage: operationally relevant data'.

7 Ibid section 1.3 'Items of interest in categorisation'.

As discussed in Chapter 2, much has been made of various prominent terror groups' abilities to master their online presence and also the eagerness by their members and supporters to share data regarding its day-to-day activities. Be it knowingly or unwittingly, such data is invaluable in terms of manufacturing such content into intelligence that produces targets for the military to hone in on. For example, in September 2015, a 20-year-old Kosovo citizen named Ardit Ferizi was arrested by Malaysian police following a tip-off from the US Government that he had allegedly hacked and released personally identifiable information relating to over 100,000 US service members and federal employees, and that he was passing the information onto ISIS in August 2015. Ferizi had used his real name on all his social media accounts and openly declared that he was the head of a Kosovo hacking collective. Despite entering Malaysia to study forensic computer science, some of the hacks he perpetrated had been done without him encrypting his internet traffic, meaning that his IP address was clearly visible to investigators. It was the digital equivalent of painting a target practice bull's-eye on his forehead.

As we will see throughout this chapter, Ferizi is not alone in his digital *faux pas*; the examples are countless. For instance, on 15 June 2015, an ISIS Twitter account posted photos of the computer command in the 'ongoing battle in jazal area', in rural Homs, Syria. In April of the same year, ISIS tweeted its cyber operations centre from which its recent attack on the Baiji oil refinery was coordinated and posted it on the pro-ISIS Shumoukh Al-Islam jihadi forum in Iraq's Salah Al-Din province. Airmen at Hurlburt Field, Florida, with the 361st Intelligence, Surveillance and Reconnaissance Group, also used a comment on a social media site as part of the intelligence gathering which facilitated an airstrike that resulted in three Joint Direct Attack Munition (JDAM) bombs destroying an Islamic State in Iraq and Syria (ISIS) headquarters building, as described by Air Force General Hawk Carlisle, head of Air Combat Command: 'It was a post on social media to bombs on target in less than 24 hours, incredible work when you think about'.[8]

Since Edward Snowden set alight a veritable internet surveillance wildfire,[9] Al-Qaeda, along with ISIS and other well known terrorist organisations, have increasingly placed focus on evading detection. However, this is only half the story as the organisations have also markedly taken more care over what they post online and sought to delete old posts that they would rather not have on their accounts (much like university undergraduates applying for jobs, who – only when

8 M Hoffman (2015), 'US Air Force Targets and Destroys ISIS HQ Building Using Social Media' *DefenceTech Magazine* (3 June) http://defensetech.org/2015/06/03/us-air-force-targets-and-destroys-isis-hq-building-using-social-media/#ixzz3siSmbir5.

9 If you are the type of reader who read the last chapter of Harry Potter before you read the first one and want to skip to the very exciting Snowden leaks, section 3.3 contains the spoiler about what the Snowden leaks were about. The rest of this chapter is very much worth taking the time, however, if you want to explore other history-making moments covering Oliver Cromwell, the Nazis and Bletchley Park.

it is too late in the day – furiously delete photos of rugby club initiations and evenings spent cow-tipping from Facebook).

In response to an article in the Washington Times concerning the future powers of the US Government with regard to bulk surveillance, Ron Hosko, president of Law Enforcement Legal Defence Fund and former assistant director of the FBI summarised the arguments for surveillance powers thus:

> ISIS is singing a siren song, calling people to their death to crash on the rocks — and it's the rocks that ISIS will take credit for. They're looking for those who are disaffected, disconnected and willing to commit murder. So if we're willing to take away tools, OK, congressman, stand behind it [and] take the credit for putting the FBI in the dark.[10] This chapter does not seek to pretend to represent a comprehensive account of the security laws governing bulk communications data collection and interception;[11] rather, it explores the changing trends of terrorists with regard to their use and understanding of surveillance techniques deployed by the security services and the unique challenges that such law enforcement and military agencies face in terms of terrorism. The reader will have to decide where they sit in terms of the debate, but when reading this chapter, no matter which side you do sit on, it is worth acknowledging that this is a *very complex debate* and to have the grace to see a little of various points of view, as ever told through the fascinating contemporary source materials themselves.

4.1 Privacy

4.1.1 The importance of privacy

Before we can fall down the rabbit hole into Wonderland, it is necessary to consider why surveillance is subject to scrutiny and the accusation that it infringes the rights of individuals. The United Nations has stated that: '[t]he promotion and protection of human rights for all and the rule of law is essential to all components of the Strategy, recognising that effective counter-terrorism measures and the promotion of human rights are not conflicting goals, but complementary and mutually reinforcing'.[12]

Clearly, surveillance and investigatory powers have the potential to impinge on a variety of human rights and interests, including: 'the right to respect for

10 M Ybarra (2015), 'FBI admits no major cases cracked with Patriot Act snooping powers' *Washington Times* (21 May) http://www.washingtontimes.com/news/2015/may/21/fbi-admits-patriot-act-snooping-powers-didnt-crack/?page=all.

11 If the reader wishes to consult a comprehensive review of this area and the challenges the current law faces, David Price QC's Report 'A Question of Trust: Report of the Investigatory Powers Review' June 2015 is a detailed and illuminating read.

12 United Nations Global Counter-Terrorism Strategy (General Assembly Resolution 60/288, annex).

. . . private . . . life, home and communications' and 'the right to protection of personal data'.[13]

4.1.2 What is 'privacy'?

Controversies over privacy have existed for centuries and have been brought into sharp focus by the advent of the internet and social media. The ethical concerns surrounding one's right to privacy have therefore been accentuated, whilst raising a whole host of legal concerns which shade into legal questions.

Concerns about privacy are, however, not *exactly* new. Concepts of privacy, including the relative freedom of the home from intrusion can be found in ancient texts such as the Code of Hammurabi of Ancient Babylonia, the laws of Ancient Greece and Rome and of Ancient China.[14] Holy texts (such as the Bible, the Koran and Jewish law[15]) are also replete with privacy guidance. The concept of privacy is closely aligned with the idea of secrecy, which is a recurring theme in this chapter. For example, one of the rewards mentioned in the Book of Revelation is: 'To him who overcomes, I will give some of the hidden manna. I will also give him a white stone with a new name written on it, known only to him who receives it'.[16] If only the author had known the reassuring nature of those words and that the modern equivalent of that white 'iStone' is an iPhone.

Although privacy is sensitive to cultural factors, most societies regard some areas of human activity as being private, even if the level of fact or degree differs.[17] The UK ranks as one of the countries least concerned by government 'spying' on internet and mobile communications, with only 44 per cent of individuals opposed to it, according to a study conducted in 2015.[18] However, research has also indicated that attitudes to privacy are very much dependent on an individual's personal environment, history and development.[19] Because of this, attitudes to privacy are highly contextual,[20] with support tending to be greater where there are

13 European Union Charter of Fundamental Rights (EU Charter), Articles 7 and 8, a formulation updated from that in the European Convention of Human Rights (ECHR), Article 8, which is 'the right to respect for . . . private . . . life . . . home and correspondence'.

14 See A Rengel (2013), *Privacy in the 21st Century* (Brill, Nijhoff) 29; Samuel Dash (2004), *The Intruders: Unreasonable Searches and Seizures from King John to John Ashcroft* (New Brunswick, NJ, Rutgers University Press) 8–10.

15 See Rengel (n 14) 29 and Dash (n 14) 8–10.

16 See the Book of Revelation 2:17.

17 See the discussion in Rengel (n 14) 28.

18 Amnesty International (2015), 'Global opposition to USA big brother mass surveillance'.

19 See Nancy Marshall (1972), 'Privacy and Environment' 1(2) *Human Ecology* 92.

20 See M Madden (2014), 'Public Perceptions of Privacy and Security in the Post-Snowden Era' Pew Research Centre http://www.pewinternet.org/2014/11/12/public-privacy-perceptions/. See also Pew, Public Perceptions; Demos, which showed a greater concern regarding 'personal information' than 'behavioural data'; Eurobarometer, which showed particular concern for financial, medical and national identity number information compared to photos, social networks, websites and tastes and personal opinions; and Wellcome Trust, which highlighted a number of distinguishing factors, including the degree of risk if it is misused/stolen, the level of security

tangible public benefits[21] such as enabling the government to protect individuals against crime, including terrorism.[22]

Even though it has been suggested that: 'a public that is unable to understand why privacy is important – or which lacks the conceptual tools necessary to engage in meaningful debates about its value – is likely to be particularly susceptible to arguments that privacy should be curtailed',[23] 71 per cent of respondents in a worldwide study[24] were strongly opposed to the US monitoring their internet usage (with 60 per cent wanting tech companies to secure their communications to prevent this).[25]

In an attempt to create a universal standard of privacy, various definitions have been proposed. According to Schoeman,[26] it has been regarded as a claim, entitlement or right of an individual to determine what information about himself (or herself) may be communicated to others, relating to the measure of control an individual has over information about himself, intimacies of personal identity, or who has sensory access to him and as a state or condition of limited access to a person, information about him, or the intimacies of his personal identity. However, this definition does not connect the impact of technology upon privacy rights.

Over 100 years ago, Warren and Brandeis[27] connected the necessity of the recognition of the right to privacy in common law with the effects of the new inventions of the age and the spreading of 'business methods' unknown up to that point. For example, one of the contemporary developments for Warren and Brandeis was the development of photography[28] and the press. According to them, newspapers invaded privacy in a negative way as '[g]ossip [wa]s no longer the resource of the idle and the vicious, but has become a trade, which is pursued with industry as well as effrontery'.[29] Given the increasing use of Facebook and Twitter

attached to the data, whether it was anonymous or personally identifiable data, the value of the data, whether it was anonymous or personally identifiable data, the value of the data, whether it was extracted by free choice or compulsion and whether the collector is governmental or private. See Wellcome Trust (2013), 'Summary Report of Qualitative Research into Public Attitudes to Personal Data and Linking Personal Data' as excerpted in 'A Question of Trust: Report of the Investigatory Powers Review' by David Anderson QC Independent Reviewer of Terrorism Legislation, June 2015.

21 TNS-BMRB Polling (23–27 January 2014), as excerpted in 'A Question of Trust: Report of the Investigatory Powers Review' by David Anderson QC Independent Reviewer of Terrorism Legislation (June 2015) n 20.

22 Wellcome Trust (n 20).

23 B J Goold (2009), 'Surveillance and the Political Value of Privacy' Amsterdam Law Forum.

24 The US, UK, Canada, Australia and New Zealand.

25 Amnesty International (n 18).

26 Ferdinand D Schoeman (ed) (1984), *Philosophical Dimensions of Privacy: An Anthology* (Cambridge: Cambridge University Press).

27 Samuel D Warren and Louis D Brandeis (1890), 'The Right to Privacy' (15 December) 4(5) *Harvard Law Review* 193–220.

28 Latterly debated in relation to privacy rights and CCTV, see *Peck v United Kingdom* (2003) 36 EHRR 41; [2003] EMLR 287.

29 See Warren and Brandeis (n 27) 196.

postings in relation to celebrities, criminal proceedings or political scandals, one wonders if little has changed at all, save for the medium by which such gossip and information is communicated and the viral qualities of those platforms compared to traditional print media.

Warren and Brandeis noted that, in relation to instantaneous photography, such advancement in technology made it possible to take a picture of someone against his or her will, whereas (prior to that time) it was necessary to sit for one portrait for lengthy periods of time. Warren and Brandeis noted that 'the law of contract or of trust might afford the prudent man sufficient safeguards against the improper circulation of his portrait',[30] whereas instantaneous photography meant that protection, in a legal sense that misuse of that image could not so easily be afforded. Warren and Brandeis reviewed the contemporaneous practices of common law courts of justice, and concluded that the rights protected were 'not rights arising from contract or from special trust, but are rights as against the world'[31] (i.e. they perceived them as absolute rights), but 'the principle which has been applied to protect these rights is in reality not the principle of private property, unless that word be used in an extended and unusual sense'.[32] They proposed that a solution would be to interpret a 'right to privacy' in a manner which would complement the right used by judges in comparisons of a casual letter or an entry in a diary with the most valuable poem or essay, or to a botch or daub with a masterpiece.[33] However, they noted that this was only one aspect of the right and that 'the law has no new principle to formulate when it extends this protection to the personal appearance, sayings, acts, and to the personal relation, domestic or otherwise'.[34] Warren and Brandeis supported the need for the acknowledgement of the 'right to privacy' with the change in the structure of publicity and the appearance of new technologies of the age. The protection of the individual gained a new background replacing proprietary rights: privacy means the protection not only of privacy, but the protection of autonomy in its wider sense, not only the protection of proprietary autonomy. The right is lost only when the author himself communicates his production to the public (in other words, publishes it[35]), which in the modern context may be through publishing a thought on Twitter. Remarkably, although it was written in 1890, there is much to be garnered from the importance of the law of contract and the emerging right of privacy, which remains applicable in the social media context, e.g. social media site terms and conditions, community standards and privacy policies.

Whilst the concept of privacy is much-debated, there is no academic consensus on the subject, leading one commentator to declare that privacy is 'a value so

30 Ibid (n27).
31 Ibid (n27) 213.
32 Ibid (n27).
33 Ibid (n27) 199.
34 Ibid (n27) 213.
35 Ibid (n27) 199–200. See also *Duke of Queensberry v Shebbeare* 2 Eden 3 329 (1758); *Bartlett v Crittenden* 5 McLean 32 4I (1849).

complex, so entangled in competing and contradictory dimensions, so engorged with various and distinct meanings, that I sometimes despair whether it can be usefully addressed at all'.[36]

4.1.3 The value of privacy

Understanding what privacy means is, of course, only half the battle. Privacy must be understood with regard to the value that is attached to it.

A good start is provided by the recent judicial description of privacy protection as 'a prerequisite to individual security, self-fulfilment and autonomy as well as to the maintenance of a thriving democratic society'.[37] It can facilitate concepts such as identity, dignity, autonomy, independence, imagination and creativity, which can be more difficult to realise and maintain.[38] It can also facilitate trust, friendship and intimacy, arguably qualities that form the essential basis for a diverse and cohesive society.[39] However, conversely, surveillance has been shown to lead to self-censorship[40] and the suppression of certain behaviour,[41] although once again, anti-social as well as pro-social behaviour may be suppressed by surveillance.[42]

Privacy can also be seen to secure other important rights such as freedom of expression and the right to a fair trial. Lord Neuberger, President of the UK Supreme Court, recently suggested that 'at least in many cases' the right to privacy is 'an aspect of freedom of expression'; as when one wishes to do or say something only privately, it is an interference with expression when one cannot.[43] In relation to anonymous speech, Lord Neuberger noted that privacy rights 'reinforce' the right to freedom of expression, both generally and particularly in relation to confidential speech.[44]

The notion of privacy only exists in contraposition to the notion of what is public. As we have seen from the discussion above, the notion of privacy has changed across time and cultures. The right to be let alone[45] has been proclaimed

36 R C Post (2001), 'Three Concepts of Privacy' 89 *Geo. L.J.* 2087.

37 *R v Spencer* [2014] 2 SCR 212 para 15, summarising the effect of previous cases in the Supreme Court of Canada.

38 See Daniel J Solove (2002), 'Access and Aggregation: Privacy, Public Records, and the Constitution' 86 *Minn. L. Rev.* 1137, 1145 and C Fried, 'Privacy' (1968) 77 *Yale LJ* 475, discussing love, friendship and trust.

39 See Goold (n 23); R Post (1989), 'The Social Foundations of Privacy: Community and Self in the Common Law Tort' 77 *Cal. L. Rev.* 957.

40 See J Kang (1998), 'Information Privacy in Cyberspace Transactions' 50 *Stan. L. Rev.* 1193, 1260.

41 A Oulasvirta and others , 'Long-term Effects of Ubiquitous Surveillance in the Home' Ubicomp *12: Proceedings of the 2012 ACM Conference on Ubiquitous Computing* (Pittsburgh, USA: ACM) 12, 41.

42 To take a practical example, whether a person reports or owns up to scraping another vehicle in a car park might depend on whether the incident is thought to have been recorded by CCTV.

43 Lord Neuberger at the Hong Kong Foreign Correspondents' Club, 'The Third and Fourth Estates: Judges, Journalists and Open Justice', 26 August 2014.

44 Lord Neuberger at 5 RB Conference, 'What's in a name? Privacy and anonymous speech on the Internet' (30 September 2014).

45 Ibid (n29) 193–205.

to be the 'most comprehensive of rights and the right most valued by civilized men'.[46] This right has been associated with human dignity,[47] with the notion of the 'inviolate personality' and with the need for beliefs, thoughts, emotions and sensations to be protected from unwanted prying.[48] The same principle has also been expressed as a positive right to conceal information, a so-called 'sphere of privacy'. However, as Bok has pointed out, there is a difference between secrecy and privacy: a secret is something kept intentionally hidden, whilst privacy is the 'condition of being alone or from unwanted access by others, physical access personal information or attention'.[49]

After studying the subject in depth, David Solove classified the different conceptions of privacy into six types:

- the right to be let alone;
- limited access to oneself;
- secrecy – the concealment of certain matters from others;
- control over personal information – the ability to control personal information about oneself;
- personhood – the protection of one's personality, individuality and dignity; and
- intimacy – control over, or limited access to, one's intimate relationships or access aspects of life.[50]

Solove's analysis concludes that conceptualising the unique characteristics of privacy is difficult, owing to the risk of narrowing or overbroad applications of the core concepts of privacy, so that they can fail to include some matters which rightly ought to be described as private or conversely fail to exclude matters which are not generally considered to be private.[51] To Solove, 'the value of privacy must be determined on the basis of its importance to society, not in terms of individual rights. Moreover, privacy does not have a universal value that is the same across all contexts. The value of privacy in a particular context depends upon the social importance of the activities that it facilitates'.[52] Therefore, Solove advances the utility of a pragmatic approach to conceptualising privacy in its historical background to contextualise the analysis.

46 Brandeis J dissenting in *Olmstead v United States*, 277 U.S. 438 (1928) 478, later upheld in *Katz v United States*, 389 U.S. 347 (1967).

47 See E Bloustein (1964), 'Privacy as an Aspect of Dignity: An Answer to Dean Prosser' 39 *NYU L. Rev.* 962, 974.

48 As enumerated by Brandeis J in *Olmstead v US* (n 46).

49 S Bok *Secrets: on the Ethics of Concealment and Revelation* (Quartet Books, 1983) 10–11.

50 Daniel J Solove (2002), 'Conceptualizing Privacy' 90 *Cal. L. Rev.* 1087.

51 Ibid.

52 Ibid 39–77.

4.1.4 Checks and balances on the right to privacy

Privacy rights also empower individuals to challenge arbitrary power exercised by the state. A state which can monitor communications offers opportunities for manipulation or control, and to respond to perceived threats to power. Profiling dissenters and minority groups can offer the capacity to control the information received or dispensed by such groups,[53] leading to the observation that intrusion on privacy is the 'primary weapon of the tyrant'.[54]

However powerful the need for privacy, it is not an absolute right and can yield to competing considerations. Therefore, in certain circumstances, public authorities can interfere with the private and family life of an individual. At the European level, these circumstances are set out in Article 8(2) of the European Convention on Human Rights (ECHR). Such interference must be proportionate, in accordance with law and necessary to protect national security, public safety or the economic well-being of the country; to prevent disorder or crime, protect health or morals; or to protect the rights and freedoms of others.

The concept of private life in UK law is based on the classic civil liberties notion that the state should not intrude into the private sphere without strict justification. In our modern system, aspects of this right are protected by several regulations and statutes, including the Human Rights Act 1998, the E-Privacy Directive, the Data Protection Act 1998[55] and the Regulation of Investigatory Powers Act 2000. The proposed Investigatory Powers Bill will be considered later in this chapter.

The regulation of social media raises collective action problems and baseline definition issues. The internet crosses may different jurisdictions, each with a different approach to privacy. Moreover, it is difficult to pass a binding treaty or convention on the use of social media by terrorists as it is harder to identify (and arguably label) it as terrorist activity, against other regulated areas of internet use. Disagreement among UN members on whether internet governance should be implemented by the international community also makes a treaty unlikely.

4.1.5 Is privacy dead?

Is privacy dead, as has been declared by some commentators?[56] It is difficult to argue against the proposition that the notion of privacy has changed in recent years. We are now apparently willing to share once-private information with online contacts (who may not necessarily be known to us in the 'real world'), service providers and the general public. All of this would tend to confirm Mark Zuckerberg, the founder of Facebook's contention that privacy is no longer a

53 Frequently cited in this regard is the comment attributed to Cardinal Richelieu: 'Show me six lines written by the most honest man in the world, and I will find enough therein to hang him'.

54 Bloustein (n 47) 974.

55 Which will soon be replaced by the General Data Protection Regulation.

56 See e.g. J Morgan (2014), 'Privacy is completely and utterly dead, and we killed it', *Forbes.com* (19 August).

social norm[57] in a world where we share our most personal thoughts, location and photos through any number of social media sites and blogs. Often we click through to services without considering the terms of use, or how our data may be shared. In the words of the well known cryptographer and writer Bruce Schneier, 'The bargain you make, again and again, with various companies is surveillance in exchange for free service'.[58] In the modern world with its tablets, smart phones, even smart fridges which can order our milk and every company we order from online wanting our email address and details about our household, it seems a virtual impossibility to engage in the mundane activities of day-to-day economic and social existence without having to pass over, willingly or unwittingly, information about ourselves. The significance of such developments is expressed in the following prediction:

> Store clerks will know your name, address, and income level as soon as you walk through the door. Billboards will know who you are, and record how you respond to them. Grocery store shelves will know what you usually buy, and exactly how to entice you to buy more of it. Your car will know who is in it, who is driving, and what traffic laws that driver is following or ignoring.[59]

However, it does not follow that privacy should not be protected, or that privacy norms will not change again over time. Indeed, in December 2014, Facebook sent an update to users promoting its new 'Privacy Basics' service, noting that 'protecting people's information and providing meaningful privacy controls are at the core of everything we do'.[60] Furthermore, there are many different types of private information, as well as different ways that it can be imparted to selected or wide audiences. Therefore, different categories of communication may attract a different level of privacy (e.g. consider Facebook wall posts or Twitter tweets compared with private messaging). Users may be mindful of the extent and degree to which that information is available to others.[61]

Moreover, the incredible development in technology means that privacy is actively sold as a feature of modern products. By way of example, iPhones offer encryption standards which mean that not even the provider of the phone will be able to decrypt its contents,[62] and in 2016 Whatsapp announced that messages will now be sent with end-to-end encryption.[63]

57 'Privacy no longer a social norm, says Facebook founder', *The Guardian* (11 January 2011).

58 B Schneier (2015), *Data and Goliath* (W W Norton & Company) ch 1.

59 Ibid ch 2.

60 Facebook update (20 December 2014).

61 See A Watts (2015), 'A Teenager's View on Social Media' (2 January).

62 See the Privacy section on the Apple website: https://www.apple.com/privacy/government-informationrequests/.

63 Whatsapp Blog, *End-to-end encryption* https://blog.whatsapp.com/10000618/end-to-end-encryption (5 April 2016).

4.1.6 The private sector's role in privacy protection

There is also a distinction to be drawn between the trust placed in private companies as opposed to the government, with research indicating that the government is trusted.[64] However, concern has been expressed regarding the government's use of data,[65] particularly in terms of recent profiling or leaks,[66] perhaps compounded by the 'Snowden effect'. A number of studies have suggested that most people had already assumed that the type of action alleged in the Snowden documents was undertaken;[67] however, this has not overcome some research indicating low levels of trust in the UK Government to use people's data appropriately,[68] with many holding the opinion that neither government nor private companies can now keep their data completely secure.[69]

The old adage that nothing in life is free very much applies to 'free online services'. Although no subscription charge may be payable, there is a value trade-off garnered from the information provided to companies offering online services. This is because data relating to our buying habits and social/lifestyle preferences is a valuable trade for big organisations being employed to different degrees to do everything from marketing to helping to determine credit scores and insurance price,[70] thereby creating 'a detailed composite of the consumer's life'.[71]

Such site providers disclose this information in their terms of service, for instance, with the aim to generate advertising revenue. For example, Google's online terms of service state that:

> Our automated systems analyze your content (including emails) to provide you personally relevant product features, such as customized search results, tailored advertising, and spam and malware detection. This analysis occurs as the content is sent, received, and when it is stored.[72]

64 See Executive Office of the President (2015), 'Big Data: Seizing Opportunities, Preserving Values' (May 2014), as excerpted in 'A Question of Trust: Report of the Investigatory Powers Review' by David Anderson QC Independent Reviewer of Terrorism Legislation, June 2015. (n 20), in which law enforcement and intelligence agencies were ranked low in terms of public trust.

65 Ipsos MORI, 'Public attitudes to the use and sharing of their data', for the Royal Statistical Society, as excerpted in 'A Question of Trust: Report of the Investigatory Powers Review' by David Anderson QC Independent Reviewer of Terrorism Legislation, June 2015. (n 20) 33–34.

66 Ibid.

67 See TNS-BMRB (n 21).

68 Polling was conduct by Ipsos MORI for the *Evening Standard* in October 2014. See 'Public backs curbs on police seeing phone records of journalists' *London Evening Standard* (21 October 2014), as excerpted in 'A Question of Trust: Report of the Investigatory Powers Review' by David Anderson QC Independent Reviewer of Terrorism Legislation, June 2015. (n 20) 33–34; Ipsos MORI: RSS; 13% had high trust in the British Government compared to 46% with low trust.

69 Ibid.

70 'How Wireless Carriers Are Monetizing Your Movements' MIT Technology Review Website (12 April 2013).

71 'Data Brokers: a Call for Transparency and Accountability' (May 2014).

72 See http://www.google.com/intl/en/policies/terms/.

Sources can include a user's IP address, Google and YouTube profiles, Google search engine results, Google map requests and apps belonging to businesses which advertise with Google. Google offers its 'partners'[73] a number of products to help manage their advertising and websites, including 'Adsense, Adwords, Google Analytics and a range of DoubleClick-branded services'.[74]

Location-based services also allow users of social media, such as Facebook, to 'check in' at a certain location (i.e. a restaurant or a cinema), so if a user's privacy settings are 'open' on the account, anyone can see this and track the user's movements; however, even if settings are set to 'private', a third party (such as the police) can still gain access to this information (i.e. as part of a criminal investigation). This came as news to user @IrinaHolmes, whose Twitter by-line reads: 'I've heard the blood of the kuffar [infidel] is delicious. I came here to enjoy it'. Users admonished her for revealing her US nationality to her followers and for posting photos; user Abu Umar Al-Ansari wrote to her, 'your photo has GPS metadata which can be traced, which means the kuffar can raid this brothers position'. Irina replied, 'This picture is not that new. Also my location is off. You don't need to worry'.[75] To which user Prince Khattab tweeted, 'Your positions can be easily found with Google Maps by someone who knows Syrian terrain and landmarks', which prompted Abu Umar Al-Ansari to write again, 'sister, high-level Dawlah [ISIS] personnel are saying not to post photos of Dawlah positions or from cities. Please respect this'. At this point, another user entered the conversation, adding, '#CIA #Pentagon have access to Twitter, they can locate you from your IP'. Taking the message on board Irina subsequently cautioned, 'Be careful about what you say on the social network sites. If you are planning to come here, don't announce it. #ISIS #IS #IslamicState'.

Social media sites are also engaged in the trading of data. According to Facebook's 2015 Data policy[76] it 'shares' information about users 'within the family of companies that are part of Facebook'[77] to 'facilitate, support and integrate their activities'.[78] Facebook's Audience Network programme provides app developers with aggregated data to target their ads. 'Facebook Services' are also covered by this data policy and include services such as 'Audience Insights'. This service is designed to provide businesses with information about the 'geography, demographics and purchasing behaviour and more' of other businesses and individuals.[79]

As approximately 90 per cent of the time spent using mobile devices is spent in apps[80] and such sites do not allow for the normal conventions of websites,

73 Listed details of partners are not provided. See http://www.google.com/policies/privacy/example/our-partners.html.

74 See https://www.google.com/intl/en/policies/technologies/ads/.

75 @Irina Holmes posted at 4:25 am (14 February 2015).

76 See Facebook's Data Policy: https://www.facebook.com/policy.php.

77 See https://www.facebook.com/help/111814505650678. There are currently ten companies listed in the family, including Whatsapp, Instagram and Atlas: https://www.facebook.com/fbprivacy/.

78 See https://www.facebook.com/help/111814505650678.

79 See https://www.facebook.com/business/news/audience-insights.

80 'Getting to Know you', *Economist* (13 September 2014).

deep-linking allows app developers to link to pages in apps and so replicate the structure of the web and enable tracking. Social plug-ins, which allow users to share third-party content with the likes of Facebook and Twitter, are also popular: examples include Facebook's 'like' button, Google+'s '+1' and Twitter's 'tweet' button. 'Passive location tracking',[81] which involves an app collecting location data even when it is not in use, is also increasingly common with popular apps such as *Angry Birds* making use of it. According to revelations in the Snowden leaks, the National Security Agency and its UK counterpart GCHQ have been developing capabilities to take advantage of 'leaky' smartphone apps.[82]

In March 2016, social networking forum Reddit removed a section from its website used tacitly to inform users that it had never received a certain type of US Government surveillance request.[83] Reddit also deleted a paragraph usually included in its transparency report known as a 'warrant canary' to signal to users that it had not been subject to so-called national security letters, which are used by the FBI to conduct electronic surveillance without the need for court approval.

This 'big brother' society has caused privacy watchdogs to scrutinise more closely the practices of big businesses. Indeed, in April 2015, the Information Commissioner's Office, which oversees data protection issues in the UK, launched an investigation into UK firms sharing pension, medical and financial data.[84] Although certain activities require user consent and users can actively opt out of certain instances of tracking, whether users are actively able to manage their privacy in practice is very much a moot point.[85] Essentially, if a user wants to use the services then the user must consent to the terms, so is our consent really freely given and informed when we just want to click yes and get access to services? They are the lifeblood of modern life, as expressed by one commentator:

> It's not reasonable to tell people that if they don't like the data collection, they shouldn't email, shop online, use Facebook or have a cell phone. I can't imagine students getting through school anymore without Internet search or Wikipedia, much less finding a job afterwards. These are the tools of modern life.[86]

81 'Location-tracking: 6 Social App settings to check', *Information Week* (26 August 2014).

82 J Ball 'Angry Birds and "leaky" phone apps targeted by NSA and GCHQ for user data' (28 January) http://www.theguardian.com/world/2014/jan/27/nsa-gchq-smartphone-app-angry-birds-personal-data.

83 D Voz), 'Reddit Deletes Surveillance "Warrant Canary" in Transparency Report' *Reuters* (21 March) http://www.reuters.com/article/us-usa-cyber-reddit-idUSKCN0WX2YF.

84 See the announcement on the ICO website: 'ICO launches investigation into firms sharing sensitive data' (1 April) https://ico.org.uk/about-the-ico/news-and-events/news-and-blogs/2015/04/ico-to-make-enquiries-about-sale-of-pension-data/.

85 V Mayer-Schonberger and K Cukier (2013), 'Big Data: a Revolution that will transform how we live, work and think' (John Murray).

86 See Schneier (n 58) ch 4.

Therefore, it is technically possible to opt out of companies using your data, but only if you live in a cave without any internet access. Furthermore, even if you try to manage your privacy setting this is no guarantee of snooping-free blissful internet surfing. By way of example, Apple's Safari Browser is set to block third-party cookies, yet Google was still able to send a third-party cookie which operated to allow the DoubleClick cookie to be sent to the user's browser for part of 2011 and 2012.[87]

The story of data sharing does not, however, stop with the data that can identify you. Companies are allowed to share your data with third parties without your consent so long as it does not contain data which can identify you individually. However, a truly anonymous data set is as rare as hens' teeth. A study of a number of these techniques in 2014 concluded that each failed to 'meet with certainty the criteria of effective anonymisation'.[88]

The above discussion is an interesting exploration of privacy rights online; however, the debate relating to communications data centres around the collection of web logs/URLs and location data. Facebook's data policy uses 'device locations, including specific geographic locations, such as through GPS, Bluetooth or WiFi' and IP addresses;[89] Twitter may receive 'log data', which includes the user's IP address and location. Twitter will either remove or delete the full IP address after 18 months.[90]

Weblogs of URL's are also an important way to track users. For instance, Google records page requests made, including the requested URL.[91] Facebook collects information 'when you visit third party sites and apps that use our services (like when they offer our Like button or Facebook Log In or use our measurement and advertising services). This includes information about the websites and apps you visit' and Twitter services may mean details of web pages are received by Twitter.

Some private sector companies have reacted to state interference in private technology. For example, Microsoft is currently suing the US Government over the right to tell its users when federal agencies want access to private data. Microsoft is also fighting a court battle in New York over the government's demand for emails of a non-US citizen that the company has stored in a data centre located in Ireland.[92]

87 *Vidal-Hall v Google* [2015] EWCA Civ 311 para 3.

88 Article 29 Data Protection Working Party, *Opinion 5/2014 on Anonymisation Techniques* (April 2014). The ICO published a Code of Practice on Anonymisation in 2012, which provides advice on good practice.

89 See Facebook's Data Policy: https://www.facebook.com/policy.php

90 See Twitter and Google's respective Privacy Policies: https://twitter.com/privacy?lang=en; https://www.google.com/intl/en/policies/privacy/key-terms/#toc-terms-server-logs.

91 See https://www.google.com/intl/en/policies/privacy/key-terms/#toc-terms-server-logs.

92 'Microsoft Suit is Latest Tech Clash with US over Privacy' *Tempo.co* (1 April 2016) http://en.tempo.co/read/news/2016/04/16/310763182/Microsoft-Suit-is-Latest-Tech-Clash-with-US-over-Privacy.

4.2 Surveillance: a potted history

Spying has always been a topic that excites the senses, but usually we think of it in terms of the rich, famous or politically exposed, traditionally thanks to our upbringing on Frederick Forsyth and Ian Fleming, which conjure up images of spies with suitcases coming to sticky ends and not as something that applies to 'Joe Public'. Whilst even just a few years ago spying would have made us think of Tosh doing an all-night stakeout on *The Bill*, it now seems synonymous with phrases such as 'phone tapping' and 'Big Brother society'. Not a day goes by when there is not some article in the papers or online news site about how the state is watching us or a jihadi bride has been caught through the monitoring of her online activity.

4.2.1 The origins of modern surveillance

Much like the contemporary vogue for 'scandi-style', surveillance feels very contemporary. However, as noted by Keith Laidler in his book *Surveillance Unlimited*: '[s]pying and surveillance are at least as old as civilization itself. The rise of city states and empires . . . meant that each needed to know not only the disposition and morale of their enemy, but also the loyalty and general sentiment of their own population'.[93]

In the late 1600s the UK postal service provided the surprising ground for plots and intrigue, which went to the very heart of government. The mail, as the main distance communications tool of the day, was ripe for spying as it was frequently used to deliver matters of national importance and thereby held the potential to uncover secret plots. Oliver Cromwell's principal secretary of state, John Thurloe, relied on regular interception of the mail for intelligence purposes and even exposed Edward Sexby's 1657 plot to assassinate Cromwell. Had he not done so, the landscape of the United Kingdom might have been considerably different today. Cromwell's son, Henry, wrote to Thurloe: 'Really it is a wonder you can pick so many locks leading into the hearts of wicked men as you do'. This sentiment could equally attach today to any number of plots that have been thwarted through the use of communications data.

Snowden has undoubtedly reignited the debate but the battle to fashion a common law constraint on the bulk collection of data goes back a long way and is entrenched in the concept of obtaining a warrant to permit a certain course of action within defined parameters. In 1762, the Home Secretary, the Earl of Halifax, issued a general warrant to search for Mr John Entick, who had rather daringly written libellous publications concerning the king and Parliament. The warrant was 'to seize and apprehend, and to bring, together with his books and papers, in safe custody before me to be examined concerning the premises and further dealt with according to law'.[94] The Lord Chief Justice, Lord Camden,

93 Keith Laidler (2008), *Surveillance Unlimited: How We've Become the Most Watched People on Earth* (Cambridge, Crow's Nest, Australia: Icon Books Ltd) 17.

94 *Entick v Carrington* 95 ER 807, 810.

declared: ' . . . we can safely say that there is no law in this country to justify the defendants in what they have done; if there was, it would destroy all the comforts of society; for papers are often the dearest property a man can have . . . '.[95]

Lord Camden was not alone in his good fight for respecting the individual right to prevent interference by the state. In another leading case of the day, Lord Chief Justice Pratt stated that: 'to enter a man's house by virtue of a nameless warrant, in order to procure evidence, is worse than the Spanish Inquisition'.[96]

These cases deserve their time in this chapter as they are much celebrated and, despite the passage of considerable time, have not been overruled. However, they were not decided on the basis of an infringement of privacy; rather, they focused on property violation through trespass. Any attempt to rely on these cases from a privacy perspective have received short shrift: a key example of this was the High Court holding in 1979 that these cases did not form a basis for a claim to privacy in respect of phone tapping.[97] The thrust of this is that the common law, independent of the influence of the ECHR, barely recognises the right to privacy or private communications.[98]

Since the daring acts of Mr Entick, the issues and the enemies of the state have become increasingly complex. In 1909, German spies were active in the UK, leading to the establishment of a secret service Bureau. By the time of the First World War, the security services began to put their focus into 'signals intelligence' (SigInt). Despite changing hairstyles and tastes in soft furnishings over the years, this type of surveillance remains very much at the heart of GCHQ's work. However, even during periods of history when counter-espionage was high on the agenda, such as code breaking at Bletchley Park to decipher the Nazi's Enigma machine, it was (to an extent) a more innocent time, where the objectives of the mission at hand were clear and the ability to mine vast amounts of data as opposed to targeting in on a particular activity were very limited indeed. Careless talk may have cost lives, but opinions, classified communications and potentially restricted information was not being blasted out on the internet and on social media.

In 1994, the Intelligence Services Act (ISA) gave a legal underpinning to the agency for the first time, but the powers conferred on GCHQ, and its objectives, remained broad and vague, describing the agency's work as 'in the interests of national security, with particular reference to the defence and foreign policies

95 Ibid 817–18.

96 *Huckle v Money* (1763) 2 Wilson 205 95 ER 768.

97 *Malone v Commissioner of Police (No 2)* [1979] 1 Ch 344, 368–69.

98 See *Kaye v Robertson* [1991] FSR 62 (Glidewell LJ), with whom Bingham and Leggatt LJJ agreed: 'It is well known that in English law there is no right to privacy and accordingly no right of action for breach of a *person's privacy*'; see *Wainwright and another v Home Office* [2003] UKHL 53; [2004] 2 AC 406 para 26 (Lord Bingham): 'All three judgments are flat against a judicial power to declare the existence of a high-level right to privacy and I do not think that they suggest that the courts should do so'; and *R (Catt) v Metropolitan Police Commissioner* [2015] UKSC 9 para 2 (Lord Sumption): 'The [US] concept of a legal right of privacy whether broadly or narrowly defined fell on stony ground in England. Its reception here has been relatively recent and almost entirely due to the incorporation into domestic law of the [ECHR]'.

of Her Majesty's government; in the interests of the economic wellbeing of the United Kingdom; and in support of the prevention and the detection of serious crime'. The tensions between the wide remit of the security services as opposed to the protection of rights really began to come to the fore at this time, with John Wadham (the then legal director of Liberty) stating that:

> [n]ational security is used without further definition. It is true the courts themselves have found it impossible to decide what is or what is not in the interests of national security. The reality is that 'national security' can mean whatever the government of the day chooses it to mean.

The same could be said for the clause referring to 'economic wellbeing'.

Whilst the activities at Bletchley Park have become the subject of misty-eyed documentaries and films starring Kate Winslet, for example, in the present day the focus is much more on the role of parliamentary scrutiny of the work of the security services. Indeed, Winslet's films would not have had the same box office appeal if she been filmed filling out comprehensive risk reports on government standard forms for her line manager. Over the past 20 years technology has changed beyond all recognition. Whilst most people in possession of the internet and internet enabled smartphones use it to look at funny pictures of cats, terrorists too have harnessed the power of the internet for far more sinister motives. In a world where private companies hosted in the far-flung corners of the globe deliver every imaginable type of social networking tool, texting and internet based communication (e.g. Whatsapp, Facebook Messenger and WeChat), in a leaked internal GCHQ memo dated October 2011 it was noted that: '[Our] targets boil down to diplomatic/military/commercial targets/terrorists/organised criminals and e-crime/cyber actors'.

4.2.2 Project Tempora

In 2014, reality TV star Kim Kardashian may have tried to 'break the internet' by baring all, but long before her flesh-revealing antics graced the virtual world, the UK security services had a far grander design in mind: to 'master the internet'.

In about 2007 *Project Tempora* was the melting pot into which all ideas for new ways to tackle the cyber threat were poured. A year later, 'Mastering the Internet' was being run out of GCHQ's outpost based in the surfers' paradise, Bude in Cornwall, exploring the uses of an 'internet buffer', in the charmingly quintessentially British-named 'Cheltenham Processing Centre'. Depending on your ideological and political point of view, this is either the equivalent of Tracy Island from Thunderbirds or Dr No's pad in the James Bond film of the same name.

In a memo dating back to 2009, written jointly by the director in charge of the 'Mastering the Internet' project and a senior member of the agency's cyber-defence team, it was pondered how the intelligence services could keep apace with intelligence in a world of endless technological possibilities:

> It is becoming increasingly difficult for GCHQ to acquire the rich sources of traffic needed to enable our support to partners within HMG [Her Majesty's Government], the armed forces, and overseas. The rapid development of different technologies, types of traffic, service providers and networks, and the growth in sheer volumes that accompany particularly the expansion and use of the internet, present an unprecedented challenge to the success of GCHQ's mission. Critically we are not currently able to prioritise and task the increasing range and scale of our accesses at the pace, or with the coherence demanded of the internet age: potentially available data is not accessed, potential benefit for HMG is not delivered.[99]

By March 2010, the NSA was granted access to the project, now going under the codename TINT, which then came to be referred to in official documents as a 'joint GCHQ/NSA research initiative' that 'uniquely allows retrospective analysis for attribution'. Essentially, this amounted to information being swept from the internet, from which analysis could be made. Around this time, GCHQ also began to start accessing the cables that carry internet traffic into and out of the country. Although when visualising this in the mind's eye this may seem as clumsy as scamming your neighbour's electricity by openly plugging into their mains, all of this activity was authorised by legal warrants.

By 2011, the NSA noted that the Cheltenham Processing Centre now produced 'larger amounts of metadata collection than the NSA'; that is to say, GCHQ had access to details of calls made and messages sent, e.g. time and duration, rather than the content. The programme was now capable of collecting, a memo explained with startling academic prowess and finely crafted mastery of the art of the written word, 'a lot of data!'.[100] *Tempora*, the document said, had shown that 'every area of ops can get real benefit from this capability, especially for target discovery and target development'.[101] Whilst such surveillance would be met with almost universal agreement that individuals such as Jihadi John or Osama bin Laden should be under detection for the 'greater good', surveillance is not always so targeted.

The UK was not alone in its surveillance efforts. In 2007, in the wake of the passage of the Protect America Act under the Bush administration, the NSA launched the sexily titled PRISM programme. PRISM is a government code name for a data-collection effort known slightly less glamorously as the SIGAD US-984XN.[102] PRISM collects internet communications from at least nine major

99 Quoted in J Ball and others (2013), 'Mastering the internet: how GCHQ set out to spy on the world wide web' (21 June) http://www.theguardian.com/uk/2013/jun/21/gchq-mastering-the-internet.

100 Ibid.

101 Ibid.

102 Bill Chappell (2013), 'NSA Reportedly Mines Servers of US Internet Firms for Data': the Two-Way (blog of NPR)' (6 June); Zack Whittaker (2013), '"PRISM: Here's How the NSA Wiretapped the Internet"' ZDNet (8 June).

US internet companies,[103] based on requests made under Section 702 of the FISA Amendments Act of 2008 to turn over any data that match court-approved search terms. (Without spoiling what is to come, as a teaser, one of these words is 'pork'.)[104]

4.2.3 The Snowden leaks

Yes, dear reader, we have finally reached the part that you were waiting for, enter stage right Mr Snowden . . .

The sheer scale of this monitoring was revealed in June 2013, by Edward Snowden, covering everything from internet searches, social-media content and, most controversially, the records (known as meta data) of phone calls (including details of who called whom, for how long and from where), which customarily has been held for years, but potentially forever. Many of the documents that continue to trickle out to this day specifically relate to GCHQ. The UK Government has stated that at least 58,000 'highly classified UK intelligence documents' were among the documents appropriated and disseminated. The principal allegations broadly concern:[105]

- bulk collection of internet and international communications data
- analytic tools enabling advanced searching of intercepted data
- cooperative relationships between governments and service providers
- methods for Computer Network Exploitation (CNE) and
- intelligence sharing.

In 2014, the *Guardian* newspaper published extracts of these secret documents, which showed that GCHQ, with aid from the US National Security Agency under a programme called Optic Nerve, intercepted and stored the webcam images of millions of internet users not suspected of wrongdoing.[106] The GCHQ files dating between 2008 and 2010 revealed images of Yahoo webcam chats in bulk and saved them to agency databases, regardless of whether individual users were an intelligence target or not. In just six months, in 2008, more than 1.8 million Yahoo user accounts globally were surveyed, many of which included sexually explicit images. Optic Nerve was based on collecting information from GCHQ's huge

103 Barton Gellman and Laura Poitras (2013), 'U.S. Intelligence Mining Data from Nine U.S. Internet Companies in Broad Secret Program' *The Washington Post* (6 June).

104 Barton Gellman and Ashkan Soltani (2013), 'NSA infiltrates links to Yahoo, Google data centers worldwide, Snowden documents say' *The Washington Post* (30 October).

105 It is important to note that the British government has adopted a 'neither confirm nor deny' approach to the allegations contained in the Snowden Documents (other than the PRISM programme, the existence of which has been acknowledged by the US Government) and only a tiny (and not necessarily representative) proportion of the Snowden Documents has been placed in the public domain.

106 S Ackerman and J Ball (2014), 'Optic Nerve: millions of Yahoo webcam images intercepted by GCHQ' *Guardian* (28 February) www.theguardian.com/world/2014/feb/27/gchq-nsa-webcam-images-internet-yahoo.

network of internet cable taps, which was then processed and fed into systems provided by the NSA. Webcam information was fed into NSA's XKeyscore search tool, and NSA research was used to build the tool that identified Yahoo's webcam traffic. Bulk surveillance on Yahoo users was begun, the documents said, because 'Yahoo webcam is known to be used by GCHQ targets'.

It must be pointed out that, whilst the UK has adopted a neither confirm nor deny approach to the Snowden disclosures, US Government officials have disputed some aspects of the *Guardian* reporting. The US has also defended the programme as surveillance that is subject to the issuing of a warrant and is independently overseen by the Federal Government's executive, judicial and legislative branches. Indeed, while it is tempting just to look at confirmation of a gross invasion into what Mr Smith at number 20 gets up to in his shed on a Friday night, GCHQ in some of the documents disclosed did note the ethical and legal minefield governing surveillance taking place under *Tempora*, stating that:

- You are in a privileged position – repay that trust.
- You have ready access to a lot of sensitive data.
- Understand your legal obligations: don't become a case study in future legalities training presentation.
- If you have legal or ethical concerns, speak to someone: they will be taken seriously.

However, the document concluded that: 'you are in an enviable position – have fun and make the most of it'.[107] The revelations of the surveillance conducted have proved to be a source of friction, resulting in much debate as to the role of the agencies and how the competing interests of privacy, freedom of expression and the state's duty of care to its citizens can be resolved. Social media, which pours out user generated content at a rate of knots, has added a new dimension to the debate. The use of home grown security software solutions has declined and reliance on Western social media apps, particularly encrypted ones, has markedly increased.[108]

In one official document considering the complexity of the issue in the face of there being two billion users of the internet worldwide and more than 400 million regular Facebook users, the author claimed 'we are starting to "master" the internet', and 'our current capability is quite impressive'.[109] In 2011, another

107 See Ball and others (n 99).

108 S Stalinsky and R Sosnow (2015), 'Al-Qaeda's Embrace of Encryption Technology Part III – July 2014-January 2015: Islamic State (ISIS) and Other Jihadis Continue to Develop their Cyber and Encryption Capabilities; Post-Snowden Fears Lead them to Test New, More Secure Technologies and Social Media Inquiry & Analysis' Series No 1143 (4 February 2015) http://www.memrijttm.org/al-qaedas-embrace-of-encryption-technology-part-iii-july-2014-january-2015-islamic-state-isis-and-other-jihadis-continue-to-develop-their-cyber-and-encryption-capabilities-post-snowden-fears-lead-them-to-test-new-more-secure-technologies-and-social-media.

109 See Ball and others (n 99).

memo revealed that: 'MTI delivered the next big step in the access, processing and storage journey, hitting a new high of more than 39 billion events in a 24-hour period, dramatically increasing our capability to produce unique intelligence from our targets' use of the internet and made major contributions to recent operations'.[110]

Snowden sent his first-ever tweet at noon on 29 September 2015, asking, 'Can you hear me now?'.[111] Within the hour, the Republican candidate in America, former New York Governor George Pataki (@Governor Pataki) responded: '[s]ome say you have courage, I saw real courage on #Sept11. You are just a traitor who put American lives at risk. https://twitter.com/snowden/status/648890134243487744 . . .'.[112] Twitter will provide Snowden an enormous platform; indeed, Twitter (@Twitter) itself posted: 'Today @Snowden joined Twitter, and here's the world's response. pic.twitter.com/d6HgVvdRsf', which linked to a visual heat map of the effect of the post across the globe.[113] So far, Snowden is only following one account: the NSA's.[114]

As we saw throughout Chapter 2, there is an expectation in Europe that communications will remain private, due to the sanctity placed in concepts such as freedom of expression and the right to privacy. Most of the cases which have come to the European courts have been concerned with interception.[115] However, as seen from the work of Cheltenham, communications data plays a crucial role in policing and counter-terrorism in the UK and authorities do not always need to have the intimate details of a conversation between two people; just as interesting is who is speaking to whom.

4.2.4 What I talk about, when I talk about surveillance

So how is all of this inception and data mining governed? To even begin to grasp that nettle we need to take a step back and consider what types of data can be monitored and how we define those categories. It may not be the raciest part of the story, but it is a very important one nonetheless.

The primary statute, pursuant to which telecommunications can be intercepted or communications data obtained, is the Regulation of Investigatory Powers Act 2000 (RIPA). RIPA sets out different mechanisms for the authorisation of interception and acquisition of communications data. The primary means by which an interception may be authorised under RIPA is via a warrant, issued under section 5 and signed by a Secretary of state or Scottish minister in person.

110 Ibid.

111 Edward Snowden @Snowden (29 September 2015).

112 S Detrow (2015), 'What Edward Snowden on Twitter Could Mean for the Presidential Race' NPR.org (29 September) http://www.npr.org/sections/itsallpolitics/2015/09/29/444531467/snowdens-twitter-account-could-put-domestic-surveillance-back-on-the-radar.

113 @twitterToday @Snowden joined Twitter, and here's the world's response pic.twitter.com/d6HgVvdRsf 8:14 pm– (29 September 2015).

114 https://twitter.com/Snowden?ref_src=twsrc%5Etfw.

115 See e.g. *Malone v UK*; *Weber v Germany*; *Liberty v UK*; *Kennedy v UK* [2010] All ER (D) 224.

The Secretary of state must believe that the warrant is necessary on grounds of national security, preventing or detecting serious crime, or safeguarding the economic well-being of the UK or for the purpose of giving effect to an international agreement.[116]

The Secretary of state must also believe it is necessary and proportionate to the objective sought. That dual requirement of necessity and proportionality is a direct import from the Article 8 case law of the ECtHR concerning the right to respect for private life. The power to apply for a warrant to intercept communications under RIPA is limited to MI5, MI6, GCHQ, the NCA, the Metropolitan Police Service (MPS), the Police Service of Northern Ireland (PSNI), the Police Service of Scotland (Police Scotland), HMRC and the MoD. There is a distinction in RIPA, which recognises that some warrants may be targeted and others may be more general in nature.

4.2.4.1 Interception

Interception is the collection of communications in the course of transmission.[117] RIPA provides that an interception takes place when 'contents of the communication [are made] available while being transmitted to a person other than the sender or intended recipient of the communication'.[118] It can include activities such as phone tapping, gathering emails or text messages as they are transmitted along communications cables. The authorities can then see the contents of that communication and also the data relating to that communication (related communications data).[119]

4.2.4.1.1 TARGETED WARRANTS

Warrants issued under section 8(1) are targeted, as they must describe either 'one person as the interception subject' or 'a single set of premises' where the interception is to take place under sections 8(1) and (2). Essentially these warrants can authorise the interception of communications between two people in the British Isles, the communications of known individuals who are communicating outside the British Isles or between two persons overseas. The Interception Code, whilst not only being a brilliant potential title for a film, sets out the elements that a section 8(1) warrant application must contain.[120] They include:

- the background to the operation in question
- the person or premises to which the application relates (and how the person or premises feature in the operation)

116 Regulation of Investigatory Powers Act 2000 (RIPA) s 5(3).

117 Ibid s 1(1).

118 Ibid s 2.

119 Ibid s 20 for the definition of related communications data.

120 See the Interception of Communications Code of Practice (Interception Code) para 4.2; 'A Question of Trust: Report of the Investigatory Powers Review' by David Anderson QC Independent Reviewer of Terrorism Legislation, June 2015. (n 20) 83.

- a description of the communications to be intercepted, details of the service provider(s) and an assessment of the feasibility of the interception operation where this is relevant
- a description of the conduct to be authorised or the conduct (including the interception of other communications not specifically identified by the warrant as foreseen under RIPA section 5(6)(a)) as it is necessary to undertake in order to carry out what is authorised or required by the warrant, and the obtaining of related communications data
- an explanation of why the interception is considered to be necessary[121]
- a consideration of why the conduct to be authorised by the warrant is proportionate to what is sought to be achieved by that conduct
- a consideration of any unusual degree of collateral intrusion and why that intrusion is justified in the circumstances. In particular, where the communications in question might affect religious, medical or journalistic confidentiality or legal privilege, or communications between a Member of Parliament and another person on constituency business, this must be specified in the application
- where an application is urgent, supporting justification and
- an assurance that all material intercepted will be handled in accordance with the safeguards required by RIPA section 15.

4.2.4.2 Communications data

Communications data, which has been the big source of debate recently, is more about what is used and when, rather than the content and generally gathered retrospectively. This aligns with the concept of communications data gathering; that it may be of use one day (much as the contents of our lofts at home), rather than an active interest in a particular subject, e.g. data about use made of a service but not the contents of the communications themselves. RIPA separates out these communications into three broad categories, namely traffic data, i.e. person, apparatus, location or address to or from which a communication is transmitted, and information about a computer file or program that has been accessed or run in the course of sending or receiving a communication. It includes things such as location data (think again when you turn your location on your phone to 'check-in' using Facebook), and information of servers visited, IP addresses (your computer's unique fingerprint) . Secondly, there is service use data, which are things such as how many times someone uses a service and what they are downloading, e.g. a call log on your phone bill. Finally, there is subscriber information, which is all other information that the service provider holds about the person that uses the service, i.e. your billing address, email, name but also bank account data when you sign up for your price plan in the mobile phone shop.[122]

121 Necessary under the provisions of RIPA s 5(3); see also 'A Question of Trust: Report of the Investigatory Powers Review' by David Anderson QC Independent Reviewer of Terrorism Legislation, June 2015. (n 20) 83

122 RIPA s 21(4)(c).

The bulk interception of communications data supports many different government activities related to foreign affairs, defence, including cyber defence, serious crime and counter-terrorism. As the ISC put it:

> GCHQ's bulk interception capability is used primarily to find patterns in, or characteristics of, online communications which indicate involvement in threats to national security. The people involved in those communications are sometimes already known, in which case valuable extra intelligence may be obtained (e.g. a new person in a terrorist network, a new location to be monitored, or a new selector to be targeted). In other cases, it exposes previously unknown individuals or plots that threaten our security which would not otherwise be detected.[123]

GCHQ considers carefully what communications channels it seeks to intercept and has to make a case to the foreign secretary to support the bulk warrant application. The selection of targets is also examined by agency analysts and controlled through an internal process, which creates a permanent auditable record. An analyst must show the target to be relevant to the requirements set out in the certificate, i.e. it must demonstrate on what grounds the processing is justified (e.g. the interests of national security). The analyst also has to consider if the access is proportionate to the aim in question and cannot simply jump to the bulk warrant if another method would achieve the same or a more favourable outcome end, for example, the likelihood that a domestic fixed telephone line will have more users than the immediate target's email account.

The ISC noted, in March 2015: '[w]e were surprised to discover that the primary value to GCHQ of bulk interception was not in the actual content of communications, but in the information associated with those communications',[124] e.g. another email address used by a subject of interest.

The furore surrounding Snowden, however, has really arisen as a result of bulk communication. Bulk collection is trickier than *The Times* cryptic crossword puzzle and is potentially problematic, from a legal perspective, owing to the huge number of people's lives that it potentially interferes with, making it more difficult to justify that the interference is 'necessary in a democratic society', or proportionate in the face of the violation of an individual's right to privacy.[125]

When it comes to decided cases on the matter, there are only a handful. The leading case was brought by a German national, Weber, who complained that the German state was monitoring communications in the absence of any 'concrete suspicion' and relying on 'catchwords' in order to analyse the data.

123 'Privacy and Security: a modern and transparent legal framework' HC 1075 (March 2015) (ISC Privacy and Security Report) para 90, as excerpted in 'A Question of Trust: Report of the Investigatory Powers Review' by David Anderson QC Independent Reviewer of Terrorism Legislation, June 2015. (n 20) 129.

124 Ibid para 80, as excerpted in 'A Question of Trust: Report of the Investigatory Powers Review' by David Anderson QC Independent Reviewer of Terrorism Legislation, June 2015. (n 20) 130

125 See e.g. the judgement in *Kennedy v United Kingdom* [2010] All ER (D) 224.

Whilst this does not seem a million miles away from Snowden, the court dismissed the application as manifestly ill-founded, stating that that 'strategic monitoring' was not, in itself, a disproportionate interference with the right to privacy[126] because it had taken into account the narrow and closely defined justifications for such collection, the safeguards that governed the authorisation of the collection, the safeguards concerning use of that material and the data protection systems in place. In another important case concerning bulk data, the court concluded that the UK legislation in question (the Interception of Communications Act 1985 (IOCA 1985)) was not in accordance with the law. The IOCA 1985 did not provide sufficient safeguards against abuse of the power to intercept or use the material in question.[127] However, the court did not consider whether the interference in question was proportionate.

Essentially, what these cases tell us is that, per se, the bulk collection of data is not a disproportionate interference with privacy, but it is subject to more stringent scrutiny than one-off interceptions of particular individuals and the state will need to ensure that there are adequate safeguards in place to protect the data.[128] In the UK, we have a system of ministerial authorisation and a raft of organisations charged with oversight that such surveillance is conducted in accordance with law, e.g. the Interception of Communications Commissioner (IOCC),[129] the Intelligence and Security Committee (ISC) of Parliament[130] and the Investigatory Powers Tribunal.

4.2.4.2.1 BULK WARRANTS

This type of warrant is issued under section 8(4) of RIPA, and is often called an 'external' warrant. Issued by the foreign secretary to GCHQ, they authorise interception of communications where one or both of the senders or recipients

126 *Weber v Germany* (n 115) paras 114–117.

127 *Liberty v UK* (n 115) para 69.

128 This is consistent with the approach adopted by the CJEU in *Digital Rights Ireland*; see 'A Question of Trust: Report of the Investigatory Powers Review' by David Anderson QC Independent Reviewer of Terrorism Legislation, June 2015. (n 20) 79.

129 The office of IOCC is constituted under RIPA to keep under review the exercise and performance by the Secretary of State and other public authorities of their functions under RIPA Part I. The IOCC must hold, or have held, high judicial office. The current Commissioner is Sir Anthony May, a former judge of the Court of Appeal. He reports to the prime minister, who lays that report before Parliament every six months.

130 The Intelligence and Security Committee of Parliament (ISC) is the parliamentary body tasked with providing oversight of the use of investigatory powers by the security and intelligence agencies (although not by other public authorities). It is a cross-party Committee, and its members are drawn from both the House of Commons and the House of Lords. It was recently reformed by the Justice and Security Act 2013 and now oversees the operational activity and wider intelligence and security activities of the government. It is not responsible for reviewing ongoing and current operations being conducted by the agencies; see as excerpted in 'A Question of Trust: Report of the Investigatory Powers Review' by David Anderson QC Independent Reviewer of Terrorism Legislation, June 2015. (n 20) para 6.113.

of a communication is located outside the British Isles.[131] Large volumes of data are carried around the world through fibre-optic cables and satellites. Section 8(4) warrants may be used to authorise the interception of all communications transmitted on a specified route or cable, or carried by a particular service provider. In order to obtain the warrant, the relevant authority must specify the following in their application:[132]

- the background to the operation in question
- a description of the communications to be intercepted, details of the service providers and an assessment of the feasibility of the operation where this is relevant
- a description of the conduct to be authorised which must be restricted to the interception of external communications, or to conduct necessary in order to intercept those external communications, where appropriate
- the certificate that will regulate examination of the intercepted material
- an explanation of why the interception is considered to be necessary for one of the RIPA section 5(3) purposes
- a consideration of why the conduct to be authorised by the warrant is proportionate to what is sought to be achieved by that conduct
- a consideration of any unusual degree of collateral intrusion, and why that intrusion is justified in the circumstances. In particular, where the communication might affect religious, medical or journalistic confidentiality or legal privilege, this must be specified in the application
- where the application is urgent, supporting justification
- an assurance that intercepted material will be read, looked at or listened to only so far as it is certified and it meets the conditions of RIPA sections 16(2)–(6) and
- an assurance that the material intercepted will be handled in accordance with the safeguards required by RIPA section 15 and section 16.

Because the potential for surveillance is significant, when granting a warrant, the Secretary of state must also issue a certificate that describes the material that may be examined within that wider body of data. The certificates reflect the Priorities for Intelligence Collection (PIC) that is approved annually by the National Security Council after consideration by the Joint Intelligence Committee (the part of the Cabinet Office responsible for directing the security and intelligence agencies).

At the time of writing, GCHQ has the capacity to intercept just a fraction of the data travelling through the 100,000 bearers and undersea cables, which make up the global communications core infrastructure,[133] of which section 8(4) warrants form a strategic role as to which of these shall be intercepted. The scope of

131 See RIPA s 20.

132 Interception Code para 5.2.

133 ISC Privacy and Security Report para 27.

the surveillance is potentially very broad indeed. With regard to terrorism, the ISC said of these certificates in its recent report:

> We note that the categories are expressed in very general terms. For example: 'Material providing intelligence on terrorism (as defined by the Terrorism Act 2000 (as amended)), including, but not limited to, terrorist organisations, terrorists, active sympathisers, attack planning, fund-raising'.

4.2.5 A wider playing-field

The surveillance of data does not stop with UK citizens: data drawn from all over the world can be of use to various governments across the globe. The courts have not directly addressed this thorny issue but, generally speaking, states do not owe duties to individuals located beyond their own shores or control. However, the cases have alluded, and the UN Human Rights Committee has made clear, that treaty obligations may extend extraterritorially.

All of the above does not, however, mean that the authorities can access data wherever and however they please. Whilst the case law coming from Europe is clear that both the collection of communications data and the interception of content interfere with the right to privacy,[134] in the *Liberty v UK*[135] case (in which the court referred to six principles from *Weber v Germany*) and concluded that they should apply to both kinds of data gathering to stop abuse of power by the state, regarding: '(1) the nature of the offences which may give rise to an interception order; (2) a definition of the categories of people liable to have their telephones tapped; (3) a limit on the duration of telephone tapping; (4) the procedure to be followed for examining, using and storing the data obtained; (5) the precautions to be taken when communicating the data to other parties; and (6) the circumstances in which recordings may or must be erased or the tapes destroyed'[136] and there are a number of powers and safeguards governing interception and communications data.

4.2.6 Safeguards

Because RIPA has the potential to infringe individuals' rights in a significant way, there are checks and balances built into it. RIPA contains a set of general safeguards concerning intercepted material. The number of persons, copies and times that that information is shared is restricted to the minimum that is necessary, i.e. it is on a 'need-to-know' basis. However, unlike intercepted material, RIPA

134 *Malone v Commissioner of the Police for the Metropolis* [1979] CLY 2098, [1979] 1 Ch 344, [1980] QB 49, [1979] 2 All ER 620; *Copland v United Kingdom* (Application no 62617/00, judgment of 03 April 2007) paras 39–47.

135 Case Nos IPT/13/77/H, IPT/13/92/CH, IPT/13/168-173/H, IPT/13/194/CH.

136 *Weber v Germany* (n 115) para 95, cited in *Liberty v UK* (n 115) para 114.

places no restrictions on the retention or use of communications data and further disclosure between authorities is not specifically addressed, either within RIPA or the Codes of Practice. The framework to keep things safe therefore largely falls back onto the Data Protection Act 1998. The Secretary of state does, however, have the power to issue a certificate excluding material from the scope of the data protection principles and from parts of the Act on national security grounds.

As noted above, data protection laws also provide limitations on the gathering and processing of data, through surveillance or any other method.[137] The 1995 Data Privacy Directive lays down the standards that govern the processing of personal data, including the collection, recording, organisation, storage, adaptation, retrieval, consultation, use or dissemination of that material throughout the Union (Article 2) for 'specified, explicit and legitimate purposes and not further processed in a way incompatible with those purposes' (Article 6(1)(b)), 'kept in a form which permits identification of data subject for no longer than is necessary for the purposes for which the data were collected . . . ' (Article 6(1)(e)).[138]

Echoing the language of the European Court in *Liberty* about safeguards, Member States also have to ensure that they put in place appropriate technical and organisational measures to protect personal data from accidental or unlawful destruction, loss or unauthorised disclosure (Article 17(1)). The e-Privacy Directive, which covers electronic communications, states that:

> Member States may adopt legislative measures to restrict the scope of the rights and obligations provided for in Article 5, Article 6, Article 8(1), (2), (3) and (4) and Article 9 of this Directive, when such restriction constitutes a necessary, appropriate and proportionate measure within a democratic society to safeguard national security (i.e. State security), defence, public security, and the prevention, investigation, detection and prosecution of criminal offences . . . To this end, Member States may, inter alia, adopt legislative measures providing for the retention of data for a limited period justified on the grounds laid down in this paragraph.

Article 15(1) of the e-Privacy Directive, required service providers to retain data generated for billing purposes concerning use of telephone, internet and email services for between six and 24 months. In Digital Rights Ireland this was challenged by the petitioner, as the scope of the data was very broad, covering data necessary to identify a sender and recipient, date, time and duration, type, equipment of communication and the location of mobile phone calls.[139] The reason why this was being challenged was that the data was, in fact, being held

137 Although it is arguable that they do not do so in all circumstances.

138 The Data Protection Directive (Directive 95/46/EC on the protection of individuals with regard to the processing of personal data and on the free movement of such data) is a European Union directive adopted in 1995 which regulates the processing of personal data within the European Union.

139 *Digital Rights Ireland* (Advocate General's opinion) [2013] Case C–293/12 (12 December 2013).

for much longer than the minimum requirements, in order to assist in the investigation and prevention of serious crime.

In the UK this did not make the newspaper headlines, but across Europe the provisions were hotly debated. The Court noted that the data gathered pursuant to the directive was a valuable tool for criminal investigations, including counter-terrorism. However, despite this the Data Retention Directive was declared to be invalid on the grounds that the interference was not proportionate for failure to comply with the principle of proportionality. The utility of the directive in the fight against serious crime was not enough to render it 'necessary' in the absence of safeguards, which the Court ruled that the EU legislator should have provided, especially since the majority of the data collected would not relate to those associated with any such crime. The lack of timescales for retention were also noted as there was no restriction on the collection by reference to particular timescales, places or persons who were likely to be involved directly or indirectly with such serious crimes, nor any objective standard to determine what is a serious crime or when access to such data would be permissible (paragraph 61). Most troubling for the Court, access was not subject to a 'prior review carried out by a court or by an independent administrative body whose decision seeks to limit access to the data and their use to what is strictly necessary . . . ' (paragraph 62).

More recently, the Grand Chamber of the Court of Justice of the European Union heard argument in a landmark challenge[140] to Member States' data retention and access laws. The case was highly unusual, taking a full day's legal argument in which 10 Member State governments made oral submissions. The case relates to Member States' laws that require telecoms companies to store data about individuals so that they can be accessed by intelligence and law enforcement agencies. These data include information about telephone calls made or received, messages and emails sent and received, the information tracking the movements of individuals, subscriber data and IP addresses. In Digital Rights Ireland the judgement ruled that the EU's 'data retention' Directive 2006/24/EC, which required telecoms companies to store such data for up to two years, was contrary to Articles 7 and 8 of the EU Charter of Fundamental Rights. This judgement gave rise to a considerable degree of uncertainty amongst Member States as to whether (and if so, how) the Charter applies to Member State laws. The final judgement is expected in July 2016

4.2.7 Powers outside RIPA

There is also a myriad of legislation governing this area far beyond European jurisprudence and RIPA.

The Wireless Telephony Act 2006 confers on the Secretary of State and

140 Joined Cases C–698/15 *R (Davis, Watson, Brice & Lewis) v Secretary of State for the Home Department* and C–203/15 *Tele 2 Sverige AB v Post- och Telestyrelsen.*

the Commissioners of Revenue and Customs a broad power to authorise the interception of wireless or other communications, one justification for this is the prevention of crime and disorder or the interests of national security, so long as it is proportionate to the overall goal.

Search orders for private or commercial premises can also be sought under the Police and Criminal Evidence Act 1984 (PACE) or the Supreme Courts Act 1981. Commonly, such an order may include the right to access and remove files from the computers on site. Production orders may also be requested requiring an individual to provide a phone, computer or certain physical files, subject to establishing reasonable grounds to make the request, as well as other conditions contained in Schedule 1 of PACE.

The Terrorism Act 2000 provides an exception to the general requirement of judicial authorisation. Schedule 7 to that Act grants port officers (generally the police) a broad power to require persons passing through ports or airports to provide their property – including a telephone or laptop – without judicial authorisation. That property may be retained for up to a week, but information downloaded is kept for much longer periods, pursuant to management of police information guidelines.

The Telecommunications Act 1984 also grants the Secretary of State (subject to considering the proportionality and content of the request sought) a power to give 'directions of a general character' to an individual, to the extent that they are 'necessary in the interests of national security or relations with the government of a country or territory outside the United Kingdom'.

4.2.8 The future of surveillance

In the UK, the Investigatory Powers Bill (Bill) will overhaul the framework governing the use of surveillance by the intelligence and security agencies and law enforcement to obtain the content of communications and communications data. The Bill followed on from important reports published in 2015, all of which concluded that the law in this area is unfit for purpose and in need of reform. Many of the capabilities for which the Bill provides have been in use for a number of years. As seen above, some are openly provided for in the Regulation of Investigatory Powers Act 2000, whereas others have been only recently avowed, having operated on the basis of vaguely drawn provisions in legislation governing the general powers of the security, intelligence and law enforcement agencies. The capabilities for which the Bill provides are:

- the interception of communications
- the retention and acquisition of communications data
- equipment interference and
- the retention and examination of bulk personal datasets.

Interception, acquisition of communications data and equipment interference powers are provided for both on a targeted basis and in bulk. The government has said that the only new capability provided for by the Bill is the ability to require retention of Internet Connection Records, a kind of communications data that reveals the websites an individual has visited.[141] The Bill will also reform the oversight regime for the use of these powers, replacing the three existing Commissioners with a single body of Judicial Commissioners led by the Investigatory Powers Commissioner, which would bring an element of judicial oversight to the process of issuing warrants to the intelligence services.

The Bill, and the powers it provides, raises questions of profound importance. These include:

- the balance to be struck between privacy and security
- the extent to which Parliament, and the public, should be aware of conduct exercised on their behalf; and the trust that should be placed in the agencies and government not to abuse powers that have the potential to be deeply intrusive.

Debate around these issues has been heated. Some believe that intrusive capabilities should only ever be exercised on the basis of reasoned suspicion, arguing that this reflects long-standing British legal convention. Others take the view that an unprecedented terrorist threat, coupled with a constantly evolving technological landscape, mean that the agencies tasked with protecting the public should be endowed with whatever capabilities they believe necessary in order to fulfil that role. The European Data Protection Supervisor, Giovanni Buttarelli, urged the EU to enhance its controls over the export of technologies that can be used for communications surveillance and interception, stating there was a 'tension between the positive use of ICT tools and the negative impact that the misuse of technology can have on human rights', which needed to be addressed in national and EU policies, most notably in relation to controls on the export of surveillance and interception technologies to third countries to be stiffened.[142]

The Joint Committee on the Draft Investigatory Powers Bill published a report of session 2015–16, making a number of detailed recommendations, including:[143]

- ensuring that the proposed new system of judicial oversight delivers the increased independence and oversight which have been promised
- ensuring there is further clarity to the proposals for what form the internet connection records (ICRs) would take and about the cost and feasibility of creating and storing them

141 See Investigatory Powers Bill, House of Commons Library (11 March 2016) http://researchbriefings.parliament.uk/ResearchBriefing/Summary/CBP-7518.

142 'EDPS issues an alert on intrusive surveillance' EDPS/2015/13, Brussels (15 December 2015).

143 Joint Committee on the Draft Investigatory Powers Bill; Draft Investigatory Powers Bill Report of Session 2015–16 (11 February 2016) HL Paper 93, HC 651 http://www.publications.parliament.uk/pa/jt201516/jtselect/jtinvpowers/93/9302.htm.

- expressing concerns over the provisions in the Bill for bulk powers to intercept and acquire communications data and to interfere with equipment and
- those aimed at ensuring that vital protections for lawyers and journalists are not compromised.

The report also calls for a code of practice to be published and a post-legislative review five years after enactment. On 9 February 2016, the Intelligence and Security Committee of Parliament published a Report on the draft Investigatory Powers Bill[144] noting that the draft Bill makes some attempt to improve transparency but does not cover all the agencies' intrusive capabilities. Various powers and authorisations remain scattered throughout different pieces of legislation, meaning that it is difficult for the Bill to achieve a clear and comprehensive legal framework to govern the use and oversight of investigatory powers. In considering the substance of the draft Bill, the report noted that the privacy protections are inconsistent and need strengthening, 'given the background to the draft Bill and the public concern over the allegations made by Edward Snowden in 2013, it is surprising that the protection of people's privacy – which is enshrined in other legislation – does not feature more prominently'.[145]

On 1 March 2016, the Bill was reintroduced with tighter privacy safeguards, according to the Home Office the Bill is now clearer, with tighter technical definitions and stricter codes of practice setting out exactly how the powers will be used, includes stronger privacy safeguards and bans UK agencies from asking foreign intelligence agencies to undertake activity on their behalf unless they have a warrant approved by a secretary of state and Judicial Commissioner. The Investigatory Powers Bill was approved by the House of Lords on 16 November 2016. The Bill will have important implications for the technology industry, on whose cooperation and expertise the exercise of investigatory powers at times depends. Industry has raised concerns about the feasibility and cost impact of the proposed measures, and the competitiveness of the UK's technology sector.

The Bill is not the only shift in privacy law. The European Commission is currently set to review the e-Privacy Directive (2002/58/EC), which was last updated in 2009. The stated objectives of the review are to assess the need to broaden the scope of the rules, ensure consistency between the e-Privacy Rules and the future GDPR, including assessing any overlaps and enhance security and confidentiality of communications throughout the EU. It is implied in the

144 Intelligence and Security Committee of Parliament (2016), 'Report on the draft Investigatory Powers Bill' (9 February) HC 795.

145 Intelligence and Security Committee of Parliament Report on the Draft Investigatory Powers Bill http://isc.independent.gov.uk/files/20160209_ISC_Rpt_IPBill(web).pdf.

consultation that there will be an assessment of the need for additional legal measures to enforce security obligations.[146]

4.2.9 Brexit

On 23 June 2016, the UK voted to leave the European Union. According to then prime minister David Cameron's resignation speech on 24 June 2016, the UK Government has indicated that Article 50 of the Treaty of Lisbon (which must be invoked to trigger the UK's breakaway from the EU) will be initiated after the Conservative Party leadership election has successfully taken place and the October party conference is held.

As seen throughout this chapter, the overseas transfer of data has been a hot topic of late, notably in light of the Snowden leaks and the case brought by a privacy lobbyist, which saw the end of the Safe Harbor regime, which legitimised transfers of personal data between the UK and USA.[147]

Under the Data Protection Directive 1995 ((Directive 95/46/EC) the current EU law which broadly is adopted into UK legislation by the Data Protection Act 1998) personal data cannot be transferred outside of the European Economic Area (EEA) unless it has been recognised by the European Commission as having 'adequate protection' to personal data.

At the moment it is not clear if the UK would become a member of the EEA if it left the EU. If it was not an EEA member it would not be automatically deemed 'safe' and would need to apply to the European Commission to be asked to be deemed as having an adequate level of protection. Without this finding, European companies would need to think about whether they can legitimise transfers of data from the EU to the UK. It is also likely that, unless the GDPR is adopted, a finding of adequacy would be unlikely to be forthcoming, especially in light of the activities of GCHQ. Indeed, the invalidation of the US Safe Harbor scheme originated as a result of the joint surveillance activities of the NSA (National Surveillance Agency in the USA) and GCHQ.

All does not, however, rest on a finding of adequacy. There are other mechanisms which can legitimise data transfers, such as the European Commission approved set of Model Clauses and Binding Corporate Rules. They can, however, add further administrative lawyers, especially where there are complex chains of processing and/or where the contracts are to be signed off by the local supervisory authority (for instance, Spain and Germany).

It is also possible that the UK may wish to follow the USA approach and adopt a mechanism which is approved by the EU as being 'essentially equivalent' to the

146 The consultation was open until 5 July 2016 and stakeholders were able to respond through the consultation on the European Commission's webpage: https://ec.europa.eu/digital-single-market/en/news/eprivacy-directive-commission-launches-public-consultation-kick-start-review.

147 Case C-362/14 *Maximillian Schrems v Data Protection Commissioner* Judgment ECLI:EU:C:2015:650.

EU regime. On 12 July 2016, the EU-US 'Privacy Shield' was formally adopted in by the European Commission. At the time of writing the privacy advocacy group Digital Rights Ireland (case ref: T-670/16) is contesting the adequacy of the Privacy Shield. The case has been published on the website of the Luxembourg-based General Court – the lower court of the Court of Justice of the European Union (ECJ) – listed as an "action for annulment".

The key issues that a UK privacy shield would need to address are:

- an ombudsman to handle complaints from EU citizens relating to surveillance
- UK security services would be required to give written commitments to the EU that it will not engage in mass surveillance activities (echoing the complaints levied at the UK Intelligence Bill)
- UK to agree to an annual review or audit to ensure that the mechanism adopted is operating as agreed.

4.3 Cat and mouse: the terrorists' response

4.3.1 #Carelesstalkcostslives

The Snowden leaks have generated an extraordinary level of paranoia among Jihadis, even causing them to go so far as to adopt a media restraint campaign called 'Himlat Takteem Ialami'. The leaks made by Edward Snowden have assisted ISIS with understanding the level of detection taking place and the methods employed by the security services, and Jihadis have likely 'learned a lot from recent unauthorized disclosures, and as many of their forces are familiar with the U.S. from their time in AQI, they have adapted well to avoiding detection'.[148] For instance, on 13 December 2014, ISIS issued an order banning all of its fighters from using devices equipped with GPS. Instead, Twitter is being used to spread the word. By way of example, on 20 May 2015 @dogmaticprocess tweeted: '#Warning, #Very_Urgent, beware . . . Oh lions of the Islamic State, Galaxy's battery has a GPS, #Retweet_To_Reach_Everyone' and 'Batteries of galaxy has gps please inspect your phone asap if you're in the Khilafah'.

In a speech before the House Armed Services Committee, Defense Secretary Chuck Hagel admitted 'ISIL fighters have been forced to alter their tactics—maneuvering in smaller groups, hiding large equipment, and changing their communications methods'. A compelling example of the use of communications by ISIS as a clever game of smoke and mirrors comes from the alleged death of ISIS leader Abu Bakr al Baghdadi, when it was announced that he had survived a U.S. airstrike, promising to 'erupt the volcanos of jihad'. The fact that he was not killed in this particular attack suggests that ISIS is practising tight controls

148 N Schatman and S Harris (2014), 'ISIS Keeps Getting Better at Dodging U.S. Spies' *The Daily Beast* (14 November) http://www.thedailybeast.com/articles/2014/11/13/isis-keeps-getting-better-at-dodging-u-s-spies.html#.

on their communications, especially at the top of the organisation. The need to have this model has partly arisen as a result of their prolific success with social media which, despite its phenomenal success during the recruitment and propaganda drives, has resulted in the inadvertent leaks of data through their online activities.

ISIS in Iraq and other widely populated ISIS areas are using commercial services to delete messages their members have sent via the Internet, and other applications such as FireChat, through which users can send messages to each other without connecting to the Internet, instead relying on Bluetooth, Wi-Fi, or Apple's Multipeer Connectivity. According to US Intelligence and counter terrorism officials this is enforced right down the ranks by ISIS officials, 'these guys have a level of discipline. They will enforce through the ranks not using cellphones'.[149] ISIS also go 'old school' through the occasional use of couriers to convey some messages in order to avoid digital communications altogether: 'we know this issue is not only tied to pictures, but to PDF files, word files and video files', it earnestly adds, noting that the meta data in files, such as who is the document author, the date the file was created/modified etc can also reveal incredibly useful information which may just make you the subject of a US airstrike. This is much more than a 'digital detox', it's a 'digital black out'. Whilst not the catchiest use of 140 characters in the history of Twitter, one particular account holder, posting in response to ISIS victories in the Anbar province of Iraq, summed the issue up like this 'Your abstention from posting details and your brothers' movements during [the] Hit camp blessed battle two days ago was the reason God granted you victory'.

As ISIS have started to pull down the shutters on their social media and are practising 'data hygiene', intelligence agencies have started monitoring the communications of the Syrian Assad official regime to find out what they are saying about ISIS. The value of this data is that it has the potential to be much more reliable, as private messages between ISIS 'officials' can be difficult to verify.

4.3.2 Of politics and policies: the Ladybird guide to online jihad

Whilst Western legislators have been busy pondering the ethics and legality of surveillance, ISIS has been busy too, announcing in the media that it has released a manual entitled 'How to Tweet Safely Without Giving out Your Location to NSA', explaining how to avoid surveillance. ISIS gives its fighters detailed instructions on how to remove meta data from content being put online. The guide begins: 'a number of security gaps have appeared that have benefited the enemy and have helped expose the identities of some brothers or identify some sites used by the mujahideen with ease', before going to explain what the gaps are and how they expose 'data that could turn your hair gray'. Perhaps

149 Ibid.

Dabiq Magazine will be featuring adverts for Just for Men soon, opposite their guides to deportment and human interest stories on snowball fights . . .

'How to Tweet Safely Without Giving out Your Location to NSA' is not the only tome dedicated to staying safe online. There is also in existence an e-book, distributed on 19 March 2015 by the Twitter account @Shahadastories via Twitter, entitled 'How To Survive In The West – A Mujahid Guide', which covers everything from hiding online identity, right through the use of TOR (a free anonymisation tool originally developed in the 1990s to protect online U.S. intelligence communications). This e-book's chapter titles include: 'Hiding the Extremist Identity', 'Earning Money', 'Internet Privacy', 'Training', 'Bomb-Making', 'Transporting Weapons', and 'What Happens When You Are Spied On And Get Raided'.

Chapter by chapter highlights include advice in relation to facial topiary:

> By not showing you're Muslim, you've already excluded yourself being in the 'Terrorist watchlist' . . . Don't make it too obvious you have become a practicing Muslim. For example: If you haven't grown a beard, don't grow it now, because you will bring unwanted attention onto yourself. Mujahideen in Muslim lands remove their beards for deceptive purposes.

It advises 'Practicing Muslims' to 'not remove their beard if they already have one. This would only draw unwanted attention to yourself from friends and family, and this will in turn lead them to spy on you'.[150]

> How to dress at the airport, . . . If you wear a hijab and go to a place where Muslims are searched (i.e. airports) then do not wear a black hijab, but a colored one instead. Muslim women who wear black hijabs are searched more in airports than those wearing other colored hijabs. This is merely due to a stereotype of fully black-clothed Muslim women being stricter in their religion.[151]

Chapter 2, entitled 'Disguise', offers etiquette and charm offensive tips, including:

> When a Muslim goes out in public, he wants to fit into society to make himself look as normal as possible. Remember this isn't because he fears his Islamic identity, but he is doing this so he is not suspected of being an outsider enemy: making yourself look more friendly and open minded to the Western public – For example: Muslims who call themselves by a Western nickname gain more acceptances by their non-Muslim colleagues.

150 See 'How to Survive in the West – a Mujahid Guide'. The guide includes tips regarding hiding online identity, evading surveillance, using TOR, continued use of TOR (see Chapter 1: Hiding the Extremist Identity).

151 Ibid.

Perhaps John should have dropped the 'Jihadi' bit . . .

All jokes aside, it also advises on the chillingly potent potential of Western recruits to be able to evade detection more easily:

> People with Islamic names get less jobs than those without Islamic names. This alias might be important if you need an important position in a specific job, i.e. Mujahideen send people to work in power plants or enemy governmental positions to spy on and leak reports to the Islamic State leadership (as double agents).

There are also specific chapters such as a chapter dedicated to internet privacy, which again highlights the party line of taking care with regard to what is posted online: 'When you browse the Internet, you want your Internet activity to look as normal as possible. You do not type anything jihadi, and possibly not even Islamic on your searches, and especially not in your computer'. The chapter also notes the value of traditional media outlets observing that:

> the safest way to get a basic overview on Jihad is to watch the news channels (such as Al-Jazeera). They do not tell the clear picture, but at least you get an overview of what is going on. This is safe because these channels are broadcasted on satellite for free, and no one can do a search on your history.

Inevitably, accidents can happen, so for a 'would-be jihadist' faced with the possibility that they may have become the subject of detection, the guidance notes that:[152]

> If the intelligence agencies or police has some suspicion that you are doing some criminal activity, you will be spied on and your house could be raided. The raid will begin within the later parts of the night (after 4 am) or in the early morning (usually before or during the Fajr prayer time). The reason why it is done at this time is to scare you and catch you unprepared because most people are asleep during this time period. Days before the raid, you may be being watched by the intelligence agencies because they want to know your habits. The best way to know if you are being followed is by doing the 'circular route' method. All secret agents do this and it becomes a mandatory security habit whereby you will do a full circle route before you go anywhere important. The circular route method: You will set off from point A and travel to different places while looking from the corner of our eye to see if you are seeing any same person following you everywhere you go. If you see someone going every place you go, you will finally reach point A again. This is a fully circular route because you have gone back to your original point. Now if you set off again to where you need to go, look from the corner of your

152 Ibid.

> eye again. Is that same person still following you? If yes, then they are no doubt a spy. They had no reason to follow your full circular route and set off in your destination again except to spy on where you go and see what you do. They will search your house for: weapons, cash (if you have a lot you will be asked where it came from), files/papers/computers which may contain terrorist information. Even anything written in Arabic or your child's small iPad will be taken and examined. You will be taken to custody and imprisoned for up to a month while they can look through the collected evidences for proof against you. Note: They will not break into your walls to look for things there, unless you have left big clues which make it look like you've put something there. Cageprisoners.com has sections on their website about what questions you have to answer, when you can say, 'no comment,' and what you can answer with a lawyer'.

The guide ends with a resources section:

> TOR Browser, Twitter.com/search, Startpage.com (anonymous searches on Google), Temp-Mail.org (to use temporary email addresses for fake registrations i.e. on Twitter) Dispostable.com, Emkei.cz (send fake emails from any fake email address of your choice), Tumblr.com (make your own blog – they do not ban jihadi blogs yet), archive.org (upload files with direct link downloads), 2shared.com, Scribd.com (share e-books).[153]

Inspire Magazine even followed the Snowden revelation closely, as well as publishing on the first page in all-capital letters, 'DUE TO TECHNICAL AND SECURITY REASONS, WE HAVE SUSPENDED OUR EMAIL ADDRESSES TEMPORARILY'.[154] As research by MEMRI has highlighted 'Prior to the leaks, *Inspire* encouraged interested parties to contact the magazine's editors via encrypted software, and via email'. The 12th issue of the magazine stated that, due to technical and security reasons, the normal methods of outreach were temporarily suspended. Snowden was lauded for his acts in the same issue and also praised in the third issue of the Taliban's English-language magazine *Azan*, which was released in August 2013.[155]

There are further guides available online also dedicated to technology such as that published on 20 May 2015 by British ISIS fighter Siddhartha Dhar, aka

153 Ibid.

154 A Kimery (2015), 'Snowden Openly Engaging with Isis, Al Qaeda Members, Supporters Via Social Media' *Homeland Security Today* (22 October) http://www.hstoday.us/industry-news/general/single-article/snowden-openly-engaging-with-isis-al-qaeda-members-supporters-via-social-media/fa5061af0c7c9fa75b4e8faaaafdd495.html.

155 'ISIS, Al-Qaeda Fighters and Supporters Take Keen Interest in Edward Snowden's Tweets' (16 October 2015) <interest-in-edward-snowdens-tweets/.

Abu Rumaysah al Britani[156] and that of Rabitat Al-Ansar (@mn_sir000), a pro-ISIS media body active primarily on Twitter, who released a series of security recommendations for Android users, as well as information on Google Play and various Android apps. A demonstration on modifying some of the permissions on the Facebook app was also included:

> Although it would be nice to assume that most of us aren't spies we cant be careless about it. USA is running thousancfs of undercover accounts on twitter for intelligence gathwering and comabattin gus. So when someone like fot instance Jwennifer/Aisha is cobiously creating a fitna to breat our binds we tajke distance from such a person like her, hwey? Because she isn't real, she probably is a man in an office somewhere following aplan. So instead of assuming that most of us aren't spies, assume the opposite, that most of us ARE spies or undercover. Ans as with a real agent you would never share:
>
> - Your name
> - Pictures of yourself
> - Pictures of people close to you (including cute babies or pets)
> - Pictures that can in any be linked to the real you
> - Your country
> - Yor city
> - Avoid talkingin DM too much where you might say personal things
> - Don't share IS mocements if you have knowledge
> - Don't share unknown military capabilities (like saying that IS has AA missiles in a location)
> - There is other stud that I haven't covered but you can figure it out, be quiet and be safe!

Some people tweet screenshots where their carriers can be seen or are not otherwise carful about concealing what country they live in:

> Guess what? Yeah you guessed right, the kuffar are tracking your account and when you get suspended they will find your new account. So what you might wonder Well when they raid your house and they link all your accounts to YOU then you will face months I your years in jail. You will face consequence that will follow you throughout your life for something as stupid as this.
>
> You think you are safe from the "consequences" because this is the critical battleground? Akh Shami mihr face life in jail, because he tweeted info and did others benign stuff while some of you are tweeting day and nigh about beheadings.

156 See MEMRI JTTM reports 'British ISIS Fighter Pens Islamic State Travel Guide' (20 May 2015) and 'British ISIS Fighter Boasts About Outsmarting British Intelligence; Moves to Syria with Family' (2 December 2014).

> To conclude everyone here is a spy and don't trust anyone with information, Muslim lives depend on it.

Every day examples come to light of the truth of these words. On 4 January 2016, a young boy featured in a new IS execution video was feared to be the son of a runaway jihadi bride, Grace 'Khadihag' Dare. Dare was identified as the boy's mother by an image posted of her son on social media in 2014, in which the child is holding a gun.[157]

4.3.3 Dear Deidre: Jihadi agony aunts

An unlikely (although not perhaps unsurprising) poster child and agony aunt to the jihadists, Edward Snowden's tweets have had marked popularity with the ISIS community. According to MEMRI:[158]

> Many loyal to either Al Qaeda's Syrian branch Jabhat Al Nusra or to ISIS follow Snowden's account. Some retweet his tips or engage him directly by asking questions, for instance an ISIS supporter named Ali Al Amrikini asked Snowden: "Good afternoon boss! Did you really say that ISIS works with USA? I hope you can clear it. Thank you" . . .

The user's Twitter banner was that of British rapper, turned ISIS fighter, Abdel Majed Abdel Bary, who you may recall from Chapter 2 is an ISIS militant who enjoys the occasional You've Been Framed moment on YouTube by engaging in snowball fights. Re-tweets of Mr Snowden's are also popular, with an Jabhat Al Nusra fighter named Abu Sufyan Al Libi re-posting 'For those asking how tracking phones and wireless devices (your laptop) from a plane works', accompanied by a link Snowden had shared in the Tweet to a longer article on the subject. The fun did not stop there. On 11 October, Snowden tweeted: 'Tech designed to fight Al Qaeda gets used to track Black Lives Matter. War front to home front', accompanied by a link to an article in the *Washington Post* and, on 12 October: 'is mass surveillance also a problem in your country? Unlike a VPN, @Torproject is free'.

But why stop with tweet-based trouble-shooting? In 2015 it was reported that[159] ISIS also, apparently, has its very own technical helpdesk that runs 24 hours a day, seven days a week to help train terrorists on good cyber hygiene and privacy

157 Nicholas Cecil, Justin Davenport and John Dunne (2016), 'Junior Jihadi Son of London I.S. Bride' *Evening Standard* (4 January) 1, 5.

158 S Salinsky and R Sosnow (2014), 'Al-Qaeda's Embrace of Encryption Technology – Part II: 2011–2014, and the Impact of Edward Snowden' MEMRI Research Foundation http://www.memri.org/report/en/0/0/0/0/0/0/7950.htm.

159 N Russon (2015), 'ISIS opens 24/7 helpdesk to teach good encryption and cybersecurity practice' *International Business Times* (18 November) http://www.ibtimes.co.uk/isis-24-7-helpdesk-terror-encryption-hotline-teaches-cybersecurity-1529328.

practices, such as using encryption services to stay undetected. The helpdesk, manned by six senior 'techies', not only offers IT support but also assists with the social media-based recruitment drive and even creates step-by-step educational tutorials exclusively for IS operatives, which are available via YouTube. Granted, the validity of the statistics cannot be verified but owners of internet cafes based in Syria have noted that there has been a big fall in the numbers of fighters using platforms such as Twitter. 'A few stayed online, but no one posts selfies next to chopped-off heads any more,[160] declared one source. Perhaps, however, the turn from the coffee shops can be attributed to greater problems, such as posts by some who have made the move to Syria who bemoan the loss of Starbucks with @GreenBirdofDabq posting: 'I know it may be shirk but sometimes I do miss Starbucks. The coffee here is beyond wretched'.[161]

Whilst the corresponding effect on sales of 'frappucinos' has not been released, what is clear is that ISIS is a sophisticated machine and is fully aware of how falling foul of Western surveillance could mean that the next air strike comes with a bomb for their top fighters who have become stars of social media in their own right. 'You don't see any of Isis's most important figures on Twitter and you see even less now of the more minor ones too ... odd the people who make big speeches are the ones that end up dead' former CIA official, Patrick Skinner, has commented.[162] However, any follower of the cause or those with a prurient interest are still not denied content from official accounts, and you can still watch an ISIS shepherd praising the group to an audience of a flock of sheep on YouTube, if that is of interest on the long winter nights.[163]

Although the jihadi blackout may look like as if it means that there is less access to data, where one door closes, well, another closes even further as, after all, if you can't make full use of the digital sphere and there are drones circling overhead, it does rather close the loop in a little: think of it as ankle curfew tags for terrorists.

4.3.4 There's an app for that

So how do terrorists spread the word? After all, they still need to communicate. The hunt for the next big 'Top of the Apps' is a never ending one. According to Khyat,[164] a number of terrorist organisations such as ISIS and Al-Qaeda in the Arabian Peninsula (AQAP), have turned to other forms of secure messaging

160 'ISIS closes the cyber blackout blinds to avoid attack' *The Financial Times* (17 October 2014).

161 GreenBirdOfDabiq (@GreenBirdDabiq) (May 12, 2015).

162 S Jones and E Solomon (2014), 'Isis closes the cyber blackout blinds to avoid attack' (17 October) http://www.ft.com/cms/s/0/e8feb224-555b-11e4-b750-00144feab7de.html#axzz3xECGxqZi, http://www.ft.com/cms/s/0/e8feb224-555b-11e4-b750-00144feab7de.html#axzz3GYo1fxrS.

163 Ibid.

164 M Khayat (2015), 'Jihadis Shift to Using Secure Communication App Telegram's Channels Service' MEMRI Inquiry & Analysis Series No 1198 (29 October).

apps[165] as well as using gmail accounts in which multiple users hold the password to go in and write/read draft emails which will never be sent, thus avoiding detection as no digital trace is created. The following tweets[166] reveal ongoing conversations about various encryption methods and recommendations to stay safe online:

> @aquaraya: @AntiCoupMU features of Telegram and why to use it cyberkov.com/p=1354 program is an alternative to WhatsApp Wickr and Surespot encryption apps
>
> @DqpDx: Alternative to WhatsApp: The program Telegram especially with SecretChat; Threema program is the best in encryption; Wickr is encrypted; Surespot is encrypted
>
> @aquaraya: @Batiel_Official the hope of contact is always on Twitter for all of the groups and by using the programs Telegram, Wickr and Surespot
>
> @7rbn7r1400: Alternative to WhatsApp: The program Telegram especially with SecretChat; Threema program is the best in encryption; Wickr is encrypted; Surespot is encrypted
>
> @alarab_2011: Alternative to WhatsApp: The program Telegram especially with SecretChat; Threema program is the best in encryption; Wickr is encrypted; Surespot is encrypted.

Messaging apps such as Telegram, Kik and Wickr allow users to send individual messaging content to be sent to a potentially unlimited number of users, who must also hold a subscription to their chosen app. There can be an unlimited number of subscribed users, joining either by invitation from the channel's administrator or by following a public URL. Its default position is encryption, rather than requiring an active opt-in to such a feature.

The Telegram website states: 'Telegram is a messaging app with a focus on speed and security, it's super fast, simple and free . . . You can send messages, photos, videos and files of any type . . . as well as create groups for up to 200 people' and boasts: '[t]hose looking for extra privacy should check out our advanced settings and rather revolutionary policy. And if you want secrecy, try our device-specific Secret Chats with self-destructing messages, photos and videos – and lock your app with an additional passcode . . . Unlike WhatsApp, Telegram is cloud-based and heavily encrypted . . . Telegram is also faster and way more secure . . . '[167]

As well as being a relatively secure way to send messages, a further advantage is that there is no content moderation in place, meaning that terrorists are difficult to identify and, consequently, it is difficult to report individual account holders for their use of the app, as well as have their content deleted from it. As the app

165 Telegram's Channels Service, launched in late September 2015.

166 Quoted in Khayat (n 165).

167 https://telegram.org/.

facilitates more freedom than Twitter (in terms of what can be posted), there is propaganda, tutorials on manufacturing weapons and calls to launch cyber warfare, targeted killing and lone-wolf attacks. Indeed, there are channels dedicated to encouraging lone-wolf attacks. One such channel, created on 18 October 2015, has 51 members and its description reads: 'Posting messages and military-related information directed at lone wolves, especially those in the place of [Islam's] revelation [i.e. Saudi Arabia]'. Whilst the number of subscribers may seem low, it only took four men to carry out 7/7 and two to plot the anniversary attack on Westfield Shopping Centre. Chillingly, the channel's photo is captioned 'Lone Wolves: Soon [will be] My Turn'.[168]

Feeling very much like a return to the heyday of the forums, a channel displays only the total number of its subscribers to other users, without disclosing their names – only the channel administrator can see the names of members. Messages shared via 'the channel' is also only transmitted by the sender, and there is no reverse interaction with the subscriber. Although this may limit interaction between subscribers, it also prevents counter-propaganda from being posted through the feeds, a common counter-terrorism tactic. However, it would be unfair to say that the site is merely a safe haven for terrorists. In October 2014, 400,000 South Koreans switched from domestic messaging application, Kakao Talk, to Telegram after investigators sought to punish people who spread rumours about the government's handling of the Sewol ferry disaster earlier that year.[169]

Nasher is currently the flagship of ISIS-related news on Telegram. Nasher was already associated with ISIS when it operated as a webpage (Nasher.me) and as an app as well.[170] It is described on its channel as 'a channel for all the official publications of the Islamic State', and the content posted is similar to that which appears on Twitter and on the Shumoukh Al-Islam forum. To accommodate the wide geography and languages of Islamic Sate's online following, it is offered in Arabic (over 10,000 members); English (998 members); French (348 members); Indonesian (1076 members); German (340 members); Bosnian (201 members); Russian (1919 members); Turkish (181 members); and Bengali (159 members).[171] Nasher is not, however, the only channel for updates: a3maqagency, an ISIS-affiliated A'maq news channel offers 24/7 updates mainly concerning military operations conducted by ISIS. A'maq's operations were driven to Telegram after its Facebook pages were consistently shut down by administrators.[172] As Telegram is a somewhat unknown entity, the terrorists still needed to use traditional social

168 Original source not provided due to sensitivity of materials.

169 M Earp (2015), 'Legal gags: Asia's online laws threaten media business' *PR Week* (11 June) http://www.prweek.com/article/1350837/legal-gags-asias-online-laws-threaten-media-business#l24LhWEodkBCuYY3.99.

170 See MEMRI JTTM report (2015), 'Jihadis Announce New ISIS App for Android' (3 August).

171 Quoted in Khayat (n 165).

172 See MEMRI JTTM report (2015), 'ISIS-Affiliated News Agency A'maq Remains Active on Facebook Despite Consecutive Shutdowns' (5 March).

networks to publicise its existence. By way of example, the English language KhilafaNews channel was promoted by user @mhistory087: '#IslamicState official and all breaking news here please joining Here is the channel link [Link to Telegram Messenger App]'.[173]

Realising that the sheer scale and reach of sites such as Twitter remains an extremely important part of the propaganda machine, the Publication Knights Workshop channel generates pro-ISIS tweets that can be copied and pasted into the user's Twitter account, without having to post the content to be re-tweeted through an official ISIS twitter account and run the risk of closure by Twitter account moderators or reporting to the site, which may result in account suspension or deletion of the content.

Similar to the forums, there is also a hierarchy appearing in Telegram. A channel entitled 'Elite Section Of IS' posts cyber-related content by a number of ISIS hackers. As well as live time postings and tutorials, ISIS is also building up a web-archive online. One such channel facilitating this is Fursan Al-Rafi', with the Indiana Jones-esque tag 'Knights of Upload', whose sole aim is to put the concept of being a librarian on steroids by uploading ISIS releases on various hosting websites, including YouTube, the Internet Archive (Archive.org) and Google Drive. Al-Qaeda is having its share of the Telegram too, and Al-Qaeda in the Arabian Peninsula's official channel has over 2700 members.

Surespot is also popular with jihadis, owing to its ability to facilitate the encryption of messages so that only the intended recipient can read it. Tantalisingly, Surespot declares on its website that:[174] 'we don't know or share anything about you . . . Surespot is about taking back your right to privacy and it is made free to provide unrestricted access for everyone'. The website explains Surespot's encryption by using the example of a postcard that anyone who touches can read:

> Typically you do not send information like a credit card number or your pin number or an intimate thought using the postcard format. Today this is what sending an email or a text message or an instant message or a picture is like. The message is the postcard which travels along many hops until it reaches its destination. At every one of these 'hops' the message could potentially be read.

Almost as if written with our coffee loving fiend @greenbirdofdabiq in mind,

> [f]or example you, are reading an email at Starbucks. To read this email the information travels from the server (gmail) through their (Google's) ISP, to Starbuck's ISP, to the Starbucks location you are at. At any one of these points the email can be read . . . Surespot solves these problems by using

173 Promotion of the KhilafaNews channel on pro-ISIS Twitter account (Source: @mhistory087 12 October 2015).

174 https://www.surespot.me/.

> end to end encryption . . . No one along the network route the message takes from one client to another, not any of the hops, not even the Surespot server, can view the contents of the data.

The site acknowledges that, like a website, it may be vulnerable to hacking: 'if an attacker were to obtain access to the Surespot database they would have access to the above information. An attacker that gained access to the Surespot database server could delete or otherwise corrupt user data, potentially disrupting the Surespot service'. To mitigate this the website suggests:

> Any discovery of a user's real identity can be mitigated by using an anonymous email account to register with Google as well as a pre-paid or no contract phone that has no ties to the user. As another mitigation strategy, an advanced user could compile their own Surespot client from source and prevent a Google Cloud Messaging ID from ever uploading to the Surespot server and completely remove this threat. This functionality could easily (and probably will) become a user setting in the client. Even if an attacker were to gain access to all of the data stored in the Surespot database there is not a way they could read the encrypted message data without the user's private key which resides on their device and is never sent to Surespot servers. Because usernames are completely arbitrary and chosen by the user the Surespot database in an attacker's hands represents an anonymous and practically useless dataset.

Because Surespot is not as well embedded in the public consciousness as Twitter and Facebook, a common way to use Surespot is to engage with individuals through for example Twitter and then lure them onto Surespot. According to newspaper reports, this method was used to groom three London schoolgirls, Kadiza Sultana, 16, Shamima Begum, 15, and Amira Abase, 15, who are thought to have taken a flight to Turkey before making the journey to Syria to join ISIS.[175]

4.4 Quantifying gain

Mr Snowden and films such as *V for Vendetta* may have made talking about counter-surveillance cool, but Al-Qaeda has been aware that it may be subject to surveillance and have been well versed in the art of obfuscation online for some time.

Since January 2007, dedicated researchers at MERMI have uncovered that Al-Qaeda has been using encryption tools for its online communication activities, often based on heavy-weight security, which is the equivalent of military standard

175 'Families of 3 missing UK girls urge "Please come home!"' *Daily Mail* http://www.dailymail.co.uk/wires/ap/article-2965083/Families-3-missing-UK-girls-urge-Please-come-home.html.

tech.[176] One such example was the extensive use of TOR. Snowden has posted about TOR: '@Snowden: Without Tor, when you walk the streets of the internet, you're always watched. https://blog.torproject.org/blog/what-tor-supporter-looks-edward-snowden . . . #SupportTor'[177] but he was not responsible for lifting the lid on this one; that was down to a combination of cyber hacks of terrorist websites by various Western government agencies. TOR announced, in 2010, that it would no longer be providing anonymous cloud browsing for technical reasons[178] and the spotlight was placed on TOR in a CNN TV report on ISIS's use of the Dark Web to recruit and plan attacks.[179] Al-Qaeda therefore needed to behave like Jamiroquai and 'go deeper underground', digitally speaking.

In one particularly fascinating letter to Shaykh Abu Abdullah on a balmy 17 July 2010, Osama bin Laden penned his thoughts on the matter thus:

> I have another recommendation which is that we should encrypt our correspondence. Is it possible for the people on your end to lean the Mujahideen secrets program? I will attach it, along with an explanation of it. Perhaps your assistants can lean it and use it in their correspondence.[180]

Following the elimination of Osama bin Laden in May 2011, the security agencies fell upon a veritable cornucopia of electronic devices and materials at his Pakistani compound, which revealed the sheer extent of the encryption and security standard employed by Al-Qaeda. Information flowed out of the compound as water gushes out of a burst dam. In a letter recovered at the compound, 'brother Azmarai' wrote:

> We should be careful not to send big secrets by email. We should assume that the enemy can see these emails and [we should] only send through email information that can bring no harm if the enemy reads it. Computer science is not our science and we are not the ones who invented it.[181]

176 Research from the MEMRI Jihad & Terrorism Threat Monitor, 'Al-Qaeda's Embrace of Encryption Technology Part III – July 2014–January 2015: Islamic State (ISIS) and Other Jihadis Continue to Develop their Cyber and Encryption Capabilities; Post-Snowden Fears Lead them to Test New, More Secure Technologies and Social Media' (4 February 2015); Al-Qaeda's Embrace of Encryption Technology – Part II: 2011-2014, and the Impact of Edward Snowden (25 April 2014); Al-Qaeda's Embrace of Encryption Technology: 2007-2011 (12 July 2011).

177 See Twitter account of Edward Snowden @Snowden (30 December 2015). Edward Snowden @Snowden.

178 Shamikh1.info (10 May 2015).

179 CNN Arabic (13 May 2015).

180 Letter from Osama bin Laden to Shaykh Abu Abdullah (17 July 2010) Dni.gov/files/documents/ubl/english2/Letter%20to%20Shaykh%20Abu%20Abdallah%20dtd%2017%20July%202010.pdf.

181 ABCnews.go.com (20 May 2015).

At that time, Nasir Al-Wuheishi, a high level AQAP member, also considered the organisation's use of encryption software and its use for talking to recruits, planning attacks, and other strategic purposes:

> For our part, we will make contact with anyone who wants to wage jihad with us, and we will guide him to a suitable means to kill the collaborators and the archons of unbelief – even in his bedroom or workplace. Anyone who wants to give support to [Al-Qaeda in the Arabian Peninsula's] operational side and to give teaths [to the organization] can contact us through a special email [set up] for this purpose, using the 'Mujahideen Secrets'[182] software and employing the proper security measures . . . [183]

The NSA has used the tracking of computers and mobiles of members of Al-Qaeda in Iraq to address its ground troops towards targets. However, it has become increasingly difficult to track ISIS militants, as they are more tech savvy than ever, turning to applications to facilitate encryption, instant messaging and social media, in a very modern war.

The technological sophistication of ISIS cannot be under-estimated, and this forms a key part of the recruitment drive for individuals not only committed to the cause, but also possessing technical capabilities that can further the cause in a digital world. A startling case in point of this is the content of an interview conducted by MERMI with a former computer science student from Madagascar, which took place in May 2015, who spoke about his decision to join ISIS:

> I was studying computer science in Antananarivo university and met some brothers from India who were Muslims . . . After reading the Koran and the Sirah i.e. biography of Prophet Mohammad, I came to this conclusion that the Islamic State have the true methodology and truth . . . I decided to join Islamic State Caliphate . . . Now I am asked by Ameer Abu Qubaisa Al-Anbari to join the IT department because I have degree in BCS.[184]

The internet is littered with examples of social media postings that have supposedly led to terrorism-related arrests. When Snowden let the cat out of the bag, the U.S. initially responded by suggesting that he had irreparably damaged the surveillance

182 Mujahideen Secrets is encryption software that was first released in early 2007 by the Global Islamic Media Front, and has since been updated. See MEMRI JTTM reports, 'GIMF Announces Imminent Release of New Software' (3 January); 'Al-Ekhlas Announces New Version of "Mujahideen Secrets" Software' (14 January 2008).

183 See MEMRI Inquiry & Analysis No. 1143, 'Al-Qaeda's Embrace of Encryption Technology Part III – July 2014-January 2015: Islamic State (ISIS) and Other Jihadis Continue to Develop their Cyber and Encryption Capabilities; Post-Snowden Fears Lead them to Test New, More Secure Technologies' (4 February 2015).

184 See MEMRI JTTM report 'Interview with Computer Science Student from Madagascar Who Joined ISIS' (5 June 2015).

projects underway. Just two weeks after the leaks went public, President Barack Obama said during a visit to Germany in support of the surveillance undertaken that the NSA 'averted . . . at least 50 threats . . . because of this information',[185] gathered through communications collection in the United States and abroad.

The preservation of life, which as you will recall from Chapter 2 is an obligation of the state to its people and which can legitimise the proportionate interference with other rights such as privacy and freedom of expression is often cited as the justification for mass monitoring: 'fifty-four times this and the other program stopped and thwarted terrorist attacks both here and in Europe — saving real lives', according to Mike Rogers, a Michigan Republican who chairs the House Intelligence Committee on the House floor in July, referring to programs authorised by a pair of post-9/11 laws, before adding: 'this isn't a game. This is real'.[186]

Although the 50 mark has been bandied about, a NSA counter-terrorism chart contains statistics on how data gathered through bulk communications surveillance, on 54 occasions, 'has contributed to the [U.S. Government's] understanding of terrorism activities and, in many cases, has enabled the disruption of potential terrorist events at home and abroad', the operative word being contributed not responsible for.[187]

There are various examples of inconsistency as to what exactly the role of this data plays and, as would be expected given the nature of the surveillance and the potential risk to ongoing surveillance, much of the information that would put the arguments to rest is classified. Only a handful of cases where surveillance has had a direct impact on investigations has been released: 'We've heard over and over again the assertion that 54 terrorist plots were thwarted' Leahy told Alexander at the Judiciary Committee hearing in December 2013. 'That's plainly wrong, but we still get it in letters to members of Congress, we get it in statements. These weren't all plots and they weren't all thwarted. The American people are getting left with the inaccurate impression of the effectiveness of NSA programs'.[188]

In one of the four of the 54 cases which the NSA has released information about, Najibullah Zazi, a man who plotted to bomb the New York subway system, was captured as a result of an email it intercepted to an account of a known Al-Qaeda figure in Pakistan, which allowed the NSA to identity and ultimately

185 'Obama on NSA Spying: "We Have Struck the Appropriate Balance" of Privacy and Security' (19 June 2013) http://www.realclearpolitics.com/video/2013/06/19/obama_on_nsa_spying_we_have_struck_the_appropriate_balance_of_privacy_and_security.html.

186 http://www.propublica.org/documents/item/803163-rogers-nsa-speech.html#document/p23/a125317.

187 See the NSA's 54 Events Chart http://www.propublica.org/documents/item/802269-untitled0001.html.

188 See K Gosztola (2013), 'Senate Hearing: US Intelligence Leaders Confronted for Misleading Public on Effectiveness of NSA Programs' Shadowproof.com (2 October) https://shadowproof.com/2013/10/02/senate-hearing-us-intelligence-leaders-confronted-for-misleading-public-on-effectiveness-of-nsa-programs/http://www.senate.gov/isvp/?comm=judiciary&type=live&filename=judiciary100213.

capture him. The only incident where bulk data plays a pivotal role is in the arrest of a San Diego man who transferred US$8,500 to al Shabaab in Somalia.

Indeed, at a Senate Judiciary Committee hearing in October 2013 Senator Patrick Leahy (D-Vt) stated that only 13 of the 54 cases 'had some nexus to the U.S.', not all were related to terror plots and the majority were more concerned with providing support by way of funds etc to terrorist organisations than direct terror attacks. In December 2013 a White House panel concluded that the NSA's bulk collection of data was 'not essential in preventing attacks'.[189]

Whether the same results could have been achieved through other means, both in this case and with regard to surveillance more generally, is being hotly contested by our friends on the other side of the pond in relation to section 215 of the Patriot Act, which allows government agents to compel businesses to turn over records and documents and justify the bulk collection of data. In a report that went before Congress in May 2015, Inspector General Michael E. Horowitz said that, between 2004 and 2009, the FBI tripled its use of bulk collection. However, the Inspector General concluded: 'the agents we interviewed did not identify any major case developments that resulted from use of the records obtained in response to Section 215 orders'; however, the material that has been gathered pursuant to the orders was described as 'valuable' in developing other leads or corroborating information. The need for continued review to ensure that data collection was lawful was also noted, with Horowitz adding: 'while the expanded scope of these requests can be important uses of Section 215 authority, we believe these expanded uses require continued significant oversight'.[190]

At the Committee on Homeland Security's 3 June 2015 hearing on 'Terrorism Gone Viral: The Attack in Garland, Texas and Beyond', House Committee on Homeland Security chairman Michael McCaul named social media apps such as Twitter, YouTube, Instagram, Justpaste.it, Ask.fm, Kik, WhatsApp, Wikr, Surespot as breeding grounds for terrorism, stating:

> Aspiring fanatics can receive updates from hardcore extremists on the ground in Syria via Twitter; watch ISIS blood-lust on YouTube; view jihadi selfies on Instagram; read religious justifications for murder on Justpaste.it; and find guides to the battlefield on Ask.fm. Jihadis and recruiters are mastering the ability to monitor and prey on Western youth susceptible to the twisted message of Islamist terror. They seek out users who have questions about Islam or to know what life is like inside the so-called 'Islamic State'. They engage established bonds of trust and assess the dedication of potential

189 M Isikoff (2013), 'NSA program stopped no terror attacks, says White House panel member' *NBC News* (20 December) http://www.nbcnews.com/news/other/nsa-program-stopped-no-terror-attacks-says-white-house-panel-f2D11783588.

190 'A Review of the FBI's Use of Section 215 Orders: Assessment of Progress in Implementing Recommendations and Examination of use in 2007 through 2009' Office of the Inspector General, US Department of Justice, FBI Oversight and Review Devising (May 2015) https://oig.justice.gov/reports/2015/o1505.pdf.

> recruits. From there, the extremists direct users to more secure apps or secure communications, to hide their messages from our intelligence agencies. Such communications can include advice on travelling to terrorist safe-havens; contact information for smugglers into Turkey; or the membership process for joining ISIS itself. I know the officials sitting before us today are disturbed by these trends. Mobile apps like Kik and WhatsApp, as well as data-destroying apps like Wikr and Surespot, are allowing extremists to communicate outside of the view of law enforcement. Equally worrisome are ISIS attempts to use the dark and deep web, these websites hide IP addresses and cannot be reached by search engines – giving terrorists covert means by which they can recruit fighters and intelligence, raise funds and potentially plot and direct attacks undetected.[191]

Whether the surveillance led directly to the arrest or not, there are numerous examples of posts made on social media being connected with terrorism-related arrests. On 18 April 2015, Sevdet Besim (aged just 18) was arrested and charged with conspiring to plan a terrorist attack on Australia's Anzac Memorial Day.[192] Even more incredibly the puppet master of the attack was a 14-year-old school boy from Lancashire.[193]

The baby-faced protagonist was radicalised by Islamic State propaganda, the court was told, after finding an online jihadi community through his first smartphone. The network 'filled a void' caused by problems at school and, within just two weeks of setting up a Twitter account, the boy held a court of 24,000 followers as he constructed a fantasy image of himself and 'quickly became a celebrity' within the jihadi Twitter community.

The contact between the two was made through Telegram,[194] during which more than 3000 encrypted messages were exchanged, and was instigated by a well known ISIS recruiter and propagandist named Abu Khaled al-Cambodi. Within

191 See Homeland Security Committee Website, Hearing 'Terrorism Gone Viral: the Attack in Garland, Texas and Beyond' (3 June 2015) Homeland.house.gov/hearing/hearing-terrorism-gone-viral-attack-garland-texas-and-beyond.

192 'Anzac Day terror plot was days from success, court hears' http://www.theguardian.com/uk-news/2015/oct/01/anzac-day-terror-plot-likely-to-have-resulted-in-deaths-court-told (Thursday 1 October 17.19 BST Last modified on Friday 2 October 2015 00.02 BST).

193 The minor's identity remains anonymous, Mr Justice Saunders explained there was also a risk that in some parts of society the 15-year-old defendant would be 'glorified for what he has done'. Saunders was responding to a press application to lift reporting restrictions. He said: 'I have decided that reporting restrictions should continue. That has not been an easy decision to reach because I accept that this is an important case which raises important questions of concern to the public. I accept the principle of open justice. This is an exceptional case because of the age of the defendant. I accept also that the public are more interested in reading about cases where the defendant and often his family are identified and attention can be drawn to the report of the case by photographs'. Full details of the reporting restrictions imposed by Mr Justice Saunders sitting at the Manchester Crown Court http://www.pressgazette.co.uk/judge-rejects-media-bid-name-child-terrorist-who-plotted-anzac-day-attack?qt-most_read_most_commentedt=1.

194 *Sydney Morning Herald* (19 April 2015).

hours of their first contact, the pair were discussing targeting police officers. 'Sounds good' and Besim allegedly replied: 'Make sure the dogs remember this as well as their fallen "heroes"'. Not long after this exchange, Paul Greaney QC, prosecuting, during the boy's sentencing hearing told the court that the defendant 'suggested that Besim should "break into someone's house and get your first taste of beheading"'. Greaney also told the court of the role of propaganda in the plot, telling the court:

> There is no doubt that there was a determination on the part of the defendant and Sevdet Besim that the plot should be carried through and the contact between the two included frequent references to the production of a martyrdom video by Besim for al-Cambodi which, no doubt, al-Cambodi intended to use for propaganda purposes. In the event, fortunately, the authorities here and in Australia intervened and a plot that would in all probability have resulted in a number of deaths was thwarted.

Matters soon took an even darker turn when it is alleged that, on 19 March 2015, the defendant said to Besim that he was going to present him with three options – a gun attack on the police, a car attack on the police or a knife attack on the police. Messages discussing the weapons to be used ensued and, by the early hours of 23 March, Besim stated he had a machete, knife, taser and a shahada (martyrdom) flag in his car. Besim sent a photograph of a knife, the defendant replied: 'Handle is perfect for tearing through throat'. On 24 March, Besim allegedly messaged the defendant: 'So far the plan is to run a cop over on the Anzac parade & then continue to kill a cop then take Ghanimah [booty] and run to Shahadah?' with the response from our baby-faced terrorist being: 'I'll give orders soon but it's looking along that line' and instructed Besim to make sure he was shot during the attack. Highlighting his extraordinary detachment from the reality of his situation by this stage in the plot, Besim replied: 'I feel like a young kid with a ticket to Disney world cant wait ahahah. Yeh I wanna make sure I get shot to. Not b4 I take out at least 1 [sic]'.

Just hours later the schoolboy was, thankfully, arrested, after concerns had been raised about his extremist behaviour at school, where classmates had nicknamed him 'the terrorist'. But Besim was still at large. On 18 April, Besim was arrested and found to be in possession of a knife, the court heard. The knives and shahada flag were recovered from his home, with a phone that contained a martyrdom message.

James Pickup QC, representing the defendant, questioned if the schoolboy was the mastermind behind the plans and Besim was already radicalised and fully aware of jihadi ideology, submitting: 'It is apparent that [the defendant] provided no more than emotional support, guidance to a limited degree, to someone who was well versed in the preparation of terrorist attacks'. The minor was sentenced to life with a minimum term of five years' imprisonment.

Regardless of the validity of this argument and the degree to which the schoolboy influenced Besim, this still demonstrates the power of online propaganda and supports the case for surveillance. Indeed, on 11 June 2015, Ali Shukri Amin (aged 17) admitted in court that he was the operator of @AmreekiWitness, an extremely active pro-ISIS Twitter account which amongst its web of propaganda also postulated how digital currency might be used to fund the Islamic State, tweeting more than 7000 times from the account, to his 4000 followers, according to his plea. He was also a regular on Ask.fm, running a page which, according to his plea, was 'dedicated to raising awareness about the upcoming conquest of the Americas, and the benefits it has upon the American people'. According to the *Washington Post*, although Amin expressed a desire online to travel, his role ultimately seemed to be that of a facilitator.[195]

The issue of surveillance is likely to be contentious for many years to come, covering (as it does) individuals' right to privacy and the protection of their personal data. In light of the Paris attacks in 2015, and with arrests tied to intelligence gathered by U.S. law enforcement authorities from Whatsapp with 16 suspected terrorists in Belgium being arrested on 8 June 2015,[196] it remains to be seen how surveillance will be perceived by individuals. As British terrorism scholar, Paul Wilkinson, put it: 'Fighting terrorism is like being a goalkeeper. You can make a hundred brilliant saves but the only shot people remember is the one that gets past you'.[197] The question to you, reader, is if surveillance increases the odds of a save and if for all the times it does not get used at all, the means and methods of collection justify the ends.

195 M Zapotosky (2015), 'Va. teen admits he was secret voice behind a pro-ISIS Twitter account' *The Washington Post* (11 June) https://www.washingtonpost.com/local/crime/northern-va-teen-admits-running-pro-islamic-state-twitter-and-helping-man-join-terrorist-group/2015/06/11/1d0cb33e-0eef-11e5-9726-49d6fa26a8c6_story.html.

196 C Oliver (2015), 'Belgian security forces arrest 16 in crackdown on Chechen groups' (8 June) http://www.ft.com/cms/s/9e06a18c-0df2-11e5-9a65-00144feabdc0,Authorised=false.html?siteedition=uk&_i_location=http%3A%2F%2Fwww.ft.com%2Fcms%2Fs%2F0%2F9e06a18c-0df2-11e5-9a65-00144feabdc0.html%3Fsiteedition%3Duk&_i_referer=&classification=conditional_standard&iab=barrier-app.

197 See R Mueller, Director at Federal Bureau of Investigation, speaking at Executives' Club of Chicago, Chicago, Illinois (12 September 2006) https://www.fbi.gov/news/speeches/fighting-terrorism-yesterday-today-and-tomorrow.

5 Let's start a #war

I will destroy ISIS.

Linda Clarke @HeyItsLindaC

On 14 November 2012, the Israel defence forces did not just kill Hamas military leader, Ahmed al-Jabari, as he was driving his car down the street in Gaza – they killed him, posted the strike on YouTube[1] and tweeted a warning to all of Jabari's comrades: 'We recommend that no Hamas operatives, whether low level or senior leaders, show their faces above ground in the days ahead'.[2]

It is not just official military forces expressing their views. Perhaps one of the tweet gems of 2015 was delivered by American stay-at-home mum, Linda Clarke, who tapped out a steely threat into her smartphone in response to the attacks on Paris in December 2015. The attacks were the worst France has seen since the Second World War, killing 129 people in six coordinated attacks across Paris. Linda's manifesto was simple – 'I will destroy ISIS'. The tweet instantly went viral owing to this Twitter warrior capturing a moment of collective emotion and grief into four words of absurd threat. She has subsequently been photoshopped in various military poses, held up as a secular icon, the antidote to the viral propaganda promulgated online by terror groups.

As we saw in Chapter 2, ISIS is waging a war of ideas on social media. Every war has at least two sides. Whilst the content on social media initially was commandeered by ISIS, in 2015 in particular, something new and rather radical emerged – so radical, in fact, that it deserves a chapter of its own. It is the community self-regulated online cyber war. This is not a strategy coming from the government, although as we will see in this chapter various official entities have tried to shape counter-propaganda online. This is self-mediated content coming from journalists, comedians and regular Joes like you and me. It may have a slight feeling of a digital *Dad's Army*, but underestimate it at your peril.

1 https://www.youtube.com/watch?v=r9yryHfVIGQ. Note, however, that this video is no longer available.

2 https://mobile.twitter.com/IDFSpokesperson/status/268780918209118208.

DOI: 10.4324/9781315668680-5

Sophisticated professional hackers have joined the battle; the war is very real and with terrorists increasingly adopting technology (and by extension reliance on it) as part of the means to facilitate their battle campaigns, it can have a direct impact on how things play out in the real world. This is all out war, quite literally, as it plays out on the very ecosystem that gave ISIS the ability to grow and crawl out of the primordial social media soup. This is the modern equivalent of King Lear's storm.

5.1 Official counter-narratives

When it comes to the post-terrorism backlash on social media, there are many different camps. Some efforts to harness the power of social media come from official channels, whilst others are waged by members of the public. This is a melting pot of individuals and groups coming together in pursuit of a common aim, which lacks a common strategy. How the range of actors in this extraordinary theatrical production play out on a global stage is best understood by reference to understanding who these players are and their respective spheres of influence.

5.1.1 'Official' postings

Admittedly, they do not have the same number of Twitter followers as Justin Bieber, Miley Cyrus or Katy Perry, but posts by official government agents do have strong followings online. There are many different species of use of social media by military forces, ranging from active posts about ongoing military campaigns right though to attempting to undermine the terrorists through counter-propaganda and even trolling.

Just as ISIS has gone beyond using social media to wage a war of opinion online, the Israeli Defence Forces (IDF) have taken things one step further and have begun actively to use social media as part of their military campaigns. 'Operation Pillar of Defence', which was intended severely to impair the command and control chain of the Hamas leadership, as well as its terrorist infrastructure, had as one of its key objectives to eliminate Ahmed Jabari, leader of Hamas's Izz al-Din al-Qassam Brigades and the mastermind behind several planned attacks in Israel, which resulted in the loss of civilian life and ordered Palestinian terrorists to fire thousands of rockets at Israel. The operation was accompanied by some of the most aggressive and ground-breaking social media offensives ever launched by any military group.

The lead up to Jalbari's elimination bore all the hallmarks of a film release campaign, with 'Operation Pillar of Defence' posts appearing on the IDF's official Facebook[3] page, alongside a Flick feed and Twitter postings[4] and live blogging

3 https://www.facebook.com/idfonline?fref=ts Official Facebook Page of the Israel Defence Forces.

4 https://mobile.twitter.com/IDFSpokesperson/status/268795866784075776 Official Twitter Feed of the Israel Defence Forces @IDFSpokesperson.

of the rocket attacks on southern Israel coming from Gaza. After neutralising Jalbari, the IDF reinforced the justification for the campaign by releasing the rationale of the mission on its blog,[5] along with photographs, embedded YouTube videos of the IDF pinpoint strike on Jalbari and details of Jalbari's alleged role in the kidnapping of young soldier, Gilad Shalit.

The Jabari campaign was not, however, piloting the use of social media. The story of the IDF and social networking has organic beginnings, not originating with the IDF itself, but rather with private individuals in the online community. In 2009, during 'Operation Cast Lead', the IDF embedded camera crews in its combat units to capture footage which was primarily recorded to prevent allegations of war crimes. The videos were shared with the press in the days following the attacks; however, this traditional outlet of reporting did not gain worldwide attention. It was only when a young Israeli soldier from Hawaii and an American Israeli with clearance from the IDF decided to create a YouTube account and share the videos on that channel that millions of views were generated.[6] The account was adopted as the official YouTube account of the IDF shortly afterwards, blogging in both English and Arabic.[7]

The use of social media during 'Operation Pillar of Defence' represented a break from the traditional official reporting styles adopted by military forces more generally, where footage relating to planned operations may not be released until months afterwards. For example, during the operation to eliminate Osama bin Laden, photographs of his body were purposely kept out of the public domain and the only contemporaneous reporting on social media came from a series of tweets made by a bystander in Abbottabad, who heard the helicopters landing:[8] 'A huge window shaking bang here in Abbottabad', tweeted Sohaib Athar, a local IT consultant. 'I hope its not the start of something nasty :-S'.[9] The need to keep such raids secret is understandable, as the risk of compromising such missions is significant. The unofficial posts by Ahthar also highlighted the risk to political and diplomatic damage through releasing information as it was not clear, from the raid, the extent to which Pakistani forces were involved with assisting the US and also how much intelligence sharing with Pakistan was going on prior to the raid. There was also discussion at the time as to whether it was US, or US and Pakistani, helicopters that were involved in the raid, with Athar tweeting 'since taliban (probably) don't have helicopters, and since they're saying it was not "ours", so must be a complicated situation'. Similarly, footage of the drone strikes

5 'Ahmed al-Jabari – The Military Chief' (21 January 2012) https://www.idfblog.com/hamas/2012/01/21/ahmed-al-jabari/.

6 N Schachtman (2009), 'Israel's Accidental YouTube War' (21 January) http://www.wired.com/2009/01/israels-acciden/.

7 https://www.youtube.com/watch?feature=player_embedded&v=2Zd55Zhj5gQ.

8 D Axe and N Shachtman (2011), 'Latest on Osama Raid: Tricked-out Choppers, Live Tweets, Possible Pakistani Casualties' (2 May) http://www.wired.com/2011/05/latest-on-the-osama-raid-tricked-out-choppers-live-tweets-possible-pakistani-casualties/.

9 https://twitter.com/#!/ReallyVirtual.

that killed Awlaki and Jihadi John have not been made public and certainly were not released contemporaneously with the events.

The IDF posts represent a key example of the use of social media as a propaganda tool and the potential for manipulation. What the blogging and posts did not post about was that Jabari has been an Israeli de facto partner and ally for several years. After Cast Lead, Israel and Hamas had agreed that Hamas would keep Gaza's array of militant movements in check, with Israel providing financial assistance and transport. Since the Jalbari operation, and as recently as January 2012, the IDF has posted on its Twitter feed about ISIS,[10] '#ISIS in #Sinai is a threat to the region, but our soldiers on the border are ready. idfblog.com/blog/2015/11/1 . . . pic.twitter.com/i5lAex6OnH'.[11]

The link to the blog provided in the tweet links to the official IDF blog, specifically a strong post about female fighters on the frontline with ISIS in Sinai.[12] The blog notes that the Caracal Battalion is responsible for defending the volatile Israel-Sinai border. Established in 2004, Caracal was the first battalion to fully integrate women as combat soldiers. The battalion is trained to deal with terrorist infiltrations, bombs on the border, shootings, smuggling and criminal events, with the blog containing statements such as: 'We are here to stand up against terrorism'. In an interesting take on the psychology of male ISIS fighters, Lieutenant Ada (a commander in the mixed sex Caracal Battalion on the Israel-Sinai border) is quoted in the blog (accompanied by a large photograph of herself) as saying: 'ISIS fighters are terrified of being defeated by a woman, it completely contradicts their radical beliefs'. The tweet to the article received 190 retweets and 261 likes within hours of being posted, with an array of responses being elicited by the audience from wishes of good luck to #FreePalestine being tagged to the replies to the post, as well as provoking further political discussion. The blog also invites users to join the international social media desk, to 'create, engage and influence'.[13]

As is common to all of the discussions in this book, the use of social media has to be placed in its political context. After Israel's political ally, the Mubarak regime in Cairo was overthrown and replaced by an Islamist government the need to forge international support and shape the debate is acute. It also sends out a message to the militants that the IDF has the capability to defend itself, and demonstrates to the Israeli public that it is defending its peoples and also shows that such attacks are not indiscriminate, focusing in on key targets rather than causing collateral loss of civilian life.

10 'Ahmed al-Jabari – The Military Chief' (21 January 2012) https://www.idfblog.com/hamas/2012/01/21/ahmed-al-jabari/.

11 https://mobile.twitter.com/IDFSpokesperson/status/690476972552626176?p=v.

12 Israeli Defence Forces Official Blog (2015), 'Female Fighters on the Frontline with ISIS in Sinai' (17 November) https://www.idfblog.com/blog/2015/11/17/female-fighters-frontline-isis-sinai/.

13 https://www.idfblog.com/about/contact-us/.

5.1.2 Counter-narratives

The development of a counter-narrative in and of itself has turned into its own cottage industry. In February 2015, at the White House's Summit on Countering Violent Extremism, the government announced new initiatives to address ISIS's social media campaign online. The factsheet issued by the White House as part of this latest strategy states that: 'the U.S. government, in partnership with foreign governments, civil society and the private sector, is working to weaken the legitimacy and resonance of violent extremist messaging and narratives, including through social media'.[14] As well as drawing upon their global network, such as partnering with the United Arab Emirates to create a 'digital communications hub', the fact sheet states that there is a further well of resource that can be tapped into, such as university students. These potential 'peer-to-peer challenges' established by the State Department would operate throughout the United States, Canada, North Africa, the Middle East, Europe, Australia and Asia, charged with creating digital content that counters the message put out by the terrorists. Running in parallel to these efforts, the government would also seek to work with the private sector to create 'technology camps' where 'social media companies will work with governments, civil society and religious leaders to develop digital content that discredits violent extremist narratives and amplifies positive alternatives'.[15]

In the US, the Centre for Strategic Counterterrorism Communications (CSCC), established in September 2011, runs more than 350 Twitter accounts for the state, plus others for the Defence Department, Homeland Security Department, and foreign governments as well. It is also active on Facebook and other platforms, with the goal of throwing a wrench into the gears of Islamic State's recruitment machine. The State Department has also set up a series of anti-ISIS accounts on Facebook, Twitter and Tumblr as part of the mission 'to expose the facts about terrorists and their propaganda'.[16] Messages have been pumped out in Arabic, Urdu and Somali for the past three years. In addition to this, the Think Again, Turn Away campaign was launched in December 2013 to dissuade impressionable jihadists from joining ISIS's cause by highlighting the realities of the brutality of the regime, with messages being posted across Twitter, Facebook, YouTube, Tumblr and Ask.fm, showing perhaps how the life offered by ISIS is 'far from the principles of Islam'.[17]

14 'Fact sheet: The White House Summit on Countering Violent Extremism' (18 February 2015) The White House, Office of the Press Secretary https://www.whitehouse.gov/the-press-office/2015/02/18/fact-sheet-white-house-summit-countering-violent-extremism.

15 Ibid.

16 https://m.facebook.com/ThinkAgainTurnAway/?_ft_=top_level_post_id.10208091316507397%3Atl_objid.10208091316507397%3Athid.447799985335217%3A306061129499414%3A3%3A0%3A1448956799%3A-6924206985315768147&__tn__=C. This page is no longer available, but was previously available at https://m.facebook.com/ThinkAgainTurnAway?hc_location=ufi.

17 P Cockburn (2015), 'Life under Isis: Why I deserted the "Islamic State" rather than take part in executions, beheadings and rape: the story of a former jihadi' *The Telegraph* (16 March)

One CSCC video production titled 'Welcome to ISIS Land', offers a poor imitation of an Islamic State recruitment video, mocking the terrorist caliphate and ending with the slogan, 'Think again. Turn away', next to the official seal of the State Department.[18] The video offers a horrifying glimpse behind the curtain of what ISIS portrays to the world, showing a mosque being blown up, followed by a photo of a body with a severed head. The idea is to use the group's own propaganda materials and show them in a different light. For instance, the video lists so-called 'useful skills' ISIS sympathisers can learn if they join the group, such as blowing up holy places of worship such as mosques, with brother Muslims inside, as well as the crucifixion and execution of fellow Muslims. The video, however, feels jarring, mixing the sombre messages of death and betrayal to peaceful civilians ending on the sarcastic note to those who would seek to join the cause: 'Travel is inexpensive, because you won't need a return ticket!'.

Whilst, on paper, the initiatives make for great reading, whether such strategies can ever be as fully effective – and if they are worth the level of investment they demand – as those conducted by the terrorists is a topic that certainly benefits from a pause for thought. As we saw in Chapter 2, Barak Obama is not going to be posting pictures of himself eating a Twix bar before engaging in air-strike activity. Anti-terrorist group messages may also have to go through an approval process before they make it to the social media platforms. ISIS is agile, staying ahead of the social media curve, delivering commentary to those who are predisposed to watch the message that they publish. By comparison, a social media camp put together by the government runs the risk of ending up along the lines of an idea that could have been lifted from the script of the BBC political comedy *The Thick of It*.

In December 2015, it was revealed that a secret review board tasked with analysing the progress of the CSCC 'had serious questions' for the State Department over a programme to undermine ISIS's use of social media. The 100-page report has not been published, but the six experts behind the report drawn from employees of Google, Twitter and other companies located in Silicon Valley, New York and Texas 'had serious questions about whether the US government should be involved in overt messaging at all', according to a US official who spoke with the *Washington Post*.[19]

The panel did have a prudent suggestion that would offer this level of posting honesty, suggesting that rather than employing overt propaganda, campaigns should focus on people who have escaped Islamic State, as well as Middle Eastern

http://www.independent.co.uk/news/world/middle-east/life-under-isis-why-i-deserted-the-islamic-state-rather-than-take-part-in-executions-beheadings-and-10111877.html.

18 See YouTube page of the Global Engagement Centre 'Welcome to the "Islamic State" land (ISIS/ISIL)' http://youtu.be/-wmdEFvsY0E.

19 G Miller (2015), 'Panel casts doubt on U.S. propaganda efforts against ISIS' *Washington Post* (2 December) https://www.washingtonpost.com/world/national-security/panel-casts-doubt-on-us-propaganda-efforts-against-isis/2015/12/02/ab7f9a14-9851-11e5-94f0-9eeaff906ef3_story.html.

allies, and share their stories. Although not potentially a message that the pro-ISIS following will want to see, the fact is that it is underpinned with integrity. It is more difficult to see the benefit of other ideas, such as sending ideological 'SWAT' teams out to ward off radicalisation in European or other hot spots. One cannot help but feel that such think tank ideas have been generated for the sake of generating them, rather than with the aim of progress.

Whilst Alberto Fernandez, coordinator of the State Department's Centre for Strategic Counterterrorism Communications, which was responsible for the programme, termed this 'participating in the marketplace of ideas', such strategies arguably drive the extremists right into the arms of ISIS as the one figure who 'understands' them, listens and gives them that missing piece of the emotional jigsaw they call life. The CSCC fails to address the crux of the issue. The key point is that it is not just about terrorist acts: it is about creating a sense of belonging to something, for those who are socially dispossessed and unmotivated to feel that they are being listened to. Mocking such content based on Western democratic understandings and casting the issue in such light runs the risk of trivialising it into a comparator of Sacha Baron Cohen's main protagonist in the film 'The Dictator', which will simply infuriate ISIS's loyal online followers, reinforcing the message that the West arrogantly dismisses their beliefs, culture and customs. To mock the very thing in which they believe undermines its importance to those individuals, rather than offering them an alternative way of thinking. The CSCC, if it had done its homework in relation to commercially successful social media campaigns, and marketing campaigns more generally, would know it is precisely when you tap into the public consciousness, generating a sense of authenticity that people begin to open up to the possibility of what your organisation is offering, which is why we all cry like babies when John Lewis releases its Christmas TV adverts, so strongly associating Christmas with Coca-Cola or, even for just a few minutes, smile and put our faith in ludicrously grand tweets posted by 'soccer-moms' like Linda Clarke.

Despite the discussion surrounding the use of counter-narrative strategies, Congress has inserted language into the National Defense Authorization Act 2016, empowering the Department of Defense to counter and degrade terror groups seeking to radicalise individuals over the internet through the development of 'creative and agile concepts, technologies, and strategies across all available media to most effectively reach target audiences, to counter and degrade the ability of adversaries and potential adversaries to persuade, inspire, and recruit inside areas of hostilities or in other areas in direct support of the objectives of commanders'.[20]

20 House report 114-270 – National Defense Authorization Act for Fiscal Year 2016 s 1056(3) 'Information Operations and Engagement Technology Demonstrations'; see also R Levinson (2015), 'The Pentagon's new weapon against ISIS: Social media Bloomberg' (2 December) http://about.bgov.com/blog/the-pentagons-new-weapon-against-isis-social-media/.

The recommendations have not been without their detractors. For instance, in a report to Congress in March 2015, which acknowledged that the state was 'affected by the growing use of cyber capabilities and social media which make it easy for our adversaries to communicate, coordinate, execute, and inspire their actions', General Joseph L. Votel, commander of US Special Operations Command, stated:

> Congress has expressed concern with DOD [Department of Defense] engaging violent extremist propaganda on the Internet, except in limited ways . . . we [US Special Operations Command] believe there is a complementary role for the Department of Defense in this space which acknowledges the need for a civilian lead, but allows the DoD to pursue appropriate missions such as counter-recruitment and reducing the flow of foreign fighters, the ability to rapidly respond to adversarial messaging and propaganda, particularly with offensive cyberspace operations to deny, disrupt, degrade, or corrupt those messages, requires an Executive Order and is limited by current U.S. government policies.

On social media specifically, he stated that: 'another gap exists in [the Pentagon's] ability to operate on social media and the Internet, due to a lack of organic capability', noting that these efforts could be outsourced, whilst military intelligence focused on ways to 'improve the department's ability to effectively operate in the social media and broader online information space'.[21]

In jolly old Blighty (UK), there has not been much traction either. On 29 August 2015, the UK set up the official Twitter account @UKAgainstISIL. The Institute for Strategic Dialogue has also used Google search results (e.g. people searching 'How do I get to Syria?') to target at-risk users, who are instead sent anti-extremist web videos that, on the face of it, look like just another piece of ISIS propaganda.[22] The account now has a total of 5369 followers and has tweeted 186 times in English, Arabic and Russian about the global coalition's efforts to defeat IS in Syria. Other initiatives include the invention of Abdullah-x.[23] Abdullah-x is a British working class Muslim with street cred clothing. On his YouTube channel[24] he appears as a cartoon character, speaking about Syria to his young

21 Hearing on National Defense Authorization Act for Fiscal Year 2016 and Oversight of Previously Authorized Programs before the Committee on Armed Services House of Representatives 114th Congress First Session (HASC No 114–24) (8 March 2015) http://fas.org/irp/congress/2015_hr/socom-2016.pdf.

22 N Kobi (2015), 'How a British Think Tank Targets Google Results to Counter ISIS Propaganda' (2 June) http://motherboard.vice.com/read/how-a-british-think-tank-targets-google-results-to-counter-isis-propaganda.

23 H Kuchler and G Dyer (2015), 'Abdullah-X takes on Isis in social media fight' *The Financial Times* (March) http://www.ft.com/cms/s/0/ce4ed632-9f8a-11e5-beba-5e33e2b79e46.html#axzz3xcMWYjOj.

24 YouTube channel of Abdullah-x https://www.youtube.com/watch?v=GrptDtDrbSU.

following. Abdullah-x emphasises responsibility, encouraging his followers to think critically about how their actions could affect their families. Although a very sensitive issue, it also addresses what the youngsters think they know about ISIS, as opposed to how – as we have seen from Chapter 2 – the organisation chooses to present itself to its loyal following: 'There is a call of duty for Syria, it is to be well informed and not misinformed', he tells them.

Abdullah-x is just one of a series of tools that is being used to diffuse radicalism online. In a column by Eric Schmidt (Google's chairman), written for the *New York Times*, he called for more tools to help cool down the tensions played out on social media, 'sort of like spell-checkers, but for hate and harassment'.[25] As part of a concerted effort to counter extremist speech, Facebook has participated in social media training sessions spanning the globe, the US Government has also sponsored technology camps, fusing the best of social media and society to brainstorm the issue. In Australia, web developers and Muslim community leaders have been called together to come up with ideas and products designed to defeat ISIS's hold on its audience, with ideas including cooperative games, special social networks for Muslim youths and a Tinder type product to meet up with mentors.

5.1.2.1 Are counter-narratives successful?

So can a counter-narrative ever be successful? The question is a difficult one, given that, as we saw in Chapter 2, there are so many strands to what ISIS is offering its current and potential following – such as acts of brutality, victimhood, belonging, war and utopianism. Getting the tone right is therefore extremely difficult. However, there is potential to pick apart the complex narrative and highlight its inconsistencies. This has not gone beyond the detection of the US, with researchers tasked with producing a white paper on ISIS's influence and Resolve highlighting the flaws and inconsistencies in the messages pumped out by ISIS; for instance, the majority of social media users rejected ISIS's framing of key issues (e.g. role of shariah, what a caliphate is and its necessity, who constitutes the ummah etc). Whilst the sheer divergence in views makes adopting any form of cohesive counter-narrative strategy a formidable task, according to the white paper, the community of ISIL supporters was significantly smaller than popular press coverage suggests, which may mean that it lacks sufficient support among regional leaders to build long-term political sustainability[26] and disagreements over its ideological justifications creates a real possibility that it may alienate large portions of the population within the region.[27] After all, when it comes to social

25 E Schmidt (2015), 'Eric Schmidt on How to Build a Better Web' (7 December) *The New York Times* Opinion pages.

26 White Paper on SMA Support to SOCCENT: 'ISIL Influence and Resolve a Strategic Multi-Layer' (SMA) Periodic Publication (September 2015) https://info.publicintelligence.net/SOCCENT-ISIL-InfluenceResolve.pdf.

27 Ibid.

media, the terrorists cannot control the conversation in the same manner as was possible within the closed confines of a moderated forum.

It is interesting to consider whether these government-led initiatives can ever successfully capture the mood on the ground, for those who may be susceptible to the propagandist material posted online. In the words of one commentator: 'I have lived on the margins. I have been spat on for being a Muslim; I have lived on one of the poorest council estates in the country and seen my parents struggle to put food on the table; I have mourned for family killed in the illegal Iraq war'. Something which legislators and commentators in the main do not have experience of, the same commentary notes that discussion surrounding radicalisation are often 'unproductive and represents everything that is wrong with the British discourse on radicalisation: the tendency is to generalise, filter our nuance and prioritise academic opinion over Muslims' feelings – the sentiment on the street'.[28] This is also coupled with a lack of understanding that there is no one base cause of radicalisation which, as seen above, is heightened by the fact that ISIS is so successful in its engagement with the online community, who are drawn to it precisely because there is diverse content, playing on the need for a sense of belonging and identity.

The UK House of Commons reports on the roots of radicalisation noted that radicalised individuals come from a wide range of backgrounds. For example, whilst the majority of individuals referred to the programme were aged between 13 and 25 and just over two-thirds of all terrorist offences since 2001 were committed by those under 30, the age of offenders ranged from 16 to 48.[29] Education levels and economic status also vary.[30] The report goes on to state that:

> Although the report stated those particularly vulnerable to radicalisation include converts to the Muslim faith, they may originate from many different ethnic communities rather than what we would regard as 'traditional' British Muslim communities. Rashad Ali, of the counter-radicalisation organisation Centri, concluded that 'I don't think there is a typical profile . . . It actually could be anybody'.[31]

When social media and terrorist content is talked about online, it often tries to put individuals into categories, or communities, identifying shared beliefs, values and

28 A Hennessy (2016), 'As a working class Muslim, I know what causes radicalisation. So why don't these rich white men believe me?' *The Independent* (11 January) http://www.independent.co.uk/voices/as-a-working-class-muslim-i-know-what-causes-radicalisation-so-why-dont-these-rich-white-men-believe-a6805976.html.

29 HM Government, *Prevent Strategy* (June 2011) para 9.23; Robin Simcox, Hannah Stuart and Houriya Ahmed, '*Islamist Terrorism: The British Connections*' Centre for Social Cohesion (2010).

30 House of Commons Home Affairs Committee, 'Roots of Violent Radicalisation' Nineteenth Report of Session 2010–12 *Volume I*, HC 1446 (6 February 2012) Q 214 (Sir Norman Bettison).

31 Ibid, Q 53.

systems that allow for the categorisation of people. There has been much debate online and in the media as to what ISIS represents and the confusion of its messages with those of Islam.

As we saw throughout Chapter 2, one of ISIS's key themes is to play on the vulnerability of those who may be persuaded to their cause and to present themselves as a marginalised group representing the true Islam. A key way in which social media challenges this powerful rhetoric is to show that ISIS's views are not representative of the Muslim faith or, in multi-cultural societies, individuals' reactions to different faiths.

Some content online, however, gives comfort to peace-loving Muslims, demonstrating that there is a global alliance of coexistence and solidarity, that is far from the image of Islam that ISIS seeks to represent. Following a knife attack in the UK at Leytonstone underground station in December 2015, perpetrated by an individual seeking to express his solidarity with Islam, in response to the attack, a bystander shouted 'You ain't no Muslim, bruv' at the alleged perpetrator, very quickly becoming a hashtag used on social media as a means to express unity against the acts of this individual. Examples include: 'Soo proud to be a Londoner. True Muslims don't try and kill innocent bystanders. Peace to true Muslims'; 'I love that #YouAintNoMuslimBruv is trending. The best response possible. So proud to be a Londoner'.

In December 2014, during a hostage siege in Sydney, perpetrated by Man Haron Monis, who declared he was representative of Islamic State and that the siege was a terrorist attack, Australians used the #I'llRideWithYou hashtag, offering to travel to work with Muslim commuters to ensure they felt safe from backlash for this individual's actions. Such hashtags demonstrate that the vast majority of the online community does not fall for the rhetoric of evil produced by the likes of ISIS, with other hashtags such as #StandWithAhmed taking hold to reclaim what Islam means for Muslims.

5.2 Responses from the social media community

5.2.1 Introduction

As we saw from the postings of Linda Clarke, the communities on which social media operate have much to say about terrorism online and communicate their views on it in a variety of different ways that go beyond mere counter-dialogue. Anti-jihad activists with names similar to the YouTube 'Smackdown Corps' 'patrol' the site, flagging material which they consider infringes the YouTube community standards. One site called 'Jihadi Smackdown of the Day',[32] which describes its activities as 'countering the cyber-jihad one video at a time . . .' encourages the online community to report videos with terrorist content: '[w]e know how valuable your time is, so we've made it simple. All you need to do

32 http://smackdownoftheday.blogspot.co.uk.

is subscribe to this feed and flag ONE video a day'. For example, many of the videos of Mr Awlaki now bear the message: 'This video has been removed as a violation of YouTube's policy'. As such accounts can be quickly recreated, such activists also create programmes that can search for similar social media handles, although these are increasingly being obfuscated by the terror groups. As noted in Chapter 3, Google, Facebook and Twitter also have 'trusted flaggers', who are utilised to identify terrorist content online.

5.2.2 Public outrage/grief

Perhaps one of the strongest counter-narratives online has been as a result of the grief expressed following terrorist activity. As much as the terrorists themselves have a right to freedom of expression, so do those who oppose their beliefs. The events of 9/11 may have drawn audiences to 24-hour TV news stations, but the shootings of liberal magazine Charlie Hebdo staff by terrorists in response to publishing cartoons of the prophet Mohammed, and the Paris attacks in December 2015, drew people to social media. Also notable was the main news channels featuring social media postings and on the ground accounts posted to social media of the events unfolding, captured on smart phones. Twitter went on fire on the day of the attacks, offering updates and support through its newsfeed. What became apparent, as the tweets unfolded, was the story of solidarity, and within 24 hours there were more than 3.4 million mentions of #JeSuisCharlie[33] (which translates as 'I am Charlie'), with many Facebook, Twitter and Instagram users posting or replacing their profile photo with a white-on-black image of the phrase. With regard to the Paris attacks, Facebook introduced a French flag filter, which could be placed over a Facebook user's profile picture.

Drawing on the free speech implications of the shootings, the events also spawned the creation of cartoons mocking the power of the pencil over the gun by numerous high profile cartoonists, which were also posted onto social media, with examples including fighters holding pencils captioned with 'where's the gun?'.[34] Among the messages of defiance were images of grief. One such tweet posted by Patrick Chappatte from the *International New York Times*. In memory of his colleagues and friends at Charlie Hebdo, the image simply said: 'without humour we are all dead', accompanied by the text[35] 'IN MEMORY OF MY COLLEAGUES AND FRIENDS FROM CHARLIE HEBDO, a cartoon for the International New York Times'. The tweet received 2205 retweets and 1246 likes within hours of its posting.

33 J Martinson (2015), 'Charlie Hebdo: A week of horror when social media came into its own' *Guardian* (22 January) http://www.theguardian.com/media/2015/jan/11/charlie-hebdo-social-media-news-readers.

34 @Newsdayopinion 'Where's the trigger? @Newsday cartoonist @MatttDavies on "mind-numbing" tragedy' http://nwsdy.li/1AtgYZ6 #CharlieHebdo Posted10:55 PM – 7 January 2015.

35 http://twitter.com/PatChappatte/status/552910782212866049/photo/1.

Magnus Shaw, a copywriter and blogger, tweeted an original Charles M Schulz image of popular cartoon character Charlie Brown, his head in his hands, sitting on a park bench. Above, he added the words 'Je suis Charlie', accompanied by the words @TheMagnusShaw: 'A terrible day for all cartoonists. #JeSuisCharlie'. He later tweeted: 'Charles M Schulz, wherever you are, I hope I didn't let you down'.[36] As well as original postings, an old *New Yorker* cartoon started to trend, which is of a blank page that the cartoonist captioned: 'Please enjoy this culturally, ethically, religiously and politically correct cartoon responsibly. Thank you'.[37] *The Telegraph*'s cartoonist, Matt, showed one gunman saying to the other: 'Be careful, they might have pens'.[38] The postings sparked expressions of support for free speech from people across the globe, with @Soshy summing it up thus: 'What Do We Have Left, if The Sound Of Silence is The Only One We Are Allowed To Make ?#JeSuisCharlie'.[39]

The Paris attacks in December 2015 also served to demonstrate the power of human kindness in the face of terrorist acts, with Parisians of diverse backgrounds and religious beliefs using the hashtag #PorteOuverte to offer their homes to those stranded in the city, or to get one of the free rides offered by taxi drivers. As well as these acts of simple human kindness, just after the Charlie Hebdo shootings, a Muslim shop assistant named Lassana Bathily showed extraordinary courage when he saved at least six people by hiding them in a walk-in freezer at the Jewish grocery store where an Islamist gunman made his final stand. Images of Mr Bathily quickly trended on Twitter, labelled Malian Muslim, as a symbol of the people united against terrorism: '@Anna_and_P Malian Muslim worker in kosher store hid Jews, saved them. Right now, Lassana Bathily is coolest man on the planet'.[40]

As counter-narratives go, this symbol of a simple act of solidarity in the face of tragedy, regardless of religion and certainly more authentic, is more potent and emotionally charged than any highly produced social media campaign ISIS can wage. It was truly a moment where modern social media met with the most primitive of human emotion and kindness. Such solidarity was again echoed on social media in the Orlando attacks of June 2016, when a gunman allegedly with some affiliation to ISIS and who had previously been investigated by the FBI[41] shot hundreds of people in a LGBT night club, killing 49 people and injuring many more.

36 http://twitter.com/TheMagnusShaw/status/552870218545238018/photo/1.

37 http://twitter.com/RamziHabre/status/552824742097719296/photo/1.

38 http://twitter.com/Telegraph/status/552947419756134401/photo/1.

39 https://twitter.com/intent/like?tweet_id=552874192199114752.

40 https://twitter.com/Anna_and_P.

41 The outcome of these investigations was that the individual in question did not present a threat. See M Mazzetti, E Lichtblau and A Blinder (2016), 'Omar Mateen, Twice Scrutinized by F.B.I., Shows Threat of Lone Terrorists' *The New York Times* (13 June) http://www.nytimes.com/2016/06/14/us/politics/orlando-shooting-omar-mateen.html?_r=0.

5.2.3 The ethics of posting graphic content and blackouts

Such outpourings raise queries as to what extent they propagate the cause they seek to denounce, as well as the ethics of posting or commenting on such graphic content. This is not something that has gone unnoticed by the social media community online. Shortly after the YouTube video 'A Message to America', featuring the beheading of journalist James Foley was released, whilst initially uploaded to YouTube, it was widely circulated over social media in full, and also in screenshots, quickly spreading across Twitter, Facebook, Instagram and other platforms. Trending terms on Twitter were #Isis, #James Foley and #Islamic State. Whilst the content was clearly shocking, as well as spurring discussion about ISIS, it also sparked debate as to the ethics of sharing a man's death online, the upset caused to Mr Foley's family and the widespread dissemination of ISIS's message. Tweets included: ' @MiaFarrow: Blackout on group that murdered James Foley. Don't share video. Give them nothing. #RespectJamesFoley',[42] '@portraitinflesh Don't share the video. Don't share the pictures. Don't work for ISIS. Share images of James Foley's life instead. #ISIS'.[43] Hend Amry, a Syrian activist and commentator, noted that: '@LibyaLiberty: you know what I think? And I know how crazy this sounds, but we need an #ISISmediaBlackout. Amputate their reach. Pour water on their flame'. Instigating the hashtag #ISISmedia Blackout, to try to starve ISIS of media coverage and limit distribution of the video, the hashtag quickly found some footing. Even Twitter's CEO became involved with the debate, tweeting: '@dickc: We have been and are actively suspending accounts as we discover them related to this graphic imagery. Thank youhttps://twitter.com/nytimes/status/501862926039654400 . . .', also posting links to its policies on offensive content and images of deceased individuals.[44]

This issue of where to draw the line when censoring content was again raised as a result of the Orlando shootings, leading to the release of copies of a deceased's SnapChat messages, which documented – in real time – the shootings that were taking place, as well as partial images of the gunman, Omar Mateen. The images that were subsequently published by the mainstream media[45] were shared many times on social media, sparking much debate, sadness, shock and outrage. The release of the content calls into question if there is a public interest in viewing such materials. In an age of instantaneous media is it inevitable that such materials will become part of news consumption as our ideas of what is and what is not acceptable are changed by the fire hydrant of information accessible to us?

42 https://twitter.com/MiaFarrow/status/501902404418535424.

43 https://twitter.com/portraitinflesh/status/501835922116079617.

44 https://twitter.com/dickc/status/502005459067625473.

45 D Franklin (2016), 'Orlando shooting victim's final moments caught on Snapchat' *NBC News* (13 June) http://kfor.com/2016/06/13/orlando-shooting-victims-final-moments-caught-on-snapchat/.

5.2.4 Spoofing

As well as expressions of grief, the ongoing spirit of Charlie Hebdo to revel in the satirical demonstrates the value that freedom of expression attracts. One way in which this has been expressed online by social media is through spoof accounts, a sort of counter-narrative which has much more freedom than posts from official channels can ever seek to enjoy.

No review of social media would be complete without a consideration of the selfie. However, when we talk of selfies in the context of terrorism, this is not about endless overly-filtered pictures of the cast of *The Only Way is Essex* and *Geordie Shore*. The Arab MBC channel has aired a TV series called *Selfie*, a satirical comedy show starring Saudi actor-comedian Nasser Al-Qasabi. The show tackles diverse issues such as extremism and domestic violence, as well as ISIS and the young Saudis who join it. Given the controversial nature of the show, it has sparked much comment online, with its opponents including Saudi bloggers, social media users, clerics and journalists, all taking to various online mediums to argue that the series ridicules Islam.[46] ISIS supporters on Twitter have issued death threats against him, using hashtags such as 'The Mujahideen Are Seeking the Head of Al-Qasabi'.[47] Many other users have, however, come to the show's defence. Sa'id Al-Suraihi, a columnist for the official Saudi daily *Okaz* wrote:

> . . . With *Selfie*'s first episodes, Al-Qasabi succeeded in restoring value to art, by linking it to affairs of the homeland, to the issues that worry people in their daily lives, and to the challenges that these issues pose. Al-Qasabi has presented [us] with quality art, by means of which he tackles issues that many artists are either unable to tackle or fear to tackle. Maybe the most obvious sign of Al-Qasabi's triumph is the direct response [to the programme] on social media, which later expanded to include articles by journalists and [statements by] Friday preachers. Al-Qasabi's show appealed to many, but many others condemned it. In Al-Qasabi's opinion, when people are divided about him, it is a victory – because if the issues he raised were not sensitive, there would have been no outrage from his opponents and no ovations from his supporters . . . Al-Qasabi was great in the episodes we saw, here plucking the string of extremism, there dancing with the wolves of ISIS. In both cases, he restored our hope that there is still someone who cares to present honorable art, and who has the courage to stick his neck out and tackle topics that many others are afraid to touch.[48]

There is also a rejection of outright hostility and generalisations made by the social media community. For instance, when Donald Trump stepped into the fray

46 Eremnews.com (19 June 2015); Alarabiya.net (19 June 2015); *Al-Madina* (Saudi Arabia) (20 June 2015).

47 https://twitter.com/hashtag/مطلوب_رأس_ناصر_القصبي_للمجاهدين?src=hash.

48 *'Okaz* (Saudi Arabia) (22 June 2015), quoted in E Ezrahi (2015), 'Selfie' – Satirical Saudi TV Show Sends Shockwaves Through the Kingdom' MEMRI Inquiry & Analysis Series Report No 1176.

and announced on Twitter that, if successful in his bid to become US president, he would defeat ISIS with 'brutal and relentless' attacks on Twitter, setting aside time to focus his efforts on an online campaign against the group: 'Of all the people running for President, I have by far the most Twitter-war experience', he boasted. 'I will declare an all-out Twitter war on ISIS, and I will win', Trump told Fox News.[49] Offering a teasing glimpse into his counter-narrative strategy, he offered some sample tweets: 'ISIS is a total joke. Has zero chance of winning. Zero!', 'ISIS leaders live in tents. Trump has TEN BILLION DOLLARS. Kicks their ass!' and 'Never see ISIS leaders with models. Why? Cannot get models. Models love Trump!'

As might be expected, the Twitter community has engaged in some excessively diverting dialogue online as a result of Mr Trump's tweets and claims that parts of 'radicalised' London are no-go areas for terrified police, sparking the hashtag #Trumpfacts. One user, John Paul (@ZooSatellite), tweeted: 'Britain so radicalised that the Queen now wears a hijab instead of a crown #TrumpFacts', accompanied by a picture of the Queen Elizabeth wearing a silk Hermes headscarf. Other online banter includes posts by Nick from Fulham (@NickFromFulham), who posted: '#TrumpFacts Duran Duran have become so radicalised they now call themselves Koran Koran'. James Doleman (@jamesDoleman) offered: 'The ancient city of Brighton is now dominated by a giant mosque', accompanied by a photograph of the exotic Royal Pavilion in Brighton, built as a seaside pleasure palace for King George IV. Alan White (@aljwhite) posted: 'the city is full of dangerous bearded radicals #Trumpfacts', alongside a photo of the UK Labour Party opposition leader Jeremy Corbyn. Despite the furore surrounding the campaign, Mr Trump went on to win the November 2016 election.

5.2.5 Islamic Bloggers

There has also been an increase in blogging activity by the Islamic community. An international network of writers, bloggers, academics, intellectuals and artists who form a resistance movement against what they see as the growing oppression, violence and political power of Islamic fundamentalists.

For example Sheikh Hamza Yusuf, an American Muslim scholar based in Berkeley, California, has made an impassioned online speech imploring Muslims not to be deceived by the 'stupid young boys' of the Islamic State. His YouTube videos have been watched by millions of users, notably excerpts from his sermon titled 'The Crisis of ISIS', in which he wept as he asked God not to blame other Muslims 'for what these fools amongst us do'.[50]

49 A Borowitz (2015), 'Trump: I Would Attack ISIS on Twitter' *The New Yorker* (11 August 2015) http://www.newyorker.com/humor/borowitz-report/trump-i-would-attack-isis-on-twitter.

50 'The Crisis of ISIS: A Prophetic Prediction' Sermon by Hamza Yusuf. Accessible via: <https://www.youtube.com/watch?v=hJo4B-yaxfk>)

Leader of the Council of Ex-Muslims of Britain, Maryam Namazie stated: 'The internet and social media is doing to Islam what the printing press did in the past to Christianity, because it's one way in which masses of people can connect with each other, can hear ideas that are taboo and forbidden.'[51] As seen from the rest of this chapter, there are numerous examples of Muslims rejecting terrorism, negative labelling, radical groups and violence of whatever means, the point is simply this, social media represents a powerful peer to peer network and the role of the wider community is an issue that cannot be ignored.

5.3 Cyber war

5.3.1 War games

In the classic 1980s film, *War Games*, baby-faced hacker David Lightman unwittingly accesses WOPR (War Operation Plan Response), a United States military super-computer programmed to predict possible outcomes of nuclear war. Lightman gets WOPR to run a nuclear war simulation, thinking it is a computer game. The simulation causes a national nuclear missile scare and nearly starts a world war. Today, we have a network of anonymous hackers, conjuring up images of Lisbet Salander in Steig Larsonn's *The Girl with the Dragon Tattoo* wearing Guy Fawkes masks like those used in *V for Vendetta*, trying to gain the upper hand against ISIS in an online war. It has all the makings to be the inspiration for a Rage Against the Machine song, with its political grass roots separatist origins.

5.3.2 Anonymous

Just a few days after the terrorist attacks in Paris, Anonymous announced #OpParis: '[t]his is only the beginning, ISIS. We will hunt you, take down your sites, accounts, emails and expose you . . . You will be treated like a virus and we are the cure', as stated by a masked crusader in a video posted on YouTube. 'We are Anonymous. We are legion. We do not forgive. We do not forget. ISIS, it is too late to expect us' and 'Anonymous from all over the world will hunt you down. You should know that we will find you and we will not let you go. We will launch the biggest operation ever against you. Expect massive cyber-attacks. War is declared. Get prepared. The French people are stronger than you and will come out of this atrocity even stronger'.

It has been argued that #OpISIS (which followed #Charlie Hebdo) was more effective than #OpParis because it had been around longer and was masterminded by a smaller team of people, rather than a vast amount of individuals scrawled across a decentralised organisation that has no externally announced chain of command. Anonymous has, however, claimed that it has foiled an attack in Italy, announcing through its Operation Paris Twitter account on Christmas

51 Exposure Documentary produced for ITV (original transmission 13 October 2016).

Day 2015: '@OpParisOfficial: In this month we are working in silence. We have already foiled 1 attack #ISIS against #Italy, we hope to block others'.[52]

As a result of the Orlando shootings, a hacker by the name of WauchulaGhost hacked an ISIS account going under the Twitter handle @gi_h_a_d35, changing the profile picture to a gay flag, accompanied by the following message: 'Hello World. It's time I share with you a little secret . . . I'm Gay and I'm Proud!! #GayPride #OrlandoWillNotBeForgotten !!! #GhostOfNoNation'.

WauchulaGhost has also been tweeting out IP addresses, phone numbers and other contact information for other hackers to get busy with. WauchulaGhost published a statement regarding the motivation for his actions:

> I did it for the lives lost in Orlando. Daesh [ISIS] have been spreading and praising the attack, so I thought I would defend those that were lost. The taking of innocent lives will not be tolerated. Our actions are directed at Jihadist extremists. Many of our own [group of hackers] are Muslim and we respect all religions that do not take innocent lives.[53]

As well as blocking accounts, Anonymous has also launched cyber-attacks on Turkey, accusing the country's leaders of supporting ISIS. In one operation, Anonymous claimed to have brought down 40,000 websites across Turkey by attacking the country's 'root servers' and threatened to sabotage servers of Turkey's airports, banks, military services and government facilities if they failed to stop aiding ISIS.

Just as there is no one agreed definition of terrorism, hacking means a variety of different things to different people. Although termed 'hacking', common techniques engaged in by online activists include distributed denial of service (DDOS) attacks, which involve tens of thousands of linked computers, termed 'botnets', designed to swap ISIS websites, causing them a tech headache or even burning out their overloaded servers. Posing as a recruit is also popular, often termed 'Doxxing', to gain confidence and then data on recruiters, which leads them to their location. This information can then be passed on to the authorities. Doxxing has resulted in the Ghost Security hactivists helping successfully to avert a terror attack in Tunisia. Sabotage has also been a fruitful avenue of hactivism; for example, the Ghost Security Group (an Anonymous affiliated group) has plunged into the dark web to find ISIS recruitment hubs and donation pages, replacing them with ads for Prozac and Viagra.[54]

The issue is that, as we have seen through this volume, ISIS has tech savvy recruits too, which means that the result is a truly modern battle, with two sides

52 Posted 7:38 am 25 December.

53 R Lee (2016), 'Anonymous hacks ISIS's Twitter, makes it as fabulously gay as humanly possible' *Techly.com* (16 June) http://www.techly.com.au/2016/06/16/anonymous-hacks-isis-twitter-makes-it-as-fabulously-gay-as-humanly-possible/.

54 M Stainer (2015), 'Ghost Sec, Anonymous affiliate, hacks ISIS site on deep web with Viagra, Prozac ad' *The Washington Times* (26 November).

going to war who have been raised on social media and the internet. The accuracy of the vigilante-gathered data that underpins the activities of such groups is questionable, not having the same scrutiny applied as official sources, such as robustly-tested FBI-gathered intelligence for instance, which may mean mixed results. The methods and modes of dissemination of data have changed, fuelled by the availability of new vehicles in which to drive forth terrorism.

6 National security and the 'fourth estate' in a brave new social media world

*Peter Coe**

For those working within security services, or operating as part of the media, whether that be as traditional journalist or broadcaster, or a blogger utilising social media, the myriad of laws and jurisprudence relating to how issues of national security, or terrorist activity, can be reported and disseminated means that navigating this area is both complex and challenging. This chapter aims to provide a road map to help to overcome some of these obstacles. It begins by considering the democratic function of the media, by virtue of its role as the 'fourth estate'. In doing so, it takes a multi-jurisdictional perspective, through recourse to a variety of international laws and jurisprudence. This acts as the foundation for the following sections, which provide analysis of the domestic and international legal principles and framework that the media are subject to, and operate within, when reporting on terrorist activity. Finally, the chapter considers how the print and broadcast media has reported terrorist activity in the past, and some of the problems that this has created. It concludes by analysing the changing media landscape, including the reasons for the demise of the traditional 'fourth estate', and the emergence, and ascendance, of citizen journalism, and an internet-based 'fifth estate'.

6.1 The media landscape: a multi-jurisdiction perspective on the purpose of the media as the 'fourth estate'

The jurisprudence of the European Court of Human Rights (ECtHR) interprets Article 10(1) of the European Convention on Human Rights (ECHR) to provide extended protection of the media, even in the absence of express provisions to that effect.[1] Thus, individuals and entities operating as part of the media enjoy a

* Senior Lecturer in Law, Aston University; Barrister, East Anglian Chambers.

[1] For example, see *Vejdeland and Others v Sweden* [2012] ECHR 242 [12]; *Jersild v Denmark* (1995) 19 EHRR 1 [31]; *Bladet Tromso and Stensaas v Norway* (2000) 29 EHRR 125 [63]; *Bergens Tidande v Norway* (2001) 31 EHRR 16 [57]; *Thorgeir Thorgeirson v Iceland* (1992) 14 EHRR 843 [67]; *Oberschlick v Austria (No 2)* (1998) 25 EHRR 357 [33]; *Prager and Oberschlick v Austria* (1995) 21 EHRR 1 [38]; *Thoma v Luxembourg* (2003) 36 EHRR 21 [45]–[46]; R. Clayton QC and H. Tomlinson QC, *Privacy and Freedom of Expression* (2nd edn, Oxford University Press, 2010) 271 [15.254].

DOI: 10.4324/9781315668680-6

privileged position within the civil liberties matrix, as they are beneficiaries of the right to media freedom.[2] This right provides protection for 'media communication' over and above that afforded to non-media, pursuant to the right to freedom of expression.[3] So, why does 'media' occupy this special position?

The contribution of the media to democracy is well documented. It has been observed, both within the UK and internationally, that as well as being a 'public educator',[4] as the 'fourth estate',[5] the primary function of the media is to act as a 'public watchdog',[6] in that it operates as the general public's 'eyes and ears' by investigating and reporting abuses of power.[7] The media's role within democratic society manifests in its dissemination of information and ideas, and its facilitation of political debate and discourse on general issues of public interest,[8] including terrorist activity, and in enabling the public's right to receive this information.[9]

This is reflected in the work of Blasi, who is a leading proponent of the movement that posits the media as a 'checking function'.[10] Blasi regards the media

2 The special position of the media in relation to the freedom of expression has been recognised by commentators such S.J. Bezanson and S.R. West. See P. Stewart, 'Or of the Press' (1975) 26 *Hastings Law Journal* 705, 707; R. P. Bezanson, 'The New Free Press Guarantee' (1977) 63 *Virginia Law Review* 731, 733; S. R. West, 'Awakening the Press Clause' (2011) 58 *UCLA Law Review* 1025, 1032.

3 For further discussion on a distinct right to media freedom, see P. Coe, 'Redefining "media" using a "media-as-a-constitutional-component" concept: An evaluation of the need for the European Court of Human Rights to alter its understanding of "media" within a new media landscape', *Legal Studies*; (2016) DOI: 10.1111/lest.12133 E. Barendt, *Freedom of Speech* (2nd edn, Oxford University Press, 2005) ch. 12.

4 In the UK see *McCartan Turkington Breen (A Firm) v Times Newspapers Ltd* [2001] 2 AC 277 [19]; for ECtHR jurisprudence, see *Bergens Tidande v Norway* (2001) 31 EHRR 16 [49]; for the US, see *Mills v Alabama* (1966) 384 US 214, 219; *Cox Broadcasting v Cohn* (1975) 420 US 469, 492. See generally A. Lewis, 'Journalists and the First Amendment' in D. Kingsford-Smith and D. Oliver (eds), *Economical with the Truth: The Law and the Media in a Democratic Society* (ECS Publishing Ltd, 1990) 1–7; D. Milo, *Defamation and Freedom of Speech* (Oxford University Press, 2008) 83.

5 P. Stewart, 'Or of the Press' (1975) 26 *Hastings Law Journal* 705, 708.

6 *The Observer and The Guardian v United Kingdom* (1991) 14 EHRR 153 [59]; *Goodwin v United Kingdom* (1996) 22 EHRR 123, [39]; *Thorgeirson v Iceland* (1992) 14 EHRR 843 [63]; *Bladet Tromso and Stensaas v Norway* (2000) 29 EHRR 125 [62]; *Bergens Tidende v Norway* (2001) 31 EHRR 16 [49].

7 *A-G v Guardian Newspapers Ltd (No 2)* [1990] 1 AC 109, 183 (Sir John Donaldson MR); see also Barendt above n 3, 418.

8 *Lingens v Austria* (1986) 8 EHRR 103 [26]; *Oberschlick v Austria (No 1)* (1991) 19 EHRR 389 [58]; *Castells v Spain* (1992) 14 EHRR 445 [43]; *Thorgeir Thorgeirson v Iceland* (1992) 14 EHRR 843; *Jersild v Denmark* (1995) 19 EHRR 1 [31]; *United Communist Party of Turkey and Others v Turkey* [1998] App. no. 133/1996/752/951 [44].

9 Article 10 ECHR includes the right to receive as well as impart information. In *London Regional Transport v Mayor of London* [2001] EWCA Civ 1491 [55], Sedley LJ described the right to receive information as 'the lifeblood of democracy'. See also *Sunday Times v United Kingdom* (1979) 2 EHRR 245 [65]; *Fressoz and Roire v France* (2001) 31 EHRR 2 [51]; *Bergens Tidande v Norway* (2001) 31 EHRR 16 [52].

10 V. A. Blasi, 'The Checking Value in First Amendment Theory' (1977) *American Bar Foundation Research Journal*, 521; V. A. Blasi, 'Journalistic Autonomy as a First Amendment Concept' in R. H. Keller, Jr (ed), *In Honour of Justice Douglas: A Symposium on Individual Freedom and Government* (Greenwood Press, 1979) 55, 68.

as a protected participant in the system of checks and balances inherent in democratic governments.[11] Consequently, investigative journalism, that is, 'finding out what is really going on in society',[12] is critical to the operation of democracy.[13] Thus, in *Reynolds v Times Newspapers Ltd*,[14] Lord Nicholls stated that a modern function of the media is investigative journalism: '[t]his activity, as much as the traditional activities of reporting and commenting, is part of the vital role of the press and the media generally'.[15] More recently, Leveson LJ in his *Inquiry into the Culture, Practices and Ethics of the Press* (*Inquiry*),[16] recognised that, in recent years, the media, and in particular the press, has played a critical role in informing the public on matters of public interest and concern.[17] This democratic function, and the extended privileges afforded to the media, has been endorsed within a number of different jurisdictions and arenas. For instance, the ECtHR has attached great importance to the role of the media,[18] and has been particularly vocal in championing media freedom, within limits, to ensure that the media can fulfil this vital purpose:

> Although the press[19] must not overstep certain bounds, in particular in respect of the reputation and rights of others, its duty is nevertheless to impart – in a manner consistent with its obligations and responsibilities – information and ideas on all matters of public interest. Not only does the press have the task of imparting such information and ideas; the public also has a right to receive them. Were it otherwise, the press would be unable to play its vital role of 'public watchdog'.[20]

Consequently, according to the Strasbourg Court, the media 'affords the public one of the best means of discovering and forming an opinion of the ideas and

11 Blasi, 'Journalistic Autonomy', ibid 69; See also R. Hargreaves, *The First Freedom: A History of Free Speech* (Sutton Publishing, 2002) 305.

12 A. Belsey, 'Journalism and Ethics: Can they Co-exist?' in M. Kieran, *Media Ethics* (Routledge, 1998) 1, 5.

13 Milo above, n 4, 82.

14 Ibid (n14) 200.

15 Ibid 200.

16 Lord Justice Leveson, *An Inquiry into the Culture, Practices and Ethics of the Press* (November 2012).

17 Ibid (n16) 455–70.

18 For example, see *Bladet Tromso and Stensaas v Norway* (2000) 29 EHRR 125 [59]; *Bergens Tidande v Norway* (2001) 31 EHRR 16 [48]; *Busuioc v Moldova* (2006) 42 EHRR 14 [64]–[65]; *Jersild v Denmark* (1995) 19 EHRR 1; *Janowski v Poland (No 1)* (2000) 29 EHRR 705 [32].

19 The jurisprudence of the ECtHR has determined that the protection afforded to the press extends to audiovisual media: *Jersild v Denmark* [1994] App. no. 15890/89 [31]; *Radio France and others v France* [2004] App. no. 53984/00 [33].

20 *Axel Springer AG v Germany (No 1)* [2012] App. no. 39954/08 [79]; *Von Hannover v Germany (No 2)* [2012] App. nos. 40660/08 and 60641/08 [102]. See further *Sunday Times v United Kingdom (No 1)* [1979] App. no. 6538/74 [65]; *Bladet Tromso and Stensaas v Norway* [1999] App. no. 21980/93 [62]; *Times Newspapers Ltd v United Kingdom (Nos 1 and 2)* [2009] App. nos. 3002/03 and 23676/03 [40].

attitudes of political leaders. It is incumbent on the press to impart information and ideas on political issues and on other subjects of public interest'.[21]

In the context of the International Covenant on Civil and Political Rights (ICCPR), the Human Rights Committee (HRC) has also recognised the media's importance to the operation of democracy. For instance, in *Bodrožić v Serbia and Montenegro* the Committee stated that 'in circumstances of public debate in a democratic society, especially in the media, concerning figures in the political domain, the value placed by the Covenant upon uninhibited expression is particularly high'.[22] Further, in *Marques de Morais v Angola*,[23] the Committee endorsed the role of the media in giving effect to Article 25 ICCPR, which provides for the right to take part in the conduct of public affairs.[24] Although not relating to the ICCPR, this endorsement by the Committee of the public affairs function of the media assimilates closely with Lord Bingham's judgement in the House of Lords case of *McCartan Turkington Breen (A Firm) v Times Newspapers Ltd*,[25] in which he stated:

> But the majority cannot participate in the public life of their society in these ways if they are not alerted to and informed about matters which call or may call for consideration and action. It is very largely through the media, including of course the press, that they will be so alerted and informed. The proper functioning of a modern participatory democracy requires that the media be free, active, professional and inquiring.[26]

Further afield, the Inter-American Court of Human Rights (IACtHR) has stated that the media plays a critical role in exercising the 'social dimension' of freedom of expression in a democracy.[27] According to the Court, journalists 'keep society informed' and play an 'indispensable' role in enabling 'society to enjoy full freedom'.[28] Consequently, journalism 'is one of the most important manifestations of freedom of expression and information'.[29] In the South African case of *Khumalo v Holomisa*,[30] the Constitutional Court held that in a democracy, members of

21 *Centro Europa 7 Srl and Di Stefano v Italy* [2012] App. no. 38433/09 [131]; *Lingens v Austria* [1986] App. no. 9815/82; *Sürek v Turkey (No 1)* [1999] App. no. 26682/95 [59]; *Thoma v Luxembourg* [2001] App. no. 38432/97 [45].

22 HRC, *Bodrožić v Serbia and Montenegro* [2005] Communications no. 1180/2003 [7.2].

23 [2005] Communication no. 1128/2002 [6.8].

24 See also General Comment no 25, [25].

25 [2001] 2 AC 277.

26 Ibid (n25) 19.

27 *Fontevecchia and D'Amico v Argentina* [2011] Case 12.524 [44]; *Ivcher-Bronstein v Peru* [2001] Case 11.762 [149]; *Herrera-Ulloa v Costa Rica* [2004] Case 12.367 [117].

28 *Ivcher-Bronstein v Peru* [2001] Case 11.762 [150]; *Herrera-Ulloa v Costa Rica* [2004] Case 12.367 [119].

29 IACtHR, Advisory Opinion OC-5/85 [71]; IAComHR, *Hugo Bustios Saavedra v Peru* [1997] Case 10.548 [71]; Office of the Special Rapporteur for Freedom of Expression with the Inter-American Commission on Human Rights, Inter-American Legal Framework Regarding the Right to Freedom of Expression 2009, CIDH/RELE/INF. 2/09, para. 165.

30 (2002) (5) SA 401 (CC).

the media 'are important agents in ensuring that government is open, responsive and accountable to the people'.[31] The media is also obliged to provide citizens with information and with 'a platform for the exchange of ideas which is crucial to the development of a democratic culture'.[32] In the US, Black J, in the Supreme Court case of *Mills v Alabama*,[33] stated that: 'the press serves and was designed to serve as a powerful antidote to any abuses of power by government officials and as a constitutionally chosen means for keeping officials elected by the people responsible to all the people whom they were selected to serve'.[34]

Media freedom, freedom of expression and democracy are inextricably and intrinsically linked with each other, as the media is an important democratic cog within society. However, as will be discussed later in this chapter, in recent years, there has, arguably, been a 'shift' in the focus of the traditional media that is, the press and broadcasting industry. Consequently, citizen journalism, through social media, has taken on some of the 'democratic responsibilities' previously associated with the 'fourth estate', including the reporting of terrorist activity. Before this is considered, the following section will look at how the media's role as the 'fourth estate' interacts with the legal framework relating to the reporting of terrorist activity.

6.2 Reporting on terrorism: legal principles and framework

The principles of freedom of expression and media freedom afford wide-ranging protection to both individuals and the media. It will come as no surprise that both protect the dissemination of information and ideas that are inoffensive or 'popular'. However, the ambit of these principles goes much further as, according to the ECtHR, they also provide protection for expression that may 'offend, shock or disturb the state or any sector of the population'.[35] Media freedom is, therefore, founded on the notion that liberal discussion on matters of public interest and concern is more conducive to the operation of democracy than the suppression of expression that may be offensive, shocking, disturbing or unpopular.[36] However, despite the protection that media freedom can provide, the media is still obliged to exercise its democratic function within a complex legal framework relating to the reporting of public order interests, including terrorist activity. Thus, very often, a balance has to be struck between what can be conflicting interests.

31 Ibid (n30) 23.
32 Ibid (n30) 24.
33 (1966) 384 US 214.
34 Ibid (n33) 219. See also *Cox Broadcasting v Cohn* (1975) 420 US 469, 492.
35 *Handyside v United Kingdom* (1976) 1 EHRR 737, [49]. See also *Éditions Plon v France* App. no. 58184/00 ECHR 2004-IV [42]–[43].
36 J. Oster, *Media Freedom as a Fundamental Right* (Cambridge University Press, 2015) 193.

6.2.1 The role of the state in protecting 'public order'

In *Sürek v Turkey (Nos 2 and 3)* and *Incal v Turkey*[37] the ECtHR stated that, because the government is in a dominant position when it comes to public discourse, it has to refrain from interfering with media freedom through governmental channels of communication.[38] Despite this, the Court made it clear in both *Sürek* cases, and in *Incal*, that in order for 'competent' government authorities effectively to exercise their function as guarantors of public order, they must be able to adopt measures which allow them appropriately, and without excess, to deal with remarks, which themselves threaten public order, by exceeding the boundaries of civilised discourse,[39] regardless of whether those remarks emanate from the media or non-media. The jurisprudence from Strasbourg reflects the qualifications imposed by Article 10(2) ECHR on the Article 10(1) right to freedom of expression. Pursuant to Article 10(2), freedom of expression (and media freedom) can be legitimately interfered with 'in the interests of national security, territorial integrity or public safety' and for the 'prevention of disorder or crime'. Consequently, the ECtHR has consistently restated that the media must not exceed the boundaries set, inter alia, 'for the protection of vital interests of the State, such as the protection of national security or territorial integrity against the threat of violence or the prevention of disorder or crime'.[40]

This position is mirrored by other international laws. For instance, Articles 19(3)(b) and 13(2)(b) of the International Covenant on Civil and Political Rights (ICCPR) and the American Convention on Human Rights (ACHR) respectively, allow freedom of expression to be restricted to protect national security or public order. Similarly, the HRC and the African Commission on Human and Peoples' Rights (AfComHPR) have stated that freedom of expression can be legitimately restricted to safeguard and strengthen national unity under challenging political circumstances,[41] and Article 27(2) of the African Charter on Human Rights states that each individual's rights and freedoms shall be exercised 'with due regard to collective security . . . and common interest'.[42]

37 *(No 2)* [1999] App. no. 24122/94; *(No 3)* [1999] App. no. 24735/94; *Incal* [1998] App. no. 41/1997/825/1031.

38 Ibid (n37) *(No 2)* [34]; *(No 3)* [37]; *Incal* [54].

39 Ibid (n38).

40 *Sürek v Turkey (No 1)* [1999] App. no. 26682/95 [59]; *Şener v Turkey* [2000] App. no. 26680/95 [41]; *Özgür Gündem v Turkey* [2000] App. no. 23144/93 [58].

41 HRC: *Mukong v Cameroon* [1994] Communication no. 458/91 [9.7]; AfComHPR: *Article 19 v Eritrea* [2007] App. no. 275/03 [108].

42 As observed by Oster, although 'public order' is not expressly referred to within Article 27(2), it is included in the term 'common interest': Oster above n 36, 193. Oster compares African Commission on Human and Peoples' Rights, *Media Rights Agenda, Constitutional Rights Project, Media Rights Agenda and Constitutional Rights Project v Nigeria* [1998] App. nos. 105/93, 128/94, 130/94 and 152/96 [73]; *Constitutional Rights Project, Civil Liberties and Media Rights Agenda v Nigeria* [1999] App. nos. 140/94, 141/94 and 145/95 [43]; *Scanlen & Holderness v Zimbabwe* [2009] App. no. 297/05 [109].

So, what does 'public order' mean, and does it cover, for instance, the dissemination or reporting of terrorist speech? According to scholars such as Grote and Wenzel, the notion of 'public order' includes the preservation of fundamental interests required by the state to guarantee public safety and to protect the interests of society generally.[43] Similarly, the IACtHR has interpreted public order to mean 'the conditions that assure the normal and harmonious functioning of [democratic] institutions based on a coherent system of values and principles'.[44] The ECtHR has recognised that the concept of 'order' includes, inter alia, order in the public sphere, such as on public streets and in public places.[45] According to the jurisprudence of the Court, the 'prevention of crime' justification, pursuant to Article 10(2) is, in essence, inherent within public order,[46] which includes the prevention of specific criminal offences, the deterrence and control of crime generally, as well as the investigation of crimes that have, allegedly, already been committed.[47] Therefore, public order encompasses expression related to terrorist activity.

There is an inextricable link between freedom of expression, media freedom, public order and democracy. As a result, public order does not only legitimise interference with freedom of expression.[48] The concept, equally, 'requires the broadest possible circulation of information, opinions, news and ideas – that is the maximum degree of exercise of freedom of expression'.[49] Thus, pursuant to a multitude of international laws, such as those discussed above, if a democratic state is concerned that public order could be threatened by discourse or the communication of information or ideas relating to, for instance, terrorism, the dissemination of that expression can be restricted. However, any such restriction of freedom of expression and media freedom, justified on the grounds of public order concerns, must be interpreted to conform strictly to the demands of a democratic society[50] and, consequently, must 'be based on real and objectively verifiable causes that present the certain and credible threat of a potentially serious disturbance of the basic conditions for the functioning of democratic institutions'.[51] Accordingly,

43 R. Grote and N. Wenzel, 'Meinungsfreiheit' in T. Marauhn and R. Grote (eds), *EMRK/GG Konkordanzkommentar zum europäischen und deutschen Grundrechtsschutz* (2nd edn, Mohr Siebeck, 2013) [85]; Oster above, n 36, 194.

44 IACtHR, Advisory Opinion OC-5/85 [64].

45 *Chorherr v Austria* [1993] App. no. 13308/87 [28].

46 Oster above, n 36, 196.

47 *Orban and others v France* [2009] App. no. 20985/05 [42].

48 Oster above, n 36, 194-5.

49 Office of the Special Rapporteur for Freedom of Expression with the Inter-American Commission on Human Rights, Inter-American Legal Framework Regarding the Right to Freedom of Expression 2009, CIDH/RELE/INF. 2/09 [81]; IACtHR, Advisory Opinion OC-5/85 [69]; AfComHPR, *Scanlen & Holderness v Zimbabwe* [2009] App. no. 297/05 [109].

50 Office of the Special Rapporteur for Freedom of Expression with the Inter-American Commission on Human Rights, Inter-American Legal Framework Regarding the Right to Freedom of Expression 2009, CIDH/RELE/INF. 2/09 [80].

51 Ibid (n50) 82.

'[m]ere conjecture regarding possible disturbances of public order, nor hypothetical circumstances . . . that do not clearly present a reasonable threat of serious disturbances' are insufficient to warrant interference with media freedom.[52]

6.2.2 The international legal framework

The public order and inherent prevention of disorder or crime rationales, which can provide legitimate justification for the interference with the rights to freedom of expression and media freedom, have become particularly important in relation to the restriction of publications, as well as orders to reveal journalistic sources for, inter alia, reasons pertaining to the fight against terrorism.[53] By virtue of its status as a Member State of, for instance, the UN Security Council, Council of Europe and the European Union (this is, of course, subject to Article 50 of the Lisbon Treaty being triggered and the formal process of leaving the EU commencing), there are a number of international legal instruments that apply to the UK and its citizens in respect to terrorism, and the reporting of terrorist activity. However, the application of these laws are subject to certain overarching principles pertaining to the operation of a democratic state, including the rights to freedom of expression and media freedom, that require a balance to be struck. The ECtHR and HRC have recognised that, on the one hand, the media has a right and duty, as the 'fourth estate', to 'convey information and ideas on political issues, even divisive ones'[54] and both inform the public on measures prescribed by the state to maintain public order, and prevent crime, including terrorism, and form public opinion on such activities. On the other hand, democracies have a right to defend themselves against abuses directed at the very democratic values that underpin them.[55]

Consequently, the jurisprudence of both the HRC and the ECtHR has affirmed that a broad margin of appreciation should be afforded to Member State authorities[56] 'to adopt, in their capacity as guarantors of public order, measures, even of a criminal-law nature, intended to react appropriately and without excess to [remarks that] incite to violence against an individual or a public official or a sector of the population'.[57] Therefore, a rather delicate 'balance' has to be struck by state authorities to determine whether proposed measures to protect, for example, national security against threats of terrorism, are suitable. To do this, the authorities embark upon careful analysis of the respective situation, and attempt to predict how it may develop. As a result, there is always a high degree of factual uncertainty with this exercise.

52 Ibid (n50).

53 Oster above, n 36, 196

54 ECtHR: *Özgür Gündem v Turkey* [2000] App. no. 23144/93 [58]; *Şener v Turkey* [2000] App. no. 26680/95 [41]; HRC, General Comment no. 34 [46].

55 Oster above, n 36, 198.

56 Ibid (n55).

57 ECtHR: *Sürek v Turkey (No 1)* [1999] App. no. 26682/95 [61]; *Şener v Turkey* [2000] App. no. 26680/95 [40]; *Erdoğdu v Turkey* [2000] App. no. 25723/94 [62]; HRC: *A.K. and A.R. v Uzbekistan* [2009] Communication no. 1233/2003 [7.2].

In applying the margin of appreciation, the courts will decide whether the aims of the state's authorities justify any potential interference with countervailing civil liberties, and that they do not disproportionately impact upon other fundamental democratic rights, such as freedom of expression and media freedom.[58] Indeed, according to the ECtHR in *Klass and Others v Germany*,[59] states are not permitted to adopt whatever measures they see fit, even to deal with terrorism: states may not undermine, or even destroy democracy, on the premise of defending it.[60]

This 'balancing act', and the HRC and Strasbourg Court's jurisprudence, is reflected by other international laws. According to its preamble, UN Security Council Resolution 1624 (2005) condemns 'in the strongest terms the incitement of terrorist acts and [repudiates] attempts at the justification or glorification *(apologie)* of terrorist acts that may incite further terrorist acts'. Article 1(a) of the Resolution '[c]alls upon all States to adopt such measures as may be necessary and appropriate and in accordance with their obligations under international law to prohibit by law incitement to commit a terrorist act or acts'.[61] However, the Resolution also refers to the right to freedom of expression, pursuant to Article 19 of the Universal Declaration of Human Rights and Article 19 ICCPR, and 'that any restrictions thereon shall only be such as are provided by law and are necessary on the grounds set out in [Article 19(3) ICCPR].

Other international instruments, including the Council of Europe Convention on the Prevention of Terrorism (CECPT) and the EU Framework Decision (EUFD) on Combating Terrorism,[62] mirror the Resolution. Article 5(2) of the Convention requires Member States to prosecute, as a criminal offence, 'public provocation to commit a terrorist offence'. Pursuant to Article 5(1), this entails 'the distribution, or otherwise making available, of a message to the public, with the intent to incite the commission of a terrorist offence, where such conduct, whether or not directly advocating terrorist offences, causes a danger that one or more such offence may be committed'. Similarly, Article 4(1) EUFD states that Member States must implement the necessary measures to ensure that inciting or aiding or abetting terrorist offences proscribed under Articles 2 and 3 are made punishable. In the same vein as Article 1(a) of Resolution 1624, Article 4(1) is also qualified by the EUFD itself. Recital 10 of the EUFD states that nothing in the Framework Decision may be interpreted as being intended to reduce or restrict fundamental rights or freedoms, including freedom of expression. Further,

58 Oster above, n 36, 198–99.

59 [1978] App. no. 5029/71.

60 Ibid (n59) 49.

61 Resolution 1624 (2005), adopted by the Security Council at its 5261st meeting, on 14 September 2005, S/RES/1624 (2005). Oster argues that, pursuant to the Resolution's preamble, Article 1 does not, therefore, require States to adopt measures to prohibit justification or glorification or terrorist acts: Oster above, n 36, 196.

62 Council Framework Decision 2002/475/JHA of 13 June 2002 on Combating Terrorism, OJ 2002, L164/3, amended by Council Framework Decision 2008/919/JHA of 28 November 2008 amending Framework Decision 2002/475/JHA on Combating Terrorism, OJ 2002, L330/21.

Article 2 of Recital 14 of the Framework Decision, amending the EUFD,[63] states that it:

> . . . shall not have the effect of requiring Member States to take measures in contradiction of fundamental principles relating to freedom of expression, in particular freedom of the press and the freedom of expression in other media as they result from constitutional traditions or rules governing the rights and responsibilities of, and the procedural guarantees for, the press or other media where these rules relate to the determination of limitation of liability.

Despite this apparent appetite to strike a balance between the adoption of measures to protect state security and the need to ensure that the right to freedom of expression and media freedom are not disproportionately interfered with, in both *Purcell and Others v Ireland*[64] and *Brind and Others v United Kingdom*[65] the European Commission of Human Rights (EComHR), allowed restrictions to be imposed on certain media organisations, in relation to their dissemination of speech associated with terrorist activity in Northern Ireland. In *Purcell* journalists and producers of radio and television programmes, employed by Radio Telfis Eireann, were instructed, pursuant to a ministerial order issued under section 31 of the Broadcasting Act 1961, to refrain from broadcasting any interview, or report of an interview, with spokesmen for the IRA or Sinn Fèin. The EComHR found that such restrictions might cause the applicants (who also included broadcasting trade unions) 'inconvenience in the exercise of their professional duties'.[66] However, despite this, it did not find that Article 10(1) was disproportionately interfered with, as live statements could 'involve a special risk of coded messages being conveyed, a risk which even conscientious journalists cannot control within the exercise of the professional judgment'.[67]

Brind also involved applicants employed as journalists and producers of radio and television programmes, as well as editors and presenters. It related to a request made by the British Home Department for the BBC and Independent Broadcasting Authority to broadcast a statement made by a representative of terrorist organisations, including Sinn Fèin, Republican Sinn Fèin and the Ulster Defence Association, only with a voice-over account spoken by an actor. The government's reason for this was to limit the impact and influence any such statements would have on the supporters of terrorist organisations in the UK. The Commission held that there was no violation of Article 10(1) as the 'limited extent of the

63 Council Framework Decision 2008/919/JHA of 28 November 2008 amending Framework Decision 2002/475/JHA on Combating Terrorism, OJ 2008, L330/21.

64 [1991] App. no. 15404/89.

65 [1994] App. no. 18714/91.

66 Ibid (n64) 17.

67 Ibid (n66).

interference' with the applicants' rights was not, in this instance, disproportionate to the measures imposed to deal effectively with the threat of terrorist activity.

It is perfectly reasonable to expect that states do not want to provide a 'soap box' for the dissemination of terrorist ideology or coded messages. However, this has to be balanced with the media's right to inform the public as to potential threats to public order, and the public's right to be informed, to enable decisions to be made on how to react.[68] Oster argues that 'a sweeping concession to the Convention States as in *Brind* constitutes a severe obstacle to public discourse on a matter of paramount importance to society'. Instead, he advocates, that rather than such a severe 'paternalistic' approach, a case-by-case analysis should be adopted.[69] This correlates closely with the jurisprudence of the ECtHR, which has suggested that such analysis would be based on whether the words used and the context within which they were written could incite criminal (including terrorist) activity or include coded messages.[70]

Oster goes on to state that, if such an approach were to be adopted, 'a publisher cannot be exonerated from any liability for the content of the third-party statements'.[71] This is because the Strasbourg Court has determined that a publisher is subject to the 'duties and responsibilities' of journalists in how they accumulate, and then communicate, information to the public. Accordingly, these 'duties and responsibilities' become even more significant during times of conflict and tension.[72] Consequently, it was held by the ECtHR in *Özgür Gündem v Turkey*[73] that 'the fact that interviews or statements were given by a member of a proscribed organization cannot in itself justify an interference with the newspaper's freedom of expression. Nor can the fact that the interviews or statements contain views strongly disparaging of government policy'.[74]

Because of its position as the fourth rstate, and the special duties and responsibilities this bestows upon the media, those operating as part of the media are under an obligation not to advocate the use of violence, glorify war, or intend to stigmatise one side of the conflict.[75] In relation to situations where it is alleged the media has actually 'advocated' terrorist activity, according to the HRC,

68 Oster above, n 36, 200.

69 Ibid.

70 *Sürek v Turkey (No 1)* [1999] App. no. 26682/95 [63]; *Şener v Turkey* [2000] App. no. 26680/95 [44 ff]; *Özgür Gündem v Turkey* [2000] App. no. 23144/93 [63], [65]; *Sürek and Özdemir v Turkey* [1999] App. nos. 23927/94 and 24277/94 [61].

71 Oster above, n 36, 200.

72 *Sürek v Turkey (No 1)* [1999] App. no. 26682/95 [63]; *Şener v Turkey* [2000] App. no. 26680/95 [42].

73 The case related to dissemination by the newspaper, Özgür Gündem, of statements made by alleged terrorists. In this instance, it concerned declarations of PKK-related organisations and an interview with Abdullah Öcalan, the PKK leader.

74 [2000] App. no. 23144/93 [63].

75 *Sürek v Turkey (No 1)* [1999] App. no. 26682/95 [62]; *Sürek v Turkey (No 3)* [1999] App. no. 24735/94 [40]; *Özgür Gündem v Turkey* [2000] App. no. 23144/93 [70]; *Balsytė-Lideikienė v Lithuania* [2008] App. no. 72596/01 [79].

offences such as 'encouragement of terrorism',[76] 'extremist activity'[77] and 'praising', 'glorifying' or 'justifying' terrorism, should be unequivocally defined to ensure that they do not unnecessarily and disproportionately interfere with freedom of expression and media freedom, but rather they fully accord with the requirement of being 'proscribed by law'.[78] The HRC has also made it clear that states must be able to specify exactly the details of the threat posed for national security if the publisher were to exercise its right to media freedom.[79] Thus, the Committee has held that 'to muzzle advocacy of multi-party democracy, democratic tenets and human rights' may not be justified, even when legitimate objectives of national security or public order are concerned.[80]

6.2.3 A view from the UK part 1: David Miranda, Glenn Greenwald, Edward Snowden and the Terrorism Act 2000

The UK's media are subject to the international laws and incorporated principles set out in the previous section. In addition, the legal matrix within which our domestic media operates includes the Terrorism Act 2000, which has impacted upon both the media's right to protect the confidentiality of its sources, pursuant to media freedom, and the role of the UK's security services.[81] A recent and high profile example of jurisprudence relating to the media's interaction with the 2000 Act is the Court of Appeal's decision in *R (David Miranda) v Secretary of State for the Home Department, Commissioner of Police of the Metropolis v Liberty, Article 19, English Pen and the Media Legal Defence Initiative*.[82] The case concerned consideration of, inter alia, section 1(1) and (2) and paragraph 2(1) of Schedule 7 of the 2000 Act, and Article 10(1) ECHR. Section 1(1) and (2), when read together, define terrorism as: (i) the use or threat of action which (ii) endangers a person's life, other than that of the person committing the action where (iii) the use of threat is designed to influence the government or an international governmental organisation or to intimidate the public or a section of the public and (iv) the use or threat is made for the purpose of advancing a political, religious, racial or ideological cause.[83]

76 HRC, Concluding observations on the United Kingdom of Great Britain and Northern Ireland (CCPR/C/GBR/CO/6) [26].

77 HRC, Concluding observations on the Russian Federation (CCPR/CO/79/RUS) [20].

78 HRC, General Comment no. 34, [46].

79 *Park v Republic of Korea* [1998] Communication no. 628/1995 [10.3]; *Kim v Republic of Korea* [1999] Communication no. 574/1994 [12.4]; *Shin v Republic of Korea* [2004] Communication no. 926/2000 [7.2].

80 *Mukong v Cameroon* [1994] Communication no. 458/91 [9.7]; see also, AfComHPR: *Article 19 v Eritrea* [2007] App. no. 275/03 [108].

81 Note that the Terrorism Act 2006 also contains provisions that may impact upon the media (see, for instance: section 1, which relates to the encouragement of terrorism, and its allied provisions). Although, at the time of writing there have been no cases involving the media in relation to these provisions, they are discussed in more detail later in section 6.2.4.

82 [2016] EWCA Civ 6.

83 Ibid [39] (Lord Dyson MR).

Pursuant to paragraph 2(1) of Schedule 7, a police officer has the power to stop and question a person at a port or border area for the purpose of determining whether they appear to be 'concerned in the commission, preparation or instigation of acts of terrorism'.

The appellant, David Miranda, is the husband of Glenn Greenwald, a journalist who, at the time, was working for the *Guardian* newspaper. In late 2012 Greenwald and another journalist, Laura Poitras, met Edward Snowden. Snowden provided the pair with encrypted data that had been stolen from the US National Security Agency. In addition, the data included UK intelligence material. Some of this material formed the basis of a number of articles published by the *Guardian*. On 12 August 2013, Miranda travelled from Rio de Janeiro to Berlin to meet Poitras. He was carrying encrypted material deriving from data obtained by Snowden, and was tasked with collecting computer drives containing further material to assist Greenwald's journalistic activity.

The UK Security Service was aware of Miranda's movements and, as a result, issued a Port Circulation Sheet informing counter-terrorism police that Miranda was knowingly carrying material, the release of which would endanger lives, and that the disclosure or threat of disclosure was designed to influence a government and was made for the 'purpose of promoting a political or ideological cause'. The police were satisfied that sufficient information had been provided by the Security Service to allow a lawful Schedule 7 stop to take place. Consequently, on 18 August Miranda was stopped by counter-terrorism police officers at Heathrow airport, whilst travelling to Rio de Janeiro, and subsequently questioned by them.[84] It is important to note at this juncture that, at the time of being stopped, Miranda did not identify himself as a journalist (as he is not a journalist), or state that he was carrying 'journalistic material'. Miranda issued judicial review proceedings. That decision of the High Court of the Divisional Court[85] was the subject of the appeal.[86] Miranda submitted that the acts of the police were unlawful for the following reasons: first, the Schedule 7 stop was exercised for a purpose that was not permitted by the 2000 Act; secondly, the use of the power contravened Article 10 ECHR; and, thirdly, in relation to journalistic material, Schedule 7 is incompatible with Article 10.

The Court of Appeal rejected the High Court's literal interpretation of the definition of terrorism, pursuant to section 1(1) and (2). Instead, the court held that Parliament must have intended for the provision to import a mental element to the definition of terrorism. This means that a defendant must intend that, or be reckless as to whether, the material that is published has the effect of endangering life or creating a serious risk to the health or safety of the public, or a section of the

84 Ibid (n82) [6]–[20] (Lord Dyson MR).

85 [2014] EWHC 255 (Admin) (Laws LJ).

86 The leading judgement was given by Lord Dyson MR, with whom Richards LJ and Floyd LJ agreed.

public.[87] Thus, in order for publication of material to amount to terrorism, the publication must satisfy the section 1(1) test, as follows: first, the defendant intended that, or was reckless as to whether, the publication of the material would endanger life or create a serious risk to the health or safety of the public, or a section thereof; secondly, the defendant intends the publication of the material to influence the government or an international governmental organisation or to intimidate the public, or a section thereof; thirdly, publication of the material is for the purpose of advancing, inter alia, a political or ideological cause. In Miranda's case, the court held that the police were entitled to consider that material in his possession might be released in circumstances falling within the definition of terrorism, and this possibility was sufficient to justify the stop and detention.[88] The court noted that Parliament has set this bar at 'quite a low level', but held that the stop and detainment of Miranda was the type of police/security activity that Parliament intended when drafting the Act.[89]

The court further rejected that the use of the Schedule 7 power was, in this instance, an unjustified and disproportionate interference with a journalist's enhanced right to freedom of expression, pursuant to media freedom. This was on the basis that compelling national security interests outweighed Miranda's Article 10(1) rights. Although the court held that the police should have known Miranda's material 'was or might have been journalistic material',[90] there was, according to the court, no reason to disagree with the security services' assessment that the material seized contained information that posed a risk to national security. Indeed, challenging such an assessment would be 'very difficult . . . in a court of law'.[91] Lord Dyson concluded by stating that he 'substantially' agreed with Laws LJ's judgement. In his Lordship's judgement, although the Schedule 7 stop was an interference with media freedom, the compelling national security interests engaged by the potential harm of the material in Miranda's possession 'clearly' outweighed his enhanced journalistic rights under Article 10.[92]

Finally, the court considered whether the Schedule 7 power, if used in respect of journalistic information or material, failed to be 'prescribed by law', pursuant to Article 10(2). *Liberty*, as interveners, argued that five principles could be derived from ECtHR jurisprudence on this point, pursuant to *Sanoma Uitgevers v Netherlands*.[93] The court rehearsed these principles,[94] which are also worthy of consideration here:

> First, the protection of journalistic sources must be attended with legal procedural safeguards commensurate with the importance of the Article 10

87 [2016] EWCA Civ 6 [53]–[55].
88 Ibid [57]–[58].
89 Ibid [58].
90 Ibid [67].
91 Ibid [82].
92 Ibid [83]–[84].
93 [2011] EMLR 4 [88].
94 [2016] EWCA Civ 6 [100].

> principle at stake . . . Secondly, first and foremost among these safeguards is the guarantee of review by a judge or other independent and impartial decision-making body of any requirement that a journalist hand over material concerning a confidential source . . . Thirdly, the judge or other independent and impartial body must be in a position to carry out the exercise of weighing the potential risks and respective interests prior to disclosure. The decision to be taken should be governed by clear criteria . . . Fourthly, the exercise of an independent review that takes place only after the handing over of material capable of revealing such sources would undermine the very essence of the right to confidentiality and cannot therefore constitute a legal procedural safeguard commensurate with the rights protected by Article 10 . . . Fifthly, however, in urgent cases, where it is impracticable for the authorities to provide elaborate reasons, an independent review carried out at the very least prior to the access and use of obtained materials should be sufficient to determine whether any issue of confidentiality arises, and if so, whether the public interest invoked by the investigating authorities outweighs the general public interest in source protection.[95]

Thus, clearly the jurisprudence of the Strasbourg Court requires prior, or at the very least, in an urgent case, immediate *post factum*, judicial oversight of interferences with Article 10 rights in situations where journalists are required to reveal their sources. Without such oversight there are no sufficiently robust safeguards to render the interference with the right 'prescribed' by law. This is not surprising when considering the importance the ECtHR has attributed to the protection of journalistic sources pursuant to media freedom.[96]

In relying on this jurisprudence, the court found that, although Miranda's case did not concern disclosure of a journalist's source, there was 'no reason in principle for drawing a distinction between disclosure of journalistic material *simpliciter* and disclosure of journalistic material which may identify a confidential source'.[97] The court held that it would be impractical to assume an average journalist would be able to obtain an emergency interim injunction following detention under Schedule 7. Further, *post factum* judicial review would not restore the confidentiality of sources or material. In line with *Sanoma*, the court held that the legal safeguards in place to avoid the risk that Schedule 7 could be exercised arbitrarily were inadequate. Consequently, the court determined that Schedule 7 was incompatible with Article 10. The court noted that, while Strasbourg has not developed an 'absolute' rule of judicial scrutiny for such cases, some form of judicial or other independent and impartial scrutiny conducted in such a way as to protect the confidentiality in the material was

95 Ibid, citing *Sanoma Uitgevers v Netherlands* [2011] EMLR 4 [88].

96 See section 2 above. See also *Sanoma Uitgevers v Netherlands* [2011] EMLR 4 [88]–[92]; *Nordisk Film & TV A/A v Denmark* ([2005] App. no. 40485/02 [10].

97 [2016] EWCA Civ 6 [107].

considered the 'natural and obvious safeguard against the unlawful exercise of . . . Schedule 7'.[98]

It remains to be seen what the impact of the decision in *Miranda* will be on the operation of media freedom in circumstances that engage conflicting security interests. Although, the court was clear in its judgement that the decision of how safeguards to protect against the arbitrary use of Schedule 7 would be implemented would be left to Parliament, clearly the decision falls down in favour of free speech and media freedom principles and, in particular, the media's right to protect the confidentiality of their sources. Indeed, the court emphasised the importance of these principles, as follows:

> The central concern is that disclosure of journalistic material (whether or not it involves the identification of a journalist's source) undermines the confidentiality that is inherent in such material and which is necessary to avoid the chilling effect of disclosure and to protect article 10 rights. If journalists and their sources can have no expectation of confidentiality, they may decide against providing information on sensitive matters of public interest. That is why the confidentiality of such information is so important.[99]

Following the decision, the Home Office stated: '[i]n 2015 we changed the code of practice for examining officers to instruct them not to examine journalistic material at all. This goes above and beyond the court's recommendations in this case'.[100]

6.2.4 A view from the UK part 2: The Terrorism Act 2006

As stated previously, the Terrorism Act 2006 also contains provisions that could impact upon the traditional media, as well as citizen journalists operating through social media.[101] For the purposes of media freedom, section 1, which relates to the encouragement of terrorism, and its allied provisions, are particularly pertinent. Although, as yet, there has been no jurisprudence in relation to the media's interaction with these previsions, they are worthy of consideration at this juncture.

Section 1 of the 2006 Act creates an offence of encouragement of acts of terrorism. The offence has been introduced to implement the requirements of Article 5 of the CECPT. As stated above, this requires states to have an offence of 'public provocation to commit a terrorist offence'.[102] The offence is committed if a person publishes, or causes a statement to be published, and either intends the public to be, or is reckless as to whether the public will be, directly or indirectly encouraged

98 Ibid (n97) [114].

99 Ibid (n97) [113].

100 'Airport stop of Snowden reporter's partner David Miranda "lawful"' http://www.bbc.co.uk/news/uk-35343852 (19 January 2016) (accessed 13 May 2016).

101 See (n81).

102 See section 3.B. 6.2.2 of the CECPT.

or otherwise induced by the statement (taken as a whole, including the circumstances and nature of its publication) to commit, prepare or instigate acts of terrorism or CECPT offences. Pursuant to section 1(5), the commission of the offence is not contingent upon the statement actually relating to an act of terrorism. Indeed, the offence can still be committed regardless of whether any body is actually encouraged or induced to commit, prepare or instigate an act of terrorism or CECPT offence.

Section 20 provides a number of definitions relating to the section 1 offence. According to section 20(4), 'publish' includes a person disseminating a statement (which, pursuant to subsection (6), means any type of communication, including without words) in any manner to the public. This includes providers and users of services that can be accessed by the public electronically. Consequently, it captures, for instance, citizen journalism via social media and blogs, as well as traditional print and broadcast media platforms.

Under section 1(3) indirect encouragement of terrorism includes a statement that glorifies the commission or preparation of acts of terrorism or CECPT offences. However, this only applies if members of the public could reasonably be expected to infer that what is being glorified (which, under section 20(2), includes praise or celebration) in the statement is conduct that should be emulated by them in existing circumstances. Section 20(7) clarifies that references to conduct that should be emulated in existing circumstances includes 'conduct that is illustrative of a type of conduct that should be so emulated'. Thus, for example, if it was reasonable to expect members of the public to infer from a Facebook or blog post glorifying an attempted suicide bomb attack on the London Underground that what should be emulated is action causing severe disruption to London's transport network, this will be caught by the section 1 offence.

This offence could impact upon freedom of expression and media freedom, in situations where a person operating as media has disseminated statements that could encourage or induce etc. terrorist activity. Section 1(6) provides limited protection for the media in these circumstances. It gives rise to a defence where it has not been proved that the publisher *intended* the statement to encourage or otherwise induce the commission, preparation or instigation of acts of terrorism or CECPT offences. However, if the publisher is found to have acted recklessly in this regard, they cannot rely on the defence. In relation to citizen journalism's facilitation of media freedom this could be problematic. Arguably, citizen journalists, that have perhaps not undergone the training associated with traditional journalism, and are less likely to have the same experience, resources and support at their disposal of, for instance, the print and broadcast media are, as a result, more likely to fall foul of having acted 'recklessly' in their dissemination of information. Consequently, in the future, it is likely that we will see prosecutions of citizen journalists relating to their 'reckless' publication of material, contrary to section 1.

For the defence to succeed the burden of proof rests on the defendant to show that: (i) the statement published neither expressed their views, nor had their endorsement, and (ii) that it was clear in all the circumstances of the statement's publication that it was not their view and did not have their endorsement. Section 3 can, in certain circumstances, add a further layer to the operation of the defence. It provides that a person cannot take advantage of the defence if they are deemed to endorse a statement because they have not complied, within two working days, with a notice, issued by a constable pursuant to subsection (3), to remove the statement from public view or alter it so that it is not related to terrorism. In situations where the defendant has complied with the notice, but the same or similar statement is posted again, they can still rely on the defence. In such a situation it may be difficult to tell if the statement is the statement to which the notice relates or a new one – a 'repeat statement'. Indeed, subsection (4) provides that the person against whom the notice was issued will be regarded as having endorsed repeat statements. However, this is subject to subsections (5) and (6), which provide a mechanism to ensure that a person is only liable for statements that he knows about.

These provisions determine that a person is not deemed to endorse a repeat statement if they can demonstrate that they have taken all *reasonable* steps to: (i) prevent such statements becoming available to the public; (ii) ascertain if the statement is available to the public; and (iii) they are not aware that the statement had been published or they were aware that it had been published but they have taken every reasonable step to ensure it is removed or modified. The Act does not specify what *reasonable* means. This could create difficulties in the context of social media and citizen journalism where issues with 'speaker control' means that a publication can be republished and therefore redisseminated at an exponential rate.[103] As the defendant bears the burden of proof in this situation, to protect media freedom, and in particular the citizen journalist, what amounts to reasonable remedial steps should be determined on a case-by-case basis, taking into account all of the circumstances surrounding the republication, how easy it is for the defendant to give effect to the section 3 notice and the efforts they have gone to in order to achieve this.

This section has illustrated the myriad domestic provisions operating at the intersection between freedom of expression and terrorist activity. As the traditional 'fourth estate' struggles, and citizen journalism, facilitated by social media, continues to go from strength to strength, it is likely that we will see an increase in cases where the activity of this new breed of journalist, operating as part of the media, potentially conflicts with the interests of national security and the security services in the name of freedom of expression and media freedom. Thus, the following section will consider the social media landscape, the diminishing fortunes of the traditional media and the continued rise of citizen journalists.

103 P. Coe, 'The social media paradox: an intersection with freedom of expression and the criminal law' (2015) 24(1) *Information & Communications Technology Law* 16–40, 26.

6.3 The demise of the traditional 'fourth estate' and the emergence of citizen journalism

6.3.1 The 'fourth estate' and the reporting of terrorist activity

Prior to the evolution of the internet into a network available throughout the world and, in particular, the social media revolution, which transformed that network into an accessible form of mass media, that has facilitated the convergence of audience and producer,[104] traditional press and broadcast companies were the only media institutions that had the ability to reach mass audiences through regular publication or broadcasts.[105] In contrast to the examples of high quality investigative public interest journalism provided by Leveson LJ's *Inquiry*,[106] there is no doubt that, in recent years, an increasing number of traditional media outlets choose to engage with 'sexy' stories that sell, as opposed to reporting on matters of public concern.[107] As a result, the traditional media's public watchdog role gradually diminished towards the end of the 20th century and, instead, the focus has shifted onto commercially viable stories.[108]

Media ownership, and the power derived from it, means that there is a constant conflict between the traditional media's 'fourth estate' role as a watchdog, or gatekeeper, and commercial reality. Indeed, during the 20th century there has been a dilution of news media ownership, which is now vested in a relatively small number of large and powerful companies. Accordingly, this ownership concentration has had a detrimental effect on investigative journalism,[109] a role of the press and wider media that Lord Nicholls considered vital in *Reynolds*.[110] Indeed, large proportions of the traditional press and broadcast media facilitate 'churnalism', that is the regurgitation of existing stories from the same source, rather than

104 See generally A. Bruns, *Blogs, Wikipedia, Second Life and Beyond: From Production to Produsage* (Peter Lang Publishing, 2008).

105 See generally J. Van Dijck, *The Culture of Connectivity: A Critical History of Social Media* (Oxford University Press, 2013) 3–23.

106 Lord Justice Leveson, *An Inquiry into the Culture, Practices and Ethics of the Press* (November 2012) 455-470.

107 Numerous examples are provided by Leveson LJ in his Inquiry: Lord Justice Leveson, *An Inquiry into the Culture, Practices and Ethics of the Press* (November 2012) 539-591. See generally N. Davies, *Flat Earth News* (Vintage, 2009).

108 For example, see C. Calvert and M. Torres, 'Putting the Shock Value in First Amendment Jurisprudence: When Freedom for the Citizen-Journalist Watchdog Trumps the Right of Informational Privacy on the Internet' (2011) *Vanderbilt Journal of Entertainment and Technology Law* 323, 341; J. Curran and J. Seaton, *Power Without Responsibility – Press, Broadcasting and the Internet in Britain* (7th edn, Routledge, 2010) 96–98; E. Cashmore, *Celebrity Culture* (2nd edn, Routledge, 2014).

109 S. L. Carter, 'Technology, Democracy, and the Manipulation of Consent' (1983–1984) *Yale Law Journal* 581, 600–607; P. Garry, 'The First Amendment and Freedom of the Press: A Revised Approach to the Marketplace of Ideas Concept' (1989) 72 *Marquette Law Review* 187, 189; See also Leveson LJ's assessment of the commercial pressures on the press: Lord Justice Leveson, *An Inquiry into the Culture, Practices and Ethics of the Press*, November 2012, 93–98.

110 See (n 14-15).

engaging with sound investigative journalism as a result of, for instance, commercial pressures and restraints.[111]

The traditional media has, undoubtedly, been responsible for some exemplary work in relation to the investigative reporting of terrorist activity. For instance, Sky News was recently at the forefront of uncovering thousands of documents detailing important information about Islamic State jihadis.[112] These 'ISIS files' were, subsequently, passed on to the security services, and will clearly help to combat the extremist activity of Islamic State. To the contrary, a number of incidents relating to the reporting of terrorist activity, both within the UK and in the US, do not just animate the demise of the traditional media, but also expose its susceptibly to bias and 'churnalism', based on commercial and political pressures. Further, they provide examples of conflict with the principles underpinning the 'fourth estate' discussed earlier in this chapter.

In Davies' wide-ranging investigation into allegations of falsehood and propaganda in the media, he considers a number of 'terror error' stories published by the UK press in the wake of the London bombings in July 2005.[113] For example, before discovering that all four bombers were British-born, the *Independent on Sunday* blamed the attack on 'white mercenary terrorists'[114] whilst, according to the *Sunday Telegraph*, the perpetrators were 'a foreign-based Islamic terrorist cell'.[115] The *Times* reported that the 'the London rush-hour bombers are alive and planning another attack',[116] before admitting that they were actually all dead. Indeed, according to Davies, Fleet Street newspapers identified four different 'masterminds' behind the bombings; the *Daily Mail* warned that a fifth terrorist was on the loose; and, after the failed attempt at bombings two weeks later, the *Sunday Times* reported that a third cell was in operation – all of which was later directly contradicted by the police and intelligence agencies.[117] Similar examples of 'terror error' stories were published by the US press after the 9/11 bombings – none of which turned out to be true. Instead, they were 'pumped into the media by official sources who either genuinely did not know the truth or did not care but hoped for some political advantage'.[118]

111 See generally Davies above, n 107.

112 S. Ramsay, 'IS Documents Identify Thousands of Jihadis' (10 March 2016) http://news.sky.com/story/1656777/is-documents-identify-thousands-of-jihadis (accessed 17 May 2016).

113 Davies above n 107, 35.

114 S. Goodchild et al, 'Police hunt "mercenary" terror gang recruited by al-Qa'ida' (9 July 2005) http://www.independent.co.uk/news/uk/crime/police-hunt-mercenary-terror-gang-recruited-by-al-qaida-5346470.html (accessed 17 May 2016).

115 P. Hennessy et al, 'Foreign terrorist cell was behind London bombings' (10 July 2005) http://www.telegraph.co.uk/news/uknews/1493717/Foreign-terrorist-cell-was-behind-London-bombings.html (accessed 17 May 2016).

116 M. Evans et al, 'Terror alert highest ever as police fear new attack' (11 July 2005) http://www.thetimes.co.uk/tto/news/uk/article1935272.ece (accessed 17 May 2016).

117 Davies above n 107, 35.

118 Ibid (n34).

This point is developed further in relation to the reporting in the US of terrorist activities relating to Abu Musab al-Zarqawi. According to Davies: '[b]y the time he was killed in Iraq in June 2006, Zarqawi had become the most notorious Islamist fighter in the world, exceeding even Osama bin Laden in the scale of the killing which was attributed to him . . . We now know that a high proportion of what was said about Zarqawi was false'.[119] It transpired that the stories published about Zarqawi were the result of 'strategic communications' – information 'campaigns' by government agencies to strategically manipulate global perception of terrorist threats through the manipulation of a weakened traditional media prone to 'churnalism'.[120]

Similarly, a high profile example from the UK of the media (in this case the *Sunday Times*) publishing politically bias stories based upon 'official communications' from government agencies, that subsequently turn out to be false, relates to the notorious shooting by the SAS of members of the IRA in Gibraltar in 1988. At 4:45pm on Sunday 6 March, the Ministry of Defence (MoD) released a statement that three suspected terrorists had been shot dead by security forces and that a 'suspected bomb' had been found. The MoD continued to provide off-the-record guidance to the media, which culminated in bulletins stating that the bomb was located in a crowded street and gunfire was exchanged between the terrorists and SAS personnel in an area containing civilians. To the contrary the three IRA terrorists had been shot dead by the SAS at 3:47pm. There had been no exchange of gunfire – as the security forces knew within minutes of the shooting – as none of the suspects carried any weapons. Further, by 7:30pm, at the very latest, the MoD knew there was no bomb. Despite this, misinformation continued to be fed to the media until 3:30pm the following day.

From a 'fourth estate' perspective, even more worrying than the MoD purposefully misinforming the media, was the now infamous reaction of the *Sunday Times*, which made no secret of its political partisanship – being allied to Margaret Thatcher's Conservative government.[121] Rather than investigate the MoD's actions the newspaper returned to the MoD to acquire further information to produce a story headlined 'SAS: Why we fired at IRA gang'. A further feature declared that this was 'another victory for Britain's security services' and reproduced, as fact, several passages of 'highly contentious' MoD briefing.[122] Following Thames Television's *Death on the Rock* documentary, which presented key witnesses casting serious doubt on the 'official' story, the *Sunday Times* published an attack on the studio, supported by official guidance from the MoD. At this point, key *Sunday Times* reporters began to become concerned that the newspaper was intent on supporting the official MoD line, rather than considering any contradictory

119 Ibid ch 6.
120 Ibid.
121 Ibid 305.
122 Ibid. See ch 8 generally.

information, to the extent that they 'disowned' the story.[123] However, the newspaper continued publicly to support the official line and attack Thames Television. Eventually, nine months after the initial story, the *Sunday Times* was forced to retract.[124]

These incidents, and the way in which they were reported by the traditional media, are symptomatic of the challenges faced by, in particular, the press industry that is not only subject to challenges posed by factors such as owner or political bias, but also by an extremely challenging financial climate, that has increasingly necessitated reporting and publishing decisions to be made based on commercial viability rather than adhering to the principles underpinning the 'fourth estate'. Although this has, arguably, always been the case, it appears that 'churnalism' is on the increase, simply because of the costs involved with running a newspaper. Clearly, the traditional media is still an excellent source of valuable information and important investigative work. However, the independence associated with citizen journalism has amplified the fact that the traditional media can no longer always be relied upon to exercise its role as the public watchdog, through, for instance, conducting sound investigative journalism.

The following section will consider the demise of the traditional 'fourth estate' media, and how its role as the public watchdog is being usurped by an internet-based 'fifth estate'.

6.3.2 The demise of the traditional media and the rise of citizen journalism: a brave new world

Citizen journalists, through the use of social media are, in many instances, replacing the traditional media as the public's watchdog, consequently giving rise to what has been described as, an internet-based 'fifth estate'.[125]

Until relatively recently, members of the public were, to a great extent, limited as to what they were exposed to reading or seeing, by what large proportions of the traditional media chose to publish or broadcast. Such decisions may have come down to editorial control, based on factors such as owner or political bias, commercial revenue, or both, rather than being based on the results of sound investigative journalism.[126] However, the emergence of social media, which has

123 Ibid 306–311.

124 The newspaper's version of events was undermined by detailed evidence given at the inquest into the shootings in Gibraltar; and from Lord Windlesham's inquiry into the *Death on the Rock* documentary. Ibid 310.

125 A. Cohen, 'The media that need citizens: The First Amendment and the fifth estate' (2011) 85 *S Cal L Rev* 1; I. Cram, *Citizen Journalists* (Edward Elgar Publishing, 2015) 39.

126 Barendt above n 3, 12. Similar issues have arisen in the print press with regard to commercial advertising. For example, in January 2015, a number of *Daily Telegraph* journalists voiced their concerns over the newspaper allegedly discouraging them from writing unfavourable stories about advertising and commercial partners. Furthermore, the journalists provided examples to *Newsnight* of how commercial concerns impacted upon coverage given to China and Russia. See: C. Cook, *More Telegraph writers voice concern* (19 February 2015) http://www.bbc.co.uk/news/health-31529682 (accessed 19 April 2016).

enabled citizen journalists to communicate with, potentially, millions of people, means that the ability to reach mass audiences is no longer something that is monopolised by traditional media institutions. Thus, social media platforms have changed the traditional media landscape forever, as they have altered our perceptions of the limits of communication, and reception of information. It is no longer the case that communication is constrained by boundaries, such as location, time, space or culture,[127] or dictated by a media organisation's ownership, political bias[128] or commercial partners.[129]

Access to multiple social media platforms 24 hours a day, that are instantaneously accessible, allows users, forming what Benkler refers to as the 'networked public sphere',[130] to transmit and receive information to one and other, via 'social networking sites' (SNS), such as Facebook or Twitter, and 'user generated content' (UGC) platforms, that include YouTube, blogs and vlogs,[131] without the need to consider, what have become the boundaries and restrictions mentioned above.[132] This is illustrated by using statistics to compare the use of social media with traditional media. For example, the *New York Times* 2013 print and digital circulation was approximately 2 million,[133] enabling it to proclaim that it was the '#1 individual newspaper site' on the internet, with nearly 31 million unique visitors per month.[134]

In contrast, YouTube, which is owned by Google, has one billion unique visitors per month[135] which, according to Ammori, equates to: 'thirty times more than the *New York Times*, or as many unique visitors in a day as the [*New York*] *Times* has every month'.[136] According to WordPress' statistics, it hosts blogs written in over 120 languages, equating to over 409 million users viewing more than 15.5 billion

127 See generally: F. Webster, *Theories of the Information Society* (4th edn, Routledge, 2014) 20; I. Barron and R. Curnow, *The Future with Microelectronics: Forecasting the Effects of Information Technology* (Pinter, 1979); G. Mulgan, *Communication and Control: Networks and the New Economies of Communication* (Polity, 1991); S. Coleman and J. Blumler, *The Internet and Democratic Citizenship – Theory, Practice and Policy* (Cambridge University Press, 2009) 27–28.

128 For example, see *Rupert Murdoch will decide Sun stance on Brexit, says its ex-political editor* (16 March 2016) http://www.theguardian.com/media/2016/mar/16/rupert-murdoch-sun-brexit-eu-referendum-trevor-kavanagh?CMP=twt_a-media_b-gdnmedia (accessed 16 March 2016).

129 For example, see C. Cook, *More Telegraph writers voice concern* (19 February 2015) http://www.bbc.co.uk/news/health-31529682 (accessed 19 May 2015); See also E. Barendt, *Freedom of Speech* (2nd edn, Oxford University Press, 2005) 12.

130 Y. Benkler, *The Wealth of Networks* (Yale University Press, 2006) 212.

131 Van Dijck above n 105, 8.

132 See generally B. Wellman, 'Physical Space and Cyberspace: The Rise of Personalised Networking' (2001) 25(2) *International Journal of Urban and Regional Research* 227–51; Coe above n 103, 21–2.

133 C. Haughney, 'Newspapers Post Gains in Digital Circulation', *New York Times* (30 April 2014) http://www.nytimes.com/2013/05/01/business/media/digital-subscribers-buoy-newspaper-circulation.html (accessed 19 May 2015).

134 New York Times Media Kit, http://perma.cc/B5KA-VMGC (accessed 12 September 2014).

135 Statistics YouTube, http://perma.cc/S8W5-ZRM4 (accessed 19 May 2015).

136 M. Ammori, 'The "new" New York Times: Free speech lawyering in the age of Google and Twitter' (2014) 127 *Harvard Law Review* 2259–95, 2266.

pages each month. Consequently, users produce approximately 41.7 million new posts and 60.5 million new comments on a monthly basis. As of December 2015, Twitter states that it has 320 million active users[137] and normally 'takes in' approximately 500 million tweets per day, equating to an average of 5700 tweets per second.[138] It has more visitors per week than the *New York Times* does in a month.[139]

Similarly, Tumblr hosts over 170 million microblogs[140] and, with 300 million visits per month, enjoys 10 times more than the *New York Times*.[141] According to Facebook, as of December 2015, it had 1.59 billion monthly active users, 934 million of which use their mobile applications to access the platform on a daily basis.[142] Late 2013 saw Instagram's global usage expand by 15 per cent, in just two months, to 150 million people.[143] Latest figures show that this has now increased to 400 million.[144] LinkedIn's current membership exceeds 400 million.[145] These established platforms are only the 'tip of the social media iceberg'. Pinterest continues to grow rapidly,[146] as do emerging platforms, such as Snapchat and WhatsApp.[147] Consequently, for many people, new media platforms have not just replaced the written word; they have become a substitute for the spoken word.[148]

This 'reach' of social media amplifies the way that the media in general envelopes our existence. Traditional media organisations simply no longer monopolise the methods we use to find and facilitate news-gathering, communication or reception, or indeed how we express opinions and ideas. As a result, social media, and citizen journalism, has become an increasingly important source of news.[149] This is demonstrated by the available evidence relating to emerging trends in

137 https://about.twitter.com/company (accessed 17 March 2016).

138 https://blog.twitter.com/2013/new-tweets-per-second-record-and-how (accessed 9 January 2015).

139 Ammori above n 136, 24.

140 Ibid 2272.

141 J. Yarow, *The Truth About Tumblr: Its Numbers Are Significantly Worse than You Think*, Business Insider, (21 May 2013) http://www.businessinsider.com/tumblrs-active-users-lighter-than-expected-2013-5 (accessed 19 May 2015).

142 https://newsroom.fb.com/key-Facts (accessed 17 March 2016).

143 http://instagram.com/press/#; UK Social Media Statistics for 2014, http://socialmediatoday.com/kate-rose-mcgrory/2040906/uk-social-media-statistics-2014 (accessed 19 May 2015).

144 http://instagram.com/press/# (accessed 17 March 2016).

145 https://press.linkedin.com/about-linkedin (accessed 17 March 2016).

146 In 2011/2012 Pinterest had approximately 200,000 users in the UK. In the summer of 2013 this had grown to over 2 million: http://socialmediatoday.com/kate-rose-mcgrory/2040906/uk-social-media-statistics-2014 (accessed 19 May 2015).

147 In February 2016 it was announced that WhatsApp had reached 1 billion active monthly users. See: 'WhatsApp reaches a billion monthly users' http://www.bbc.co.uk/news/technology-35459812 (1 February 2016) (accessed 17 March 2016).

148 Coe above n 103, 24.

149 See generally: L. Durity, 'Shielding Journalist-"Bloggers": The Need to Protect Newsgathering Despite the Distribution Medium' (2006) 5 *Duke Law & Technology Review* 1; J.S. Alonzo, 'Restoring the Ideal Marketplace: How Recognizing Bloggers as Journalists Can save the Press' (2006) 9 *New York University Journal of Legislation and Public Policy* 751, 754.

how news content is generated and disseminated in both the US and the UK. In September 2012, the *Pew Research Centre* published a report that analysed trends in news consumption by US citizens between 1991 to 2012.[150]

The report confirmed that print newspaper sales were declining,[151] and that a younger demographic of news consumers, comprising of adults under 30 years old, were turning to online and social media news sources, rather than television news. Indeed, between 2010 and 2012, the percentage of US citizens, across all age groups, receiving their news from social media, and in particular SNSs, increased from 9 per cent to 19 per cent. Accordingly, the report states that SNSs were the preferred source of news for 33 per cent of the under-30s age group; with just 13 per cent of this group obtaining their news from either the print or digital formats of newspapers. These figures are reflected in a more recent report from *Pew*,[152] which confirms that 'millenials' (persons born between 1981 and 1996) are most likely to obtain information about the 2016 presidential election via social media (Facebook is the most used platform, followed by Twitter and YouTube). The report states that, of the 91 per cent of all US adults who 'learned' about the election between 12 and 27 January 2016, 14 per cent claimed social media was the 'most helpful' source of information. Similarly, 13 per cent claimed that news websites and mobile applications were the most helpful. However, in comparison, only 3 per cent and 2 per cent felt that local and national print newspapers respectively fell into the 'most helpful' source category.

As Cram suggests, the *Pew Centre*'s figures are indicative of a broader trend outside the US and, significantly, in the UK.[153] Between March 2014 to March 2015 average national daily newspaper sales fell by half a million – from 7.6 million to just over 7 million per day. During this period, the *Daily Mail* and *The Times* were the 'best performers', but even they recorded significant losses in circulation. The *Mail*'s year-on-year circulation decreased by 4.7 per cent, whereas *The Times* saw its sales decline by 0.9 per cent.[154] According to the most recent

150 Pew Research Centre, 'In Changing News Landscape, Even Television is Vulnerable' (27 September 2012) http://www.people-press.org/2012/09/27/in-changing-news-landscape-even-television-is-vulnerable/ (accessed 16 March 2016).

151 This particular trend has been detected by the Pew Research Centre in a report which considers the diminishing financial viability of newspapers in the US is evidenced by regular occurrences of ownership change as successive owners tried and failed to prevent declining circulation levels that, sequentially, generate less advertising revenue. See Pew Research Centre, 'The declining value of US newspapers' (22 May 2015) http://www.pewresearch.org/fact-tank/2015/05/22/the-declining-value-of-u-s-newspapers/ (accessed 16 March 2016; see generally I. Cram, *Citizen Journalists* (Edward Elgar Publishing, 2015) 1.

152 Pew Research Centre, 'The 2016 Presidential Campaign – a News Events That's Hard to Miss' (4 February 2016) http://www.journalism.org/2016/02/04/the-2016-presidential-campaign-a-news-event-thats-hard-to-miss/; See also Pew Research Centre, 'News Habits on Facebook and Twitter' (14 July 2015) http://www.journalism.org/2015/07/14/news-habits-on-facebook-and-twitter/ (both accessed 16 March 2016).

153 Cram above n 151, 2.

154 J. Jackson, 'National daily newspaper sales fall by half a million in a year', *Guardian* (10 April 2015) http://www.theguardian.com/media/2015/apr/10/national-daily-newspapers-lose-more-than-half-a-million-readers-in-past-year (accessed 17 March 2016).

Audit Bureau of Circulations' (ABC)[155] report, this overall decline is continuing, at a rather rapid rate. It suggests that the overall daily newspaper market is shrinking by more than 8 per cent per year, and the Sunday market by a little over 9 per cent, with daily and Sunday red-tops falling faster than the rest. In a year, the *Sun*, *Daily Mirror* and *Daily Star* have seen their circulation fall by more than 370,000, or 10.9 per cent. The four Sunday red-tops (the *Sun*, *Mirror*, *Star* and *People*) have, collectively, seen a 12.3 per cent decline in circulation since 2014; a fall in sales of 400,000. Broadsheets have not been immune to the fate suffered by the red-tops. For instance, ABC statistics show that the *Independent* and the *Guardian* have suffered year-on-year decreases in circulation of 8.1 per cent and 7.6 per cent respectively.[156]

The decline of the traditional media and the ascendency of social media has been a catalyst for the growth of citizen journalism, and the emergence of an online 'fifth estate'. Indeed, the importance attributed to citizen journalism is demonstrated by this breed of journalist being officially recognised as press.[157] As Cram observes, these conditions have allowed social media and citizen journalism to transform: '. . . the average citizen's hitherto largely passive experience of political debate led by elite opinion formers into something much more vibrant and more participative'.[158] Other scholars, who have made this democratisation argument,[159] have emphasised the empowerment[160] of what Volokh has referred to as 'cheap speech': 'The new technologies . . . will, I believe, both democratize the information marketplace – make it more accessible to comparatively poor speakers as well as the rich ones – and diversify it'.[161]

This ability of social media to create a democratised digital public sphere has also been acknowledged by the US Supreme Court in *Reno v ACLU*,[162] in which Justice Stevens stated that online chatrooms would enable anyone to become a 'town crier with a voice that resonates further than it would from a soap box',[163] a situation animated by the following examples. The death of Osama bin Laden was leaked on Twitter, before being published by any newspaper.[164] Syria's

155 http://www.abc.org.uk.

156 R. Greenslade, 'Are national newspaper sales heading for a cliff? Not quite yet . . .', *Guardian* (9 October 2015) http://www.theguardian.com/media/greenslade/2015/oct/09/are-national-newspaper-sales-heading-for-a-cliff-not-quite-yet (accessed 17 March 2016).

157 See the High Court of Ireland case of: *Cornec v Morrice* [2012] IEHC 376; K. Q. Seelye, *White House Approves Press Pass for Blogger*, New York Times (7 March 2005) http://www.nytimes.com/2005/03/07/technology/07press.html?_r=0 (accessed 19 May 2015).

158 Cram above n 151, 3.

159 For example, see the comments of Joe Trippi, cited in M. Hindman, *The Myth of Digital Democracy* (Princeton University Press, 2009); ibid (Cram).

160 Ibid (Cram) 3–4.

161 E. Volokh, 'Cheap speech and what it will do' (1995) 104 *Yale LJ* 1805, 1833. See also P. Schwartz, 'Privacy and democracy in cyberspace' (1999) 52 *Vand L Rev* 1609; J. Rowbottom, 'Media freedom and political debate in the digital era' (2006) *Modern Law Review* 489.

162 (1997) 521 US 844.

163 ibid 862.

164 B. Shelter, 'How the Bin Laden Announcement Leaked Out' *New York Times* (1 May 2011) http://mediadecoder.blogs.nytimes.com/2011/05/01/how-the-osama-announcement-leaked-out/?_php=true&_type=blogs&_r=0 (accessed 19 May 2015).

President, Bashar al-Assad, and his opposing rebels have distributed competing propaganda on Instagram.[165] Chelsea Manning, the US soldier convicted in 2013 for, inter alia, offences pursuant to the Espionage Act, leaked classified documents to WikiLeaks, as opposed to a traditional media outlet.[166] The value of citizen journalism has been summarised by the Council of Europe's Committee of Ministers, which stated:

> Citizens' communication and interaction in online environments and their participation in activities that involve matters of public interest can bring positive, real-life, social change. When freedom of expression and the right to receive and impart information and freedom of assembly are not upheld online, their protection offline is likely to be undermined and democracy and the rule of law can also be compromised.[167]

Despite the fact that, never before has a form of media changed the scale, pace or pattern of human affairs to such an extent, within such a short period of time as social media has, this section will conclude with a caveat. Although social media platforms are now a vital, and often the preferred method of imparting and receiving news,[168] citizen journalism's contribution to matters of public interest cannot be overrated, just as traditional journalism should not be underestimated.[169] This is because social media can facilitate the instantaneous, and often spontaneous, expression of opinions and venting and sharing of emotions, thoughts and feelings.[170] Consequently, the internet is saturated with poorly

165 N. Gaouette, 'Assad on Instagram Vies with Rebel Videos to Seek Support' *Bloomberg* (19 September 2013) http://www.bloomberg.com/news/2013-09-19/assad-on-instagram-vies-with-rebel-videos-to-seek-support.html (accessed 19 May 2015).

166 Benkler above n 130, 348.

167 Para. 3, *Declaration by the Committee of Ministers on the protection of freedom of expression and information and freedom of assembly and association with regard to Internet domain names and name strings* (Adopted by the Committee of Ministers on 21 September 2011) https://wcd.coe.int/ViewDoc.jsp?id=1835805 (accessed 17 March 2016).

168 According to Ofcom's report, 'The Communications Market 2013', at [1.9.7], 23% of people use social media platforms, such as Facebook and Twitter, for news: http://stakeholders.ofcom.org.uk/binaries/research/cmr/cmr13/UK_1.pdf (accessed 19 May 2015). For a US perspective, see the following *Pew Research Centre* reports: 'In Changing News Landscape, Even Television is Vulnerable' (27 September 2012) http://www.people-press.org/2012/09/27/in-changing-news-landscape-even-television-is-vulnerable/; 'The 2016 Presidential Campaign – a News Events That's Hard to Miss' (4 February 2016) http://www.journalism.org/2016/02/04/the-2016-presidential-campaign-a-news-event-thats-hard-to-miss/; 'News Habits on Facebook and Twitter' (14 July 2015) http://www.journalism.org/2015/07/14/news-habits-on-facebook-and-twitter/all (accessed 16 March 2016).

169 J. Oster, 'Theory and Doctrine of "Media Freedom" as a Legal Concept' (2013) 5(1) *JML* 57–78, 63.

170 Indeed, in April 2014 Facebook emailed its users to inform them that the messages function would be moved out of the Facebook application, due to its Messenger application enabling users to reply 20% faster than using Facebook.

researched, biased and meaningless material. For instance, in his Inquiry, Leveson LJ refers to Popbitch that, in his Lordship's opinion, is: 'clear in its ambition to entertain and understands itself to "poke fun" and comment on the "lighter" side of celebrity culture'.[171]

Despite the best intentions of some serious citizen journalists, they may still lack the education, qualifications and experience to distinguish themselves from professional journalists. Indeed, bloggers post information despite being uncertain as to its provenance and without verifying it for reliability, and instead, rely on readers to judge its accuracy.[172] To the contrary, a blog by a professional journalist may include spontaneous comments and conversation, whilst being supported by professional experience and resources.[173] Ultimately, there exists a symbiosis between citizen journalism and the traditional media that has been articulated by a number of commentators. Essentially, this relationship is mutually beneficial because professional journalists and traditional media entities research and cover the findings of citizen journalism that, sequentially, adds credence to the citizen journalist's work and facilitates the wider dissemination of their research.[174]

6.4 Conclusion

It is clear from the prevailing sections that striking a balance between the interests of national security and freedom of expression and media freedom, particularly in the context of social media and citizen journalism is, and will continue to be, challenging. It remains to be seen what impact the ascendance of citizen journalism will have on some of the existing laws and principles relating to the dissemination of publications regarding national security and terrorism. Only time, and case law, may paint a clearer picture – if that is ever possible in a world where media is developing at such an incredible pace. It is unlikely that the law will ever actually catch-up with today's, let alone tomorrow's, technology. Ultimately, we may always be faced with having to 'make-do' with a 'square-peg-round-hole' regime. Consequently, in order for an appropriate balance to be struck, those operating at the intersection of these interests and rights must ensure that they remain attuned to, not only the complex laws that govern this area, but also the constantly evolving social and media environment.

171 Lord Justice Leveson, *An Inquiry into the Culture, Practices and Ethics of the Press* (November 2012) 168 [4.3].

172 J.S. Alonzo, 'Restoring the Ideal Marketplace: How Recognizing Bloggers as Journalists Can save the Press' (2006) 9 *New York University Journal of Legislation and Public Policy* 751, 755.

173 Rowbottom argues for a high and low level distinction for speech that is based on the context within which the expression is made, as opposed to a value based distinction deriving from the content of the expression. See: J. Rowbottom, 'To rant, vent and converse: protecting low level digital speech' (2012) 71(2) *C.L.J.* 355–83, 371.

174 Oster above n 169, 64. C. Calvert and M. Torres, 'Putting the Shock Value in First Amendment Jurisprudence: When Freedom for the Citizen-Journalist Watchdog Trumps the Right of Informational Privacy on the Internet' (2011) *Vanderbilt Journal of Entertainment and Technology Law* 323, 345; J. Curran and J. Seaton, *Power Without Responsibility – Press, Broadcasting and the Internet in Britain* (7th edn, Routledge, 2010) 286.

Index

For Product Safety Concerns and Information please contact our EU representative GPSR@taylorandfrancis.com
Taylor & Francis Verlag GmbH, Kaufingerstraße 24, 80331 München, Germany

www.ingramcontent.com/pod-product-compliance
Ingram Content Group UK Ltd.
Pitfield, Milton Keynes, MK11 3LW, UK
UKHW011011180926
475701UK00004B/671

* 9 7 8 0 3 6 7 8 7 4 9 9 5 *